NEAR-DEATH EXPERIENCES

AFTERLIFE JOURNEYS AND REVELATIONS

JIM WILLIS

DETROIT

ABOUT THE AUTHOR

Having earned his master's degree in theology from Andover Newton Theological School, **Jim Willis** has been an ordained minister for over 40 years. He has also taught college courses in comparative religion and cross-cultural studies. In addition, Willis has been a professional musician, high school orchestra and band teacher, arts council director, and even a drive-time radio show host. His background in theology and education led to his writings on religion, the apocalypse, cross-cultural spirituality, and the mysteries of the unknown. His books include Visible Ink Press' *Armageddon Now: The End of the World A to Z; Supernatural Gods: Spiritual Mysteries, Psychic Experiences, and Scientific Truths; The Religion Book: Places, Prophets, Saints, and Seers;* and *Censoring God: The History of the Lost Books (and other Excluded Scriptures).* He also published *Faith, Trust & Belief: A Trilogy of the Spirit.* Willis resides in the woods of South Carolina.

NEAR-DEATH EXPERIENCES

AFTERLIFE JOURNEYS AND REVELATIONS

JIM WILLIS

DETROIT

OTHER BOOKS BY JIM WILLIS FROM VISIBLE INK PRESS

American Cults: Cabals, Corruption, and Charismatic Leaders
ISBN: 978-1-57859-800-7

Ancient Gods: Lost Histories, Hidden Truths, and the Conspiracy of Silence
ISBN: 978-1-57859-614-0

Armageddon Now: The End of the World A to Z
ISBN: 978-1-57859-168-8

Censoring God: The History of the Lost Books (and other Excluded Scriptures)
ISBN: 978-1-57859-732-1

Hidden History: Ancient Aliens and the Suppressed Origins of Civilization
ISBN: 978-1-57859-710-9

Lost Civilizations: The Secret Histories and Suppressed Technologies of the Ancients
ISBN: 978-1-57859-706-2

The Religion Book: Places, Prophets, Saints, and Seers
ISBN: 978-1-57859-151-0

Supernatural Gods: Spiritual Mysteries, Psychic Experiences, and Scientific Truths
ISBN: 978-1-57859-660-7

ALSO FROM VISIBLE INK PRESS

The Afterlife Book: Heaven, Hell, and Life after Death
By Marie D. Jones and Larry Flaxman
ISBN: 978-1-57859-761-1

Angels A to Z, 2nd edition
By Evelyn Dorothy Oliver and James R Lewis
ISBN: 978-1-57859-212-8

Celebrity Ghosts and Notorious Hauntings
By Marie D. Jones
ISBN: 978-1-57859-689-8

Demons, the Devil, and Fallen Angels
By Marie D. Jones and Larry Flaxman
ISBN: 978-1-57859-613-3

The Dream Encyclopedia, 2nd edition
By James R. Lewis and Evelyn Dorothy Oliver
ISBN: 978-1-57859-216-6

The Dream Interpretation Dictionary: Symbols, Signs and Meanings
By J. M. DeBord
ISBN: 978-1-57859-637-9

Earth Magic: Your Complete Guide to Natural Spells, Potions, Plants, Herbs, Witchcraft, and More
By Marie D. Jones
ISBN: 978-1-57859-697-3

The Encyclopedia of Religious Phenomena
By J. Gordon Melton, Ph.D.
ISBN: 978-1-57859-209-8

Everyday Magic: How to Live a Mindful, Meaningful, Magical Life
By Marie D. Jones and Denise Agnew
ISBN: 978-1-57859-721-5

The Fortune-Telling Book: The Encyclopedia of Divination and Soothsaying
By Raymond Buckland
ISBN: 978-1-57859-147-3

The Handy Bible Answer Book
By Jennifer R. Prince
ISBN: 978-1-57859-478-8

The Handy Christianity Answer Book
By Stephen A. Werner, Ph.D.
ISBN: 978-1-57859-686-7

The Handy Islam Answer Book
By John Renard, Ph.D.
ISBN: 978-1-57859-510-5

The Handy Mythology Answer Book
By David Leeming, Ph.D.
ISBN: 978-1-57859-475-7

The Handy Religion Answer Book
By John Renard, Ph.D.
ISBN: 978-1-57859-379-8

Haunted: Malevolent Ghosts, Night Terrors, and Threatening Phantoms
By Brad Steiger
ISBN: 978-1-57859-620-1

The New Witch: Your Guide to Modern Witchcraft, Wicca, Spells, Potions, Magic, and More
By Marie D. Jones
ISBN: 978-1-57859-716-1

Nightmares: Your Guide to Interpreting Your Darkest Dreams
By J. M. DeBord
ISBN: 978-1-57859-758-1

Real Ghosts, Restless Spirits, and Haunted Places, 2nd edition
By Brad Steiger
ISBN: 978-1-57859-401-6

Real Miracles, Divine Intervention, and Feats of Incredible Survival
By Brad Steiger and Sherry Hansen Steiger
ISBN: 978-1-57859-214-2

Real Visitors, Voices from Beyond, and Parallel Dimensions
By Brad Steiger and Sherry Hansen Steiger
ISBN: 978-1-57859-541-9

The Spirit Book: The Encyclopedia of Clairvoyance, Channeling, and Spirit Communication
By Raymond Buckland
ISBN: 978-1-57859-790-1

The Witch Book: The Encyclopedia of Witchcraft, Wicca, and Neo-Paganism
By Raymond Buckland
ISBN: 978-1-57859-114-5

Please Visit Us at visibleinkpress.com

NEAR-DEATH EXPERIENCES:
AFTERLIFE JOURNEYS AND REVELATIONS

Visible Ink Press®
43311 Joy Rd., #414
Canton, MI 48187-2075

Visible Ink Press is a registered trademark of Visible Ink Press, LLC.

Most Visible Ink Press books are available at special quantity discounts when purchased in bulk by corporations, organizations, or groups. Customized printings, special imprints, messages, and excerpts can be produced to meet your needs. For more information, contact Special Markets Director, Visible Ink Press, www.visibleinkpress.com, or 734-667-3211.

Managing Editor: Kevin S. Hile
Cover Design: John Gouin, Graphikitchen, LLC
Page Design: Mary Claire Krzewinski
Typesetting: Marco Divita
Proofreaders: Christa Brelin and Suzanne Goraj
Indexer: Shoshana Hurwitz
Cover and chapter images: Shutterstock.

ISBNs
Paperback: 978-1-57859-846-5
Hardcover: 978-1-57859-856-4
eBook: 978-1-57859-857-1

Cataloging-in-Publication data is on file at the Library of Congress.

Printed in the United States of America.

10 9 8 7 6 5 4 3 2 1

TABLE OF CONTENTS

PHOTO SOURCES

PREFACE

WHAT EXACTLY IS AN NDE?

I don't mind saying that after talking with over a thousand people who have had these experiences and having experienced many times some of the really baffling and unusual features of these experiences, it has given me great confidence that there is a life after death. As a matter of fact, I must confess to you in all honesty, I have absolutely no doubt, on the basis of what my patients have told me, that they did get a glimpse of the beyond.

—Raymond Moody

The phrase "near-death experience," or NDE, was coined by Raymond Moody (1944–) in his 1975 best-selling book, *Life after Life* (the above quote is from his interview with Jeffrey Mishlove for Intuition Network's *New Thinking Allowed*). Born in 1944, Moody earned doctoral degrees in both philosophy and psychiatry as well as a medical degree, but is best known for popularizing his conviction (based on years of research and thousands of interviews with patients) that death is not the end.

In his book and in countless interviews, he has recounted story after story of those who died—often in a hospital under carefully scrutinized conditions—and then, after being revived, returned with stories about unique but somehow very similar experiences of a spiritual nature.

The stages of those experiences are now well known, consisting of detachment from the physical body; a sense of peace, unconditional acceptance, and love; a tunnel leading upward or outward; a bright light; a welcoming, comforting, radiant being; a vision of loved ones or entities of some kind; a life review; and a final, usually reluctant, decision to return.

In some cases, patients were able to describe with extreme accuracy the conditions and activities in the operating room, usually from the vantage point of being near the ceiling. Many were even able to pinpoint specific features outside of the room, features that were later verified.

In one now-famous account, a patient spotted an old sneaker outside on the hospital roof. It was impossible to see it from inside and had probably been deposited there years before by a construction worker. But when a curious researcher crawled onto the roof to confirm the story, there was the sneaker.

Time after time, Moody heard stories about an experience that can only be described as a feeling of physical excitement, which led to a totally different kind of sense perception and a totally different kind of communication. This experience abruptly ceased when the patient returned to the world of the living.

But the lack of ability to accurately portray what was an entirely new existence doesn't mean these people came back to life unchanged. Whatever their religious affiliation—or despite a complete lack of one—everyone testified that they were now believers. They were not converted to a particular religious tradition, mind you, but rather to a certainty that life does not end in death.

They no longer feared the end of life on Earth. Indeed, most looked forward to it. They had undergone a profound moral, ethical, and spiritual transformation. They felt their life now had purpose and meaning, all wrapped up in the idea of love. Love is the most-used word that they used to describe what they felt life was now all about for them.

All these stories ultimately convinced Moody that death is not an end but rather a transformation of consciousness. The material body is left behind as human consciousness morphs into a totally different kind of body—often called a "spiritual" body—that, since it is outside our normal perception realm, cannot be described with any language that was invented to talk about experiences in our material reality.

After 1975, when Moody's book became a best seller, thousands of people felt free of public ridicule to at last describe what they had experienced, sometimes after years or even decades of silence. Most hospitals now routinely interview patients who have died and been revived. Countless YouTube videos fill the internet.

Medical professionals who don't believe that there is life outside of their materialistic pedagogy often do their best to explain such stories as an illusion brought on by lack of oxygen to the brain, or memories of prebirth trauma and a passage through the birth canal. Some insist that the stories are induced by autosuggestion and a desire to believe we somehow survive death. But their voices are increasingly drowned out by example after example of facts that cannot be denied.

This book is about those examples.

Are They Real?

Before we proceed, we must address the concern that will, like it or not, probably be on everyone's mind: "Great stories! Encouraging stories! The people who tell them are obviously sincere. They really believe them. But are NDEs real or imaginary?"

Since Dr. Bruce Greyson co-edited *The Handbook of Near-Death Experiences* in 2009, the whole field of NDE research has turned into a legitimate field of empirical study. Can they be considered bona fide experiences that point to a reality outside material, biological, and physiological reality? In other words, can we put NDEs under a microscope, so to speak, and study them in a systematic fashion consistent with the scientific method?

Here's where it gets tricky. So-called mystical experiences can be induced under the right conditions. Ingesting psychoactive substances from a class of hallucinogens linked to the neurotransmitter serotonin—including psilocybin, the active ingredient in what are called "magic mushrooms"; LSD; DMT, often called the "spirit molecule"; and 5-MeO-DMT, sometimes referred to as the "God molecule"—has been a part of religious, spiritual, or recreational practices for thousands of years.

Neurologists have documented similarities between NDEs and epileptic events known as complex partial seizures. They are often localized in brain regions specific to one hemisphere. Sometimes patients who experience one of these seizures tell of seeing an aura, or light, just before such an attack. They also report sensations involving perceived tastes, smells, or feelings, often described as déjà vu or ecstasy.

U.S. test pilots and NASA astronauts sometimes describe experiences while training in centrifuges that sound similar to NDEs.

The problem, though, is that the vast majority of NDEs don't occur at five or more times the force of gravity. Although it might be said that tunnel vision, bright lights, a feeling of awakening from sleep, a sense of peaceful floating, out-of-body experiences, sensations of euphoria, and conversations with family members can be construed as the *source* of NDEs, it might just as well be true that these extreme experiments and training sessions simply *mimic* the experience.

What makes NDEs so hard to study is that they are not amenable to well-controlled laboratory experimentation. The fact that during an MRI they can be observed in the same part of the brain as epileptic seizures doesn't really prove anything.

In my book *The Quantum Akashic Field*, I wrote about this dilemma from a personal standpoint. By 2012 I had been troubled by epileptic seizures for a few years. They were probably brought on by stress. But this was also the same time period in which I began to seek out-of-body experiences actively. I was aware of the fact that MRI studies—which show similarities in what is often called the shamanic experience or the OBE—affect the same portion of the brain that is lit up during epileptic seizures. As I wrote back then:

> I was afraid to take meds or even see a doctor. My feeling was, strange and egotistical as it may sound, that there was a good possibility that the seizures were happening for a reason. I felt that the seizures might be re-wiring a section of my brain that I, through a lifetime of left-brain, analytical, religious, and theological thought, might have, by habit and misuse, allowed to atrophy. In short, I was afraid that if I chemically closed the door to the "bad guys" of epileptic seizures, I might also be closing the door to the "good guys" of spiritual entities.

There are those who deliberately seek out ecstatic feelings by engaging in dangerous activities such as high-altitude climbing, flying, and sexual practices involving choking or fainting. But even though these experiences mimic some NDE effects, there is no scientific evidence that they are the same thing.

It is difficult to explain actual sightings from an elevated perspective in a hospital room or the phenomenon known as "shared NDEs" in which people standing around a hospital bed sometimes experience the same NDE as the patient they had come to visit. It is also difficult to figure out how some people come back from an

NDE with specific knowledge of external events that cannot be explained by lack of oxygen to the brain.

Because of these questions, we are forced to confront a very common problem found in the typical human approach to any study of this nature that involves questionable scientific data. The scientific method is a very successful approach in matters involving material significance. *But*—and this is a very big "but"—it only works with material-based evidence. If something exists *outside* such evidence, if *meta*physical or *super*natural evidence exists, it cannot be detected with a typical microscope, telescope, or any other kind of instrument.

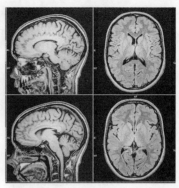

When scanned in an MRI machine, doctors can observe the activity in a brain. Studies show similarities in brain activity between epileptic seizures and spiritual experiences such as OBEs.

This leads to a highly argumentative conclusion that is not often acknowledged but nevertheless exists. The truth is that most people come at a problem of this nature with one of two previously arrived at prejudices:

1. If they have already decided, for whatever cultural reasons they have adopted, that there is no life after death; they consider NDEs to be illusions and immediately go about trying to find a physical reason, such as oxygen deprivation, to explain them away.

2. If they are open to the idea that life may exist outside our perception realm, they are willing to consider the kinds of evidence that cannot be tracked and codified by laboratory-based, materialistic tools of the trade, such as personal testimonies from those who have had NDEs and report them in vivid detail.

This second option can be abused, however. When, for example, a Christian considers the resurrection of Jesus Christ as proof of life after death, it flies in the face of those who question whether such an event actually transpired. German theologian Erich Sauer famously said, "The cross is the victory, the resurrection is the triumph.... The resurrection is the public display of the victory, the triumph of the crucified one."

If that works for the believer, it's a comforting thing, but in no way does it "prove" anything. What about those who do not believe in Christianity? Or any religion, for that matter? Their near-death experience comes right out of the blue, with no previous religious training, but is still valid.

On the other hand, personal testimony is notoriously unreliable. Any police officer who questions four eyewitnesses to a crime is apt to receive four different perspectives, some of which may even be contradictory.

The challenge, then, is to look for indications of empirical proof that might exist within the boundaries of the scientific method. This immediately separates the whole field of NDE research from those who operate only within their belief system.

Secular scientists may scoff, smirk, and go back to their laboratories. Religious folks will "take it on faith." But is there a middle ground? Can we accept personal testimonies if we try to back up their premise with firm, logical, supportive facts? Is there both subjective *and* objective evidence that life continues after death?

That's what this book is about. After all, "proof" of life after death is the single most important fact of human experience. It colors all of our activities and can affect life on Earth like no other subject.

The reason serious study in this field has begun only recently is an accident of history. For the vast amount of time humans have existed on Earth, life after death were accepted as normal and obvious. Virtually everyone believed this to be the case.

Even our distant Neanderthal cousins buried their dead with tools they thought the dearly departed would need in the next life.

Only recently in our scientific age has this traditional belief been questioned. A few hundred years ago it might have been accepted on faith, but now we require empirical facts before we believe anything to be true.

This takes us back to our previous comments about the two types of people who approach the subject of NDEs.

If you are a Christian and believe in the resurrection of Jesus Christ, you already believe in life after death and probably would have no issues with NDEs, either.

Many scientists—although by no means *all* scientists—fall into the first category of people who have previously decided that materialism defines reality. Whatever life after death is, it is certainly not materialistic in the sense that it obeys any physical laws we currently understand. It might be that a deeper understanding of quantum reality will change that idea, but it hasn't done it yet. For these folks, physical death brings oblivion. It's nothing to fear. After all, we're not conscious of it any more than we were conscious of the passage of time before we were born. We simply cease to exist.

Most religious folks fall into the second category of those whose faith demands belief. Even if they secretly harbor doubts, they usually keep those doubts to themselves because almost every major religion demands a certain amount of public declaration of accepted doctrine. That's why many of those who do not practice a particular religion still want clergy to lead their loved one's funeral service. A modicum of comfort goes a long way in assuaging grief and loss.

But what about the people who fall somewhere in between these two categories? Is there a middle ground? Can we believe in life after death without subscribing to a particular religion? Is acceptance of a traditional and personal concept of God necessary to believe that life does not end with physical death? Can we satisfy our natural curiosity without becoming *either* overly religious *or* unduly materialistic?

Spoiler Alert!

I want to make perfectly clear right here at the beginning that I fall into the second category of researchers. I have come to believe, through a lifetime of personal experience working with people who have had NDEs and from my own history with out-of-body experiences, many of which I shared in *The Quantum Akashic Field*, that consciousness, called by many names ("God" being only one of them), is the basis for our being. Our sense perceptions, consisting of smell, sight, taste, touch, and hearing, have evolved to filter out this basic truth in order to protect us from a flood of information that our brains simply cannot handle. The computer in our head would freeze up were it not so.

In this scenario, our brains do not *manufacture* consciousness. They are not *generators* as much as they are *receivers*. Consciousness does not emerge from electrical and chemical processes produced by our bodies. It is the permeating presence of all that is. Physical life springs from consciousness, not the other way around.

This is by no means an established fact. Arguments galore exist in the debate over the meaning of consciousness. No one understands what it is, where it comes from, or how it operates, but cutting-edge studies in the field of quantum physics invoke the presence of an observer to bring about physical reality, so physicists are more and more opening to the idea that consciousness exists independent of human existence.

Indeed, consciousness itself may be the creator that people have worshipped by many names down through the years. I well remember a seminary professor who sought to instill in his students the idea that "Whatever else God is, God is certainly mind." That's just another way of saying consciousness came first.

Read, for instance, these words in *The Holotropic Mind* by Stanislav Grof, a psychiatrist with over 60 years of experience in researching of non-ordinary states of consciousness and one of the founders and chief theoreticians of transpersonal psychology:

> *I now firmly believe that consciousness is more than an accidental by-product of the neurophysiological and biochemical processes taking place in the human brain. I see consciousness and the human psyche as reflections of a cosmic intelligence that permeates the entire universe and all of existence. We are not just highly evolved animals with biological computers embedded inside our skulls; we are also fields of consciousness without limits, transcending time, space, matter, and linear causality.*

The study of life after death implies that we return to this field of consciousness when we die. That, in essence, is what an NDE is. It consists of a return to the nonmaterialistic consciousness that created and permeates the physical cosmos, whether that cosmos consists of a universe or a multiverse. It constitutes a parting of the veil and a glimpse of the other side. It is a momentary return to reality.

Materialism, therefore, is simply a temporary illusion. The song that we all learn as children might be correct: "Life is but a dream." An NDE happens when we momentarily wake up from that dream. We soon fall back to sleep when we re-enter our bodies and return to materialistic existence. But for the rest of our lives, we usually long to return to the embrace of the Dreamer.

That is the basis that forms the rest of this book.

INTRODUCTION

NEW WINE IN NEW WINESKINS

No one pours new wine into old wineskins. Otherwise, the wine will burst the skins, and both the wine and the wineskins will be ruined. No, they pour new wine into new wineskins.

—Mark 2:22

The woman was sharp as a tack, full of vibrant life, but physically old and frail, approaching the end of her life in what has become the modern way of dying. She was not at home, surrounded by family and friends. No, she was in a hospital, following a lengthy stay in a hospice unit, where she had received excellent care. I visited her almost daily for a few weeks. When I learned about her love of old and familiar hymns, I had formed the habit of bringing my guitar with me so I could sing some of her favorites. "In the Garden" and "The Old Rugged Cross" were at the top of the list. Sometimes a nurse or two would stop by to listen and occasionally join in. Sometimes they would wheel in another patient or two to enjoy the concert. It had become an enjoyable part of my routine, if you could call any hospital visit enjoyable.

On this day she seemed especially buoyant and happy to see me. She was half sitting up and smiling to herself when I walked into her room. After a preliminary conversation and a few songs, I packed up my guitar and prepared to leave, assuring her I'd be back the next day. But before I got out the door, she asked what seemed to be a strange question.

"Who did you bring with you?" she said.

I looked around. "There's no one in the room but me," I replied.

"They're out in the hallway," she responded. "They won't come through the portal until you've gone. That's what usually happens."

I was struck by her use of the word "portal," and glanced toward the door. I could see out into the hallway because I was standing at the foot of her bed. But her view was blocked by a partially drawn curtain and the corner of a small bathroom next to the entrance of her room. No one was there.

"Who do you see?" I asked. "Are they hospital staff?"

"Oh, no," she responded. "They come from outside. I think they must like the singing."

She was obviously confused and I didn't want to upset her, so I just nodded, told her I'd come to see her again soon, and walked out of the room. I found only an empty hallway, so I was curious. Before I left the floor, I stopped by the nursing station and talked with a nurse who sometimes joined in the singing.

"Does Hanna get many visitors?" I asked.

"Just a few. Usually family. Most of her friends have passed on."

"Who are the people she said she saw out in the hall?"

"She's been mentioning them for the last few days. I think she's not quite herself. It probably won't be long now."

She died quietly in her sleep a few hours later.

Hanna sensed the presence of spirits outside the door, waiting in the hallway for her.

At her funeral, my wife and I sang "In the Garden," one of Hanna's favorites. But I couldn't help but wonder who, if anyone, was visiting her during her last remaining days on Earth.

For most of my adult life, I have been a clergyman. I was thus supposed to believe in heavenly beings and angelic visitors. In a way, I did. But confession is good for the soul. Or at least they say it is, so this is my confession.

The truth is that during most of my career I was a typically educated, perhaps *overly* educated, left-brained, rational, systematic theologian and teacher who thought such concepts were a bit primitive and a vestige of outdated thinking. I kept such ideas compartmentalized; believing they were probably best left alone so as to comfort those members of my congregation who needed a spiritual crutch to lean on from time to time. And, I must admit, I kind of liked the music about angelic entities. Bach, Handel, and Mendelssohn had made a good living from them, and Christmas wouldn't be the same without old favorites such as "Angels We Have Heard on High" and "Hark! The Herald Angels Sing."

Recently, however, I was visited by a former parishioner who had kept in touch with me after my retirement from ministry. I knew that his mother had recently died, and we spent some time reminiscing about it. I asked him about her final moments.

"It was strange," he recalled. "I was just about to leave her room when she asked who I had brought with me. She definitely saw someone else in the room, even though we were all alone, and she wanted to know who it was."

Alarm bells went off in my head. I had sung this song before, and in the same key.

"Who did you bring with you?" Hanna had asked. My mind went back to other, similar moments over my last 50 years of ministry—memories that I had previously attributed to self-delusion or vivid imagination.

Over the last decade, I have undergone quite a personal transformation, the substance of which I have written about in previous books. Without going into a lot of detail here, I will say that my mind has become open to the concepts of parallel dimensions and out-of-body travel. In terms of life and death, I often look forward to what comes next. Not in a morbid way, certainly, but rather couched in awe-inspired questions about what the journey after death might entail. I have remarked in many podcasts and radio shows that I regret the lost learning experiences I had encountered at deathbeds, when the people undergoing NDEs revealed that they had encountered loved ones or spiritual entities. When I was young and a victim of modern education, I closed my mind to such experiences. Maybe they happened in the past, but they certainly weren't a part of *my* life experience, so I chalked them up to illusions couched in a familiar cultural mythology.

Now, for whatever reasons, I believe. What could I have learned had I been ready to be taught by those who were dying right before my eyes?

Although I am truly sorry for lost opportunities, it's never too late to learn. This book is part of that process. I have come to believe— not only through my own experiences with those who may have glimpsed the other side of the veil, but through solid study of the latest science-based evidence lurking in laboratories filled with measuring devices, charts, and peer-reviewed studies, as well as the complex math of those who seek to penetrate the illusion of daily life through the study of quantum physics, the science of the very small—that there is much more to life and death than we usually acknowledge in our busy, noisy, and fast-paced lives.

How would our existence be different if we could, finally, with the tools of our intellect, pierce the veil between life and death that has been the intuitive, faith-based experience of our race for so many thousands of years? And even more, what if somehow our intellect could substantiate an intuitive acceptance that death is not THE END?

Stories and science. It takes a marriage of both ways of experiencing life and death, but such a marriage, and perhaps *only* such a marriage, can produce a faith that affects every moment of our days.

I'm not talking about religious faith here. I'm not insisting on "becoming" a Buddhist or a Christian or anything else. I'm talking about a faith that takes us beyond the fear of death and stamps its imprint on our daily lives. I'm talking about a faith that stands up to the vicissitudes of problems that infest our waking hours and haunt our sleeping ones. I'm talking about a faith that gives meaning and purpose to every moment. It is based on the sure and certain knowledge that we are much more than physical beings.

In Mark 2:22, the Bible talks about the danger of pouring new wine that has not yet fermented into old, cracked, and brittle wineskins. As the fresh brew begins to work, the old dried-out skins will not be pliable enough to contain the process. They are too rigid and unyielding, ultimately bursting apart and spilling their contents, thus losing the sweet, beneficial potential of the finished batch.

That is a useful metaphor when it comes to examining near-death experiences. Stories about people who have died and come back to life with descriptions about what they experienced are as old as the human race. We've all heard them. But when these stories are recounted in a modern cultural context, which is steeped in scientific fact and the latest medical explanations, they sometimes sound rather fantastic and, to put it simply, unbelievable. The "old wineskins" of mythology, oral history, and ancient religious texts did their job in the past, encompassing fresh, yeasty experiences, but they are often insufficient to handle the new personal stories of people who nowadays often die in hospital rooms while connected to measuring devices that are able to pinpoint exactly what is happening to both brain and body during the death process.

The old oral history and mythology of the past is rather like the old wineskin mentioned in the Bible into which new wine should not be poured. Similarly, new tales of NDEs should be couched within our modern experiences and beliefs.

The new way of death and dying hasn't stopped the stories. Modern medical journals are filled with examples of people who were, without question and by any definition, "dead" according to their charts, but who nevertheless came back to life with vivid recollections of what they experienced beyond the veil that separates this dimension from the next. These journals form "new wineskins," with up-to-date language that propels such experiences into the contemporary age of scientific language and inquiry. Thus, we are no longer left with "old" stories told around a campfire or written into mythologies and religious texts. They are now examined at symposiums, peer-reviewed for accuracy and substance.

In short, we live in an age when old stories of a universal human experience are now being "wedded" to new technologies and insights. We are witnessing the "marriage" of an ancient, intuitive, mystical experience with modern, scientific, measurable principles.

Hence, the outline of this book is couched in advice from an old 19th-century English rhyme that is often given to brides before a marriage ceremony. They are told to celebrate the coming union with "something old, something new, something borrowed, and something blue."

We'll look at "old" stories that have stood the test of time—stories familiar to all of those who have ever seriously considered the "valley of the shadow" that every one of us, without exception, must travel someday.

But we'll also consider the "new" stories of those who have died while hooked up to the latest data-gathering instruments, which deal with facts and statistics that eliminate any possibility of human error when it comes to determining whether a person, in fact, died. This section will examine more recent near-death experiences found in medical journals and discussed by peer-reviewed panels convened for just this purpose. It will also contain chapters detailing recently declassified reports from U.S. Army programs that studied the subject. It will include the latest scientific studies produced at institutions such as the Institute of Noetic Sciences (IONS), a research center and direct-experience lab specializing in the intersection of science and human experience, and The Monroe Institute (TMI), an education and research organization devoted to the exploration of human consciousness. We will glance into the workings of the International Association for Near-Death Studies (IANDS), as well, and view the main clearinghouse for NDE research.

Moving on to "something borrowed," we will highlight how various fields of academic study, such as the study of quantum physics, religion, neurology, biology, anthropology, and dream research, are "borrowing" from each other as their parameters overlap and combine.

Finally, we will consider "something blue." The chapters in this final section will deal with the unexplained phenomenon of waking dreams and intuitive visions that come to us "out of the blue." It will delve into the insights and information that people who underwent NDEs bring back as a result of their experience and examine the field of universal consciousness that seems to be at the core of the whole subject.

Hopefully, this will leave us open to utilizing new wineskins or a new framework of modern language and science-based thinking to describe an old experience that is forever new and vibrantly active because death will undoubtedly happen to every one of us.

NDEs are not just a mystical experience. They are a connection with the very ground of our being—the essential reality that forms the basis for life itself. If a theory of everything is to be found and articulated, it will very likely have to involve a definition of consciousness. Only then will we arrive at the under-standing that we are more than just our physical bodies and begin to explore our full human potential.

PART I
SOMETHING OLD

Scholars have analyzed mystical and historical possible experiences of NDE in ancient civilizations (Pharaonic Egypt, Mesopotamia, Vedic India, Greco-Roman Antiquity, pre-Buddhist China, Himalayan Buddhism, pre-Columbian Meso-America).

—Philippe Charlier,
Resuscitation Journal, May 28, 2014

Near-death experiences, or NDEs, are often triggered during life-threatening episodes when the body is injured by a heart attack, shock, or blunt trauma such as a car accident or fall. People who have undergone these experiences describe being detached from the body, becoming pain-free, seeing a bright light at the end of a tunnel, or experiencing dreams or visions that are not just different from normal perception but more vivid and more "real" than usual reality.

These phenomena are sometimes explained away by saying they are brought on by a loss of blood flow and oxygen to the brain, but why this should happen has never quite been justified. Why feelings of bliss, peace, and love, rather than pain or panic, would result from trauma still remains a mystery, but, on average, one out of every 10 patients who experience cardiac arrest in a hospital setting undergoes such an episode. After they are revived, they tell stories of leaving their bodies behind and encountering a realm beyond everyday existence. The boundaries of space and time no longer confine them. The overwhelming consensus is that the experience felt not only powerful but mystical, and their lives are almost always transformed.

In the vast majority of cases, the experience is positive. Those are the ones that are usually reported. But it cannot be denied that negative experiences are recalled as well. A few are frightening, marked by intense terror, anguish, loneliness, and despair. We might simply assume that social stigma and pressure to conform to the prototype of the typical peaceful, blissful NDE make some people keep their negative experience to themselves, much like trying to forget a particularly uncomfortable nightmare. It's easy to dismiss such experiences as flights of unfettered fancy, but their commonalities and universality, spanning broad cultural differences, are as old as the human race.

Dreams and imaginative visions are usually soon forgotten, but the vivid details of an NDE are often remembered in perfect clarity for decades. Indeed, the phrase "more real than real" is a very common one used by those who often struggle with words that just can't describe the event.

The experience of seeing through the veil is as old as humans who have been able to recount them. Here are some examples from antiquity.

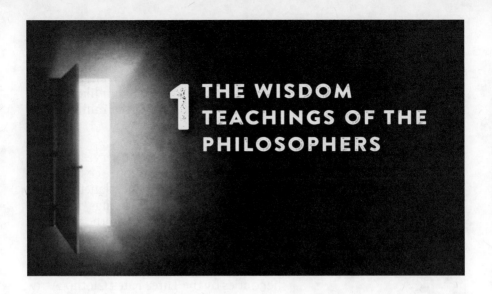

1 THE WISDOM TEACHINGS OF THE PHILOSOPHERS

For the mind does not require filling like a bottle, but rather, like wood, it only requires kindling to create in it an impulse to think independently and an ardent desire for the truth.

—Plutarch

Toward the middle of the 4th century B.C.E., a trio of the world's best-known teachers lived in ancient Greece. They were the founders of modern-day philosophy. Any philosophers who lived before them were called "pre-Socratics." Most people, even if they know nothing about the field of philosophy, know the names of Socrates, his pupil Plato, and Plato's student, Aristotle. Aristotle went on to become the private tutor of Alexander the Great.

In Plato's *Republic*, he mentions a speech by Socrates, in which Socrates remembers the near-death experience of a "warrior bold" who went by the name of Er the Pamphylian.

According to Socrates, Er was killed in battle. Tradition has it that his body was placed on a funeral pyre after a period of some 12 days. Before the fires were lit, however, Er came to life with quite a story to tell. His "soul went forth from his body" and "journeyed with a great company" to a "mysterious region where there were two openings side by side in the earth." He observed disembodied people traveling either up or down in space, depending on the kinds of lives they had lived. After seven days they were told they

The Greek philosopher Socrates related a tale of a warrior named Er, who was thought to be dead, only to spring to life 12 days later to tell about his experiences in the afterlife.

must journey on, and after another four days they saw "a straight light like a pillar, most nearly resembling the rainbow, but brighter and purer."

This pillar seemed to serve as a kind of hinge or pivot for the entire cosmos. The movements of the stars and planets, as well as the fates of all living beings, revolved around this central pivot. In the words of Socrates, it was if the central pivot was the shaft of a spindle that "turned on the knees of Ananke," a goddess who was assisted in her duties by the Three Fates: Clotho, Atropos, and Lachesis.

As Er watched, many souls who had died prepared to reincarnate to another life on earth.

One man, for instance, had died before experiencing any of the terrors of the underground. Because he had been rewarded in heaven, he decided to live his next life in complete opposition to his previous one, so he chose to be a powerful dictator. When he studied the implications of his choice, however, he discovered that among the atrocities he had chosen to commit, one was that he was to eat his own children.

Er learned that this often happened. People who were punished for their past sins often chose a better life next time. But those who had lived good lives wanted to experience something different, so they chose evil. Animals were even part of the process. Most chose to return as humans, while humans often chose the apparently easier lives of animals.

After making a choice about how to live their next life, each soul was assigned a guardian spirit to help them in their journey. They then passed before the throne of Ananke, also called Lady Necessity, before journeying to the Plain of Oblivion, through which flowed the river Lethe, or the River of Forgetfulness. There, each soul was required to drink some of the water, after which they forgot everything about their past lives and what had happened in the afterlife. After drinking the water, they lay down at night to sleep. During the night, they were lifted up and carried off to begin their new life.

Er, however, was suddenly drawn back to his body before he had a chance to drink any water, therefore returning to life with his memory intact. He recovered in time to see his body laid out on a funeral pyre. Thus, he was able to sit up and draw attention to himself before being burned to death, and he told those gathered for his funeral what he had experienced.

It's a fascinating story, to be sure. Most professors teach their students that this is merely a story invented by Plato and attributed to Socrates, similar to his even more famous myth about the lost continent of Atlantis. Its purpose, so they claim, is to teach students about the importance of living a good, moral life and to explain why evil exists in the world.

This may, indeed, be true. But the problem encountered with this explanation is the same as that surrounding the legend of Atlantis. Plato presents more detail than is necessary to make his point. Yes, the story of Er the Pamphylian is an entertaining way to teach the importance of living a good, ethical life, just as the story of Atlantis is an entertaining allegory about human hubris.

But Plato nowhere declares this to be only allegory. Could it be based on the experience of an actual person, just as Atlantis might be based on a historical incident? At the very least, the story illustrates the fact that even more than 2,300 years ago, the Greeks were familiar with the typical aspects of a modern NDE.

Er, the hero of the story, experiences an out-of-body sensation, a landscape foreign to normal human experience, judgment involving a life review, and a sudden return to earthly life. These are all aspects of a classic NDE. Either Plato must have been aware of the stages of the process in order to utilize them in this fashion or he somehow made up a series of events that would later become standardized all around the world.

We often think that concepts of reincarnation came from India, but here is a fully formed example of the doctrine found in ancient Greece. Pythagoras, who lived before Plato and coined the term *philosophy*, had been teaching his students about reincarnation as a matter of course. He claimed to have remembered eight

Plato, the student of Socrates, explained that we could have past lives that we simply forget all about in our current lives.

previous lives himself and taught his pupils techniques whereby they could recall their own past lives.

Democritus, who invented the term "atom," meaning "uncuttable," back in 400 B.C.E., believed that all matter was reducible down to small particles he called *atomos*. Obviously, the Greeks knew as much about the material aspects of life as we do today.

Plato even dealt with the idea of forgetting the details of past lives. He used the phrase "event boundary." His definition is somewhat akin to someone today going to the kitchen to get something out of the refrigerator, and then forgetting what it was that prompted the trip. We can all identify with that.

He believed that all of life was a choice. His story about Er suggests this very belief. Did he make it up, or did he hear it from people who had undergone a near-death experience? His teaching is so matter-of-fact that it seems obvious he didn't need to go into a lot of explanation, implying his students were already familiar with the process.

Another example can be found in the works of Plutarch, who lived some four hundred years after Plato. In his work *On the Delay of the Divine Justice*, he tells the story of a man from Cilicia originally named Aridaeus, but whose name was changed to Thespesius after his brief sojourn in the "other world."

Thespesius, it seems, had fallen from a great height and sustained a concussion, killing him instantly. On the third day after the accident, at his funeral, he came back from the dead, and related a strange story of having a sensation of "his intelligence being driven from his body." He claimed he could see in all directions, "as if his soul was a single eye."

This is a common testimony of people today who experienced an NDE. They claim to see in a complete 360-degree arc. It took him a while to get used to what his new body could do in terms of movement and awareness, but when he did, he "recognized one soul, that of a kinsman, though not distinctly, as he was but a child when the kinsman died. It drew near and said: 'Greetings, Thespesius.'" The kinsman became a guide to help Thespesius view the various regions of the afterlife.

This account is very similar to testimonies today, when people claim that after death they are met by long-lost relatives who usher them into their new experience.

Four centuries after Plato, another Greek, Plutarch, related another return-from-death tale in the form of Thespesius of Cilicia, who died of a concussion but recovered three days later.

The guide showed Thespesius "a great chasm extending all the way down ... called the place of Lethe ... and another deep chasm in the ambient which was a large crater with streams pouring into it, one whiter than sea-foam or snow, another like the violet of the rainbow, and others of different tints, each, when seen from afar, having a luster of its own. These regions were the abode of those who were suffering punishment."

The "final spectacle of his vision" was a view of "souls returning to a second birth, as they were forcibly bent to fit all manner of living things and altered in shape by the framers of these." There he met a woman who suddenly pulled him away with a cord. He felt a "strong and violent gust of wind upon his body," opened his eyes, and found he was back in his body at his grave site.

There is, obviously, no way to interview these people. They died a few thousand years ago. And we can't enter the minds of Plato and Plutarch to see what they were thinking. But at the very least, their words illustrate that even back then, people were familiar with typical near-death experiences that show an uncanny similarity to those found down through the ages and into today.

But there is another good source of material about NDEs that goes back a long way. It is probably familiar to many people who have never studied ancient philosophical texts, and who might even consider it a more reputable source of information. It consists of letters written by a man who came to be known as Paul the Apostle.

2 FROM THE PAGES OF THE BIBLE

Then some Jews came from Antioch and Iconium and won the crowd over. They stoned Paul and dragged him outside the city, thinking he was dead. But after the disciples had gathered around him, he got up and went back into the city.

—Acts 14:19-20

Three times in the Hebrew Scriptures—that portion of the Bible Christians call the Old Testament—and seven times in the New Testament, people were raised from the dead. The stories of Elijah and Elisha performing this feat are told in First and Second Kings. The story of Jesus coming back from the dead is well known, thanks to the accounts given in the Gospels. Those same books tell us that Jesus himself, during his earthly life, brought people back from the dead. His followers Peter and Paul were said to have performed the same feat.

But arguably the most detailed account of this happening is found in the story of the Apostle Paul.

Twelve miles (20 km) inland from the Mediterranean Sea lies the Adana-Mersin metropolitan area of Turkey. With a current population of some 3 million people, it is the modern country's fourth-largest city.

Two thousand years ago it was a major trade center called Tarsus, a city in eastern Cilicia that was part of the Roman province of Syria. It has become famous for one of its most important citizens, a man named Saul.

His parents, being devout Jews, named him after the first great king of Israel, no doubt hoping he would grow into such an august moniker. He did just that, but at the height of his fame and power, he changed his name to Paul, which means "little," "small," or "tiny."

Young Saul wanted to be a Jewish scholar but prudently developed a day job that he could fall back on. In his own words from one of his letters (1 Corinthians 4:12), he worked "with his own hands" at the tent-making trade. Even after his famous conversion to Christianity he continued his occupation at least part-time. He traveled with a few leather-working tools so he could set up shop anywhere to help support himself.

He seems to have been born into a middle-class family who managed to provide him with an excellent education. They sent him to Jerusalem to study with the famous Pharisee scholar Gamaliel, and he emerged from his schooling as a fully accredited Pharisee.

In his own words, Saul was "the best Jew and the best Pharisee of his generation" (Philippians 3:4–6; Galatians 1:13–14). He sought to make his teachers proud by persecuting the early Christian Jesus cult that had sprung up throughout the area.

While on a journey of about 135 miles (218 km) from Jerusalem to Damascus, he had an encounter that changed not only *his* life, but the future of the whole world.

> Saul ... went to the high priest and asked him for letters to the synagogues in Damascus, so that if he found any there who belonged to the Way, whether men or women, he might take them as prisoners to Jerusalem. As he neared Damascus on his journey, suddenly a light from heaven flashed around him. He fell to the ground and heard a voice say to him, "Saul, Saul, why do you persecute me?"
>
> "Who are you, Lord?" Saul asked.
>
> "I am Jesus, whom you are persecuting," he replied. "Now get up and go into the city, and you will be told what you must do."

The men traveling with Saul stood there speechless; they heard the sound but did not see anyone. Saul got up from the ground, but when he opened his eyes, he could see nothing. So they led him by the hand into Damascus. For three days he was blind, and did not eat or drink anything.

In Damascus there was a disciple named Ananias. The Lord called to him in a vision, "Ananias!"

"Yes, Lord," he answered.

The Lord told him, "Go to the house of Judas on Straight Street and ask for a man from Tarsus named Saul, for he is praying. In a vision he has seen a man named Ananias come and place his hands on him to restore his sight."

"Lord," Ananias answered, "I have heard many reports about this man and all the harm he has done to your holy people in Jerusalem. And he has come here with authority from the chief priests to arrest all who call on your name."

The conversion of St. Paul was a popular subject for many works of art over the centuries (pictured is *The Conversion of Saint Paul* [1690] by Luca Giordano). The description of what happened to Saul has some things in common with near-death experiences. In a metaphorical way, it indeed was about death and rebirth.

But the Lord said to Ananias, "Go! This man is my chosen instrument to proclaim my name to the Gentiles and their kings and to the people of Israel. I will show him how much he must suffer for my name."

Then Ananias went to the house and entered it. Placing his hands on Saul, he said, "Brother Saul, the Lord Jesus, who appeared to you on the road as you were coming here, has sent me so that you may see again and be filled with the Holy Spirit." Immediately, something like scales fell from Saul's eyes, and he could see again. He got up and was baptized, and after taking some food, he regained his strength.

—Acts 9:1-19

Ever after, Saul was known as the Apostle Paul. Because he was converted after Jesus had died and only met him in a vision after the resurrection, he thought of himself as being somewhat different from the disciples who followed Jesus in life: "And last of all he appeared to me also, as to one abnormally born."

> **What makes his letter to the Corinthians so important is that Paul apparently underwent an NDE that changed his life.**

In other words, Paul came to his faith by a different road. These verses don't specifically say that Paul's experience was an NDE, but we can assume it was because of something he said 14 years later when he wrote his second letter to the Christian church that met at Corinth.

I know a man in Christ who fourteen years ago was caught up to the third heaven. Whether it was in the body or out of the body I do not know—God knows. And I know that this man—whether in the body or apart from the body I do not know, but God knows—was caught up to paradise and heard inexpressible things, things that no one is permitted to tell.

—2 Corinthians 12:2-4

It's possible that in this passage Paul was remembering another time he was left for dead. That experience is quoted at the beginning of this chapter. Although the time frame seems to indicate that he was referring to his initial experience on the road to Damascus, *when* it happened isn't as important to our study as *what* happened.

What makes his letter to the Corinthians so important is that Paul apparently underwent an NDE that changed his life. He waited for 14 years to reveal it. That's a common tendency for those who have such an experience. They often wait for the passage of time before they are ready to tell their story. His testimony involves trauma, a bright light, an out-of-body experience, a meeting with a being of light, and a return, complete with his discovery that language is inappropriate for a real description of what he experienced. These are all classic, indeed, common, recollections of a modern NDE.

Paul was left with physical scars from this experience. He apparently lost much of his vision, a fact that he might be referring to when he much later called it "a thorn in the flesh."

> *To keep me from becoming conceited because of the surpassing greatness of the revelations, a thorn was given me in the flesh, a messenger of Satan to harass me, to keep me from becoming conceited. Three times I pleaded with the Lord about this, that it should leave me. But he said to me, "My grace is sufficient for you, for my power is made perfect in weakness" … for when I am weak, then I am strong.*

—2 Corinthians 12

What this infirmity consisted of is a matter of debate. The best guess is that he was left partially blind. He freely admits that he had to dictate his letters, and when he signed them himself to verify their authenticity, he often remarked about the big letters he was forced to use: "See what large letters I use as I write to you with my own hand!" (Galatians 6:11).

For our purposes, the religious implications of this story aren't as important as a fact often overlooked when theologians explore these texts. They are, by their very nature, religious scholars, so they quite reasonably look for spiritual lessons. But

Paul wrote of his miraculous experiences in his epistles to the Corinthians, including his out-of-body experience (*Paul Writing His Epistles* by 17th-century painter Valentin de Boulogne).

in doing so they often miss something very important. Paul's story may seem highly significant, couched as it is in words straight from the Bible, but what people often overlook is that when compared to the vast storehouse of near-death experiences now on record, it is very ordinary.

Think about the various steps in the account:

· A man is involved in what, up until then, is his usual daily activity.

· He undergoes a violent episode of some kind. In Saul's case, he falls from his horse, probably bringing about some kind of physical trauma that his companions did not immediately understand. The head trauma leaves him blind, and he seems to have been in a coma that lasted for three days, during which he "did not eat or drink anything."

· He encounters a great light and hears a loud voice.

- During this experience, he sees a being of light that somehow communicates with him. In Saul's case, he asked what now seems like a very silly question: "Who is it?" The question is comical because Saul answers it himself even before the final question mark: "Who is it, Lord?"

- He later was unable to find words that described what he had experienced: "[I] heard inexpressible things, things that no one is permitted to tell."

- Upon regaining his senses, Saul's life and belief system is so radically altered that he even changes his name from Saul to Paul—from a rather grandiose name to one that signifies humbleness. It's hard to think that St. Paul's nickname was "tiny," but that's exactly what happened.

- He comes back from his NDE with a changed attitude and a changed life. From a theology of exclusion and hatred he became a missionary of inclusion and love.

As we shall soon see when we read more NDE accounts, collected from stories of people down through the ages, this follows the pattern of a rather typical NDE. And it comes not from the pages of modern books and YouTube videos. It has been right in front of us for 2,000 years, available to anyone who opens a Bible.

3 SACRED TEXTS FROM GREAT RELIGIONS

You will never understand the meaning of actual reality.

—Tibetan Book of the Dead

NDEs have been known ever since ancient times. In his book *Anecdotes de Médecine*, Pierre-Jean du Monchaux, an 18th-century French military doctor, was probably the first medical journalist to report on them, but the *Tibetan Book of the Dead* goes back to the mid-14th century and seems to have been written from experience. It attempts to show how to achieve liberation in the moment of death and thus fulfill our potential as spiritually awakened beings.

It is difficult to imagine how the references in the book could have been simply made up out of someone's imagination. They are much too specific. Instead, they sound very much like first-person accounts. They also echo the familiar stages of even modern NDEs, including the past-life review:

> *Death holds up an all-seeing mirror, "the mirror of past actions," to our eyes, in which the consequences of all our negative and positive actions are clearly seen and there is a weighing of our past actions in the light of their consequences, the balance of which will determine the kind of existence or mental state we are being driven to enter.*

> —Graham Coleman,
> president of the Orient Foundation

In commentating on these instructions, Robert Thurman, author of many books that have popularized Buddhism in Western culture, offers this advice from Guru Padmasambhava, also known as Guru Rinpoche ("precious master"):

> There is no reason for a sound faith to be irrational. A useful faith should not be blind, but should be well aware of its grounds. A sound faith should be able to use scientific investigation to strengthen itself. It should be open to the spirit not to lock itself up in the letter. A nourishing, useful, healthful faith should be no obstacle to developing a science of death.

> —Padmasambhava and Robert A. F. Thurman

People using an old expression, often used in jest, sometimes say: "My life flashed before my eyes!" But this is a common feature found in many religious texts.

Ancient Jewish sources seem to echo modern NDE testimonies with uncanny accuracy. The Babylonian *Talmud*, written somewhere around 400 C.E., tells us: "For three days the soul hovers over the body and observes." It assures us that even people who died what appears to be a violent death, and are then resuscitated, report their death was amazingly calm and peaceful.

The Talmud records that

> at the hour of a person's departure to his eternal home, all his deeds are enumerated before him and are rendered visible to him once again, and the deeds themselves say to him: You did such and such, in such and such a place, on such and such a day, and he says: Yes, that is exactly what happened.

Other Jewish sources tell of meeting friends and loved ones who have spiritual bodies, and Christian hymnals contain songs about angelic beings or some kind of divine presence. Here is only one example:

> Oh, 'tis a glorious land,
> That land above;
> There is no sorrow there,

All, all is love.
There tears shall never start,
But love shall warm each heart,
And friends shall never part;
No, nevermore.

—"Angel Band," J. William Suffern

One of the most vivid descriptions of a trip into a totally different reality comes from the Quran:

The Talmud contains passages that relate testimonies of those whose experiences could easily be described as NDEs.

After the Prophet took this night jour-
ney from Masjid al-Haram to Masjid al-
Aqsa, he ascended to the upper heavens.

When the Prophet and Jibril arrived at the first heaven,
Jibril requested the gate to be opened. The angel assigned
to that gate asked Jibril, "Who is with you?" Jibril an-
swered, "It is Muhammad."

The angel asked Jibril, "Was he dispatched? Is it time for
him to ascend to the heaven?"

Jibril said, "Yes."

So, the gate was opened for him, and Prophet Muham-
mad entered the first heaven.

The text goes on to describe a series of visions Muhammad had after he had been "dispatched." He ascended through various stages of being called heavens, in which he was able to identify well-known biblical characters such as Adam, some of the patriarchs of Judaism, and the prophets Enoch and Moses, all of whom welcomed him with love and joy.

Finally, he reached the "seventh heaven":

Then the Prophet ascended to the seventh heaven, and
that is where our Messenger saw Prophet Abraham. The
Prophet saw Prophet Abraham with his back against al-
Bayt al-Ma'mur. To the inhabitants of the skies, al-Bayt
al-Ma'mur is like the Ka'bah is to us, the inhabitants of

the Earth. Every day 70,000 angels go there; then exit from it, and never return. The next day another 70,000 angels go, come out, and never return. This will continue until the Day of Judgment. In this, there is an indication as to the greatness of the numbers of the angels—their numbers are far more than the numbers of the humans and the devils together.

In the Quran, the Prophet Muhammad is transported by the winged Buraq, which also allows him to travel from Mecca to Jerusalem in one night. He then was accompanied by the archangel Jibril on a trip to Heaven.

As his vision continued, he entered what he called Paradise, giving some of us hope, because most of the inhabitants who lived there were poor during their earthly lives:

He saw examples of the inhabitants of Paradise and how their situation would be. He saw most of the inhabitants of Paradise are the poor people.

The Quran continues his story in great detail, but it is interesting to note the many similarities between the experience of Muhammad and many modern accounts of NDEs in contemporary literature. At the very least, it is proof that these experiences seem to be almost identical, despite geographical and cultural differences. In other words, people who live at different times, come from different cultures, speak different languages, and have different levels of education all seem to have the same experience.

Sometimes they use different words to describe what happened to them. That is to be expected. As we have already seen, language was invented to describe things on *this* side of the material fence.

If a Christian sees a being of light, he or she would be expected to describe that being as Jesus. A Muslim would be inclined to see Allah, and a Jew, Moses or Elijah. An atheist would describe a spiritual entity without a particular name, while a Buddhist would incline toward a particularly revered enlightened guru.

The importance of an NDE is not that it describes what is *actually* on the other side of the veil. It lies instead in the fact that there *is* another side, and sometimes we can see it. We might not be able to say with complete accuracy "This is what it is there," but we can say "This is what it is like."

The founders of all the great religions of the world had an initial numinous, shamanic-like experience. It shaped their lives, as well as the lives of those who would come later. Problems developed when their followers, over the course of many years, dogmatized that initial experience and fenced in their ranks with doctrines and rules. But when we return to the initial experiences, we find them very similar in nature.

A Buddhist traveling to the other side might describe seeing a being of light as a guru, an enlightened being who may also serve as a mentor.

Those who study out-of-body phenomena, including NDEs, estimate that some 2% of the earth's population, at any given moment in history, possesses the ability to spontaneously see through the veil of our perception fence—that is, the barrier that has evolved to allow us to experience our material surroundings. People such as Albert Einstein and Thomas Edison have contributed to sudden, some might even say quantum, intuitive leaps of understanding.

If this is true now, it seems probable that it is a trait that has been with us from our beginnings as a species. It might even be possible that this is an ability that has somewhat atrophied lately because of the technological, left-brained tendencies that have increased exponentially over the last few centuries. If that is the case, our ancestors might very well have experienced this phenomenon to a greater degree than we do today.

Whatever the case may be, we know from the fields of anthropology and archaeology that at least 40,000 years ago, and probably much earlier, humans experienced the biggest single evolutionary leap we ever took. We "got religion." Scientists call it symbolic thinking. We began to draw pictures on cave walls and rock outcroppings that indicate knowledge of parallel worlds or, as some might say, spiritual dimensions. We haven't been the same since.

The question now becomes rather obvious. Did our ancestors "discover" supernatural realities, or did those realities discover us?

Are gods the invention of ancient humans, or did the gods learn how to break through to us? Did intelligent beings from a parallel reality see some potential in us? Could it be possible that these beings even manipulated our DNA so as to begin the process of making us over "in their image"?

Alternatively, was DNA manipulation somehow programmed by evolution to automatically kick in when we evolved to a certain stage? If so, might this happen again in the future? Are there more hidden messages lying dormant in so-called "junk" DNA, ready to awaken when the time is right?

In other words, are we yet a work in progress? Did that process begin some 40,000 years ago, or even 4 billion years ago when life sprang into existence out of non-life? Was that process revealed to those who underwent near-death experiences that were later recorded and preserved in religious texts that have become part of our culture?

If so, we might be tempted to conclude that NDEs are a product of religious imagination. If we do so, however, we would be mistaken. Sometimes religious training has nothing to do with them.

As we shall soon see, previous religious experience isn't necessary to experience an NDE, but an NDE is almost always perceived as a religious experience.

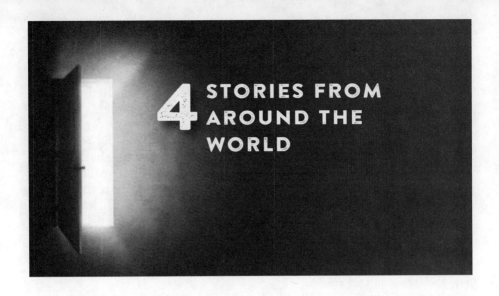

4 STORIES FROM AROUND THE WORLD

My breath was out and I died. All at once I saw a shining light—great light—trying my soul. I looked and saw my body had no soul—looked at my own body—it was dead.

—Squ-sacht-un, the founder
of the Indian Shaker Church

In 1881, a man named Squ-sacht-un, of the Squaxin Island Tribe in what was then known as Washington Territory, became very ill. Eventually he was pronounced dead, and his wife, Mary, began funeral preparations. She sent for a casket, which was eventually delivered by canoe. The casket was just sighted coming down river when Squ-sacht-un revived and began to recount a curious story.

His soul, he said, had ascended to a house where a man asked him if he believed in God. Inside the house he was shown a picture of himself. Somehow that picture illustrated all the bad deeds he had committed in life. He then witnessed people he knew being burned in a furnace. After many similar experiences he met God and was given a choice between returning to earth or going to the hell of fire he had witnessed.

He was then shown a beautiful, light-filled world and experienced feelings of peace and comfort. He was forever transformed by the experience, later claiming, "I have seen a great light

Squ-sacht-un (John Slocum) built his first Indian Shaker Church in Mud Bay, Washington, in 1892 after experiencing an NDE in which he had visions of heaven and hell.

in my soul from that good land. I now understood all Christ wants us to do. Before I came alive, I saw I was a sinner."

After returning from his NDE, Squ-sacht-un fulfilled the promise he'd made in the spirit world. He began to teach Christianity as interpreted through his Native American culture. This was the foundation of the Indian Shaker Church. The name was derived from the curious ecstatic shaking that became the hallmark of prayer for the new church.

Unlike other Christian denominations, the new religion was not centered around the Bible. Their guiding light came from the experience of Squ-sacht-un, who was named John Slocum by the white culture that surrounded him.

Things were not easy, especially at the beginning. There was a lot of opposition and hostility from whites who feared an Indian uprising. For a while, all Indian religious practices, including those of the Shakers, were banned from any kind of worship. Some members were arrested and spent time in prison.

This notice, for instance, was posted by the U.S. Indian Service at the Quileute Reservation:

> *Notice to the Shakers: You are hereby permitted to hold meetings ... under the following conditions: on Sundays not longer than three hours at one time and on Wednesdays not longer than two hours at one time.*

> *The following REGULATIONS to be observed: First, keep windows or a door open during all meetings. Second, use only one bell to give signals. Not continuous ringing. Third, do not admit school children at night meetings. It has been reported that there are some women who are violating the Rules and that they shake at all hours of the day and night. You will therefore tell the women quietly to stop shaking at any other times than the times specified in the rules. If they do not stop, you will lock them up until they agree to stop. Shaking of the sick must*

not be allowed. We do not want any trouble in this matter if it is possible to avoid it, but continual and private shaking must be stopped.

Nevertheless, the beginning of the 21st century found some 20 congregations and about 2,000 members still practicing. Back in the 1960s, they even proved their Christian tendencies by suffering a rupture in their church, a common trait of Protestant denominations through the years. The conservatives continued to reject written religious material. The liberals wanted to include the Bible and some other texts. But the two denominations still exist side by side, like Methodists and Presbyterians, practicing their faith on the Northwest Coast in Washington, Oregon, California, and British Columbia.

It all began with an NDE. In 1893, Louis Yowaluch, then the head of the church, recognized the initial experience that inspired it: "We heard from John Slocum that there was a God. We had never heard of such a thing as a man dying and bringing back the word that there was a God."

This wasn't just a local phenomenon. There are other examples of early North American Indians reporting how NDEs shaped their culture and belief system.

In 1634, the Innu of eastern Quebec and Labrador, a century and a half earlier than the Indian Shaker Church and on the other side of the continent, were visited by Paul Le Jeune, a French Jesuit missionary. He was told that what they know about the afterlife was revealed to them by two of their own people who had traveled to the "spirit world" and returned. They objected to Le Jeune's teachings concerning heaven and hell. According to the Innu, based on the evidence of their people who had had NDEs there is only one realm waiting for those who die. Everyone goes there, without judgment.

The Innu people of Quebec and Labrador (Innu traders shown here in 1903) traditionally believe that all people go to the same spirit world after they die.

On the other side of the world, the religions that make up Hinduism share a long, long history. Oral legends can be traced back for 6,000 years, and written accounts that are almost that old tell about the fantastic after-death journeys of various gurus and mystics. Given this kind of culture, it could logically be assumed that any account of a near-death experience coming out of India might have been influenced by an exposure to such teaching from an early age.

But what about the curious childhood experience of American Colton Burpo? He was just shy of four years old when he experienced the events that led him to be the featured star of both a book and a movie called *Heaven Is for Real*. The author was his father, who may be accused of bias, but he certainly had a first-row seat for what transpired. He did not report secondhand information. He was there when it happened.

The three-year-old Colton not only had a near-death experience made up of all the usual trappings that supposedly could have been brought about by biology, chemicals, and electrical impulses in the brain. Those could be explained away. But how could Colton possibly have known *after* his experience about things that had happened *before* it and that had never been told to him?

For example, when Colton came back to life after an emergency appendectomy, he told everyone that he had met his second sister. His parents had never told him about the sad episode of his mother's miscarriage. He also said he had met his great-grandfather, who had died 24 years before Colton was born. Despite the

The 2014 movie adaptation of *Heaven Is for Real*, Greg Kinnear (right) is the father of a little boy who describes heaven and the people in it after a near-death experience.

fact that a quarter of a century separated them, Colton could describe him as he looked in his 20s down to the smallest detail.

We can expect someone who has been born and raised in a culture that honors after-death realities to be open to such experiences. But how was young Colton able to recognize and know about two people he had never met or, in the case of his sister, had never even known about?

It's a mystery. The value of such stories is found not only in their detail and content but in the fact that they all point to something beyond material life. We are reminded of the faith-filled final words of the great composer Johann Sebastian Bach: "Don't cry for me. I go where music is born."

Apparently, near-death experiences go way back in time and are told in virtually every culture. Gregory Shushan, in his book *Near-Death Experience in Indigenous Religions*, reaffirms the fact that near-death experiences are not a new discovery:

> *NDEs have been popularly recognized in the West since the mid-1970s, but people from the largest empires to the smallest hunter-gatherer societies have been having them throughout history. Accounts are found in ancient sacred texts, historical documents, the journals of explorers and missionaries, and the ethnographic reports of anthropologists. Among the hundreds I've collected are those of a 7th-century B.C.E. Chinese provincial ruler, a 4th-century B.C.E. Greek soldier, a 12th-century Belgian saint, a 15th-century Mexican princess, an 18th-century British admiral, a 19th-century Ghanaian victim of human sacrifice, and a Soviet man who'd apparently killed himself but was revived during resuscitation experiments. NDEs can happen to followers of any religion, and to those of none.*

It is worth noting how exposure to these stories often leads to dramatic life changes. Even in ancient times, as reported by Sandra Ingerman and Hank Wesselman in their book *Awakening to the Spirit World: The Shamanic Path of Direct Revelation*, shamans have traditionally been people who have had a near-death experience. Sometimes that experience marks the beginning of a shamanic career.

In another of her books, the 1991 *Soul Retrieval*, Ingerman commented on her own such experiences. As quoted by psychologist J. Timothy Green in his article "The Near-Death Experience as a Shamanic Initiation: A Case Study," Ingerman said:

> *In my own near-death experience in 1971, I too was received by the light. For me, this light represented the Father and Mother God. I started thinking about God's being pure light. The Bible says that God created man in his own image. What that means to me, then, is that we are really balls of light. I started to experience myself as being light surrounded by matter, the body. We are a body; we have a mind; and we have this beautiful light that shines in us that is Spirit, which connects us to the divine.*

Having opened the door to NDEs being a mark of the initial shamanic initiation experience, we need to examine this subject in more depth.

Many of us grew up with an idea of shamanism that was shaped at least partially by old copies of *National Geographic* magazine. Until the last few decades, it was assumed that shamans were primitive, superstitious—and, let's face it, stoned—savages who lived in Peru, South Africa, or Siberia.

The word "shaman," properly used, should only apply to indigenous practitioners of medicine in Russia's Siberian region. So, for example, a medicine man in North America is technically not a shaman.

Make no mistake, some still do, and they are among the best in their field. But many modern shamans live very comfortably in modern society. You may have friends who practice the craft and never let on to you that they do so. Being a shaman is almost always a part-time position. They can't go to the metaphysical landscapes they visit and stay there. It would probably drive them mad. After a shamanic journey, no matter how vivid and spectacular the trip, they must come home and do the laundry, like everyone else.

The definition of the word "shaman" has changed in the last few decades. It was originally a Siberian term but has since been attached to indigenous practitioners who were once called medicine men, priests, or even witch doctors. It is now a catchall, universal term that is usually employed by outsiders who haven't caught up to the latest usage. It might not be a fully accurate label, but it's used as such anyway. So, what is a shaman?

In 1980, Michael Harner wrote a groundbreaking book called *The Way of the Shaman*. It was not written, as many such books are now, from the perspective of someone who has studied the field from the comfort of his easy chair or computer terminal. Harner didn't learn by studying. He learned by doing.

Most anthropologists before him were trained within an academic doctrine that insisted researchers must observe and not participate. They were, according to the rule of their day, to remain objective, because that was the only way to report accurately.

Harner, to be sure, was a scientist. But he soon realized that a real understanding of shamanism could only come about by participation. How could he possibly provide a physical description of someone who was experiencing an inward journey? Traditionally, shamans didn't write anything down. They felt that the written word polluted the experience. From the very beginning, shamanism has been an oral tradition. Perhaps it was even the very first religious experience.

The genius of Harner's work was that he was the first to find a way to convey the essence of shamanism to a modern audience in words people could understand. Once having accomplished that feat, he didn't write anything more until 2013, when he published his follow-up book, *Cave and Cosmos*. The only reason he wrote the second book at all was that he considered the inevitable approach of death and felt it would be advantageous to share some of the work in core shamanism he had accomplished at his Foundation for Shamanic Studies in Mill Valley, California.

Anthropologist Michael Harner revived interest in traditional shamanism with his 1980 book, *The Way of the Shaman: A Guide to Power and Healing.*

In Michael Harner's *Cave and Cosmos* he said:

While the work of shamans encompasses virtually the full gamut of known spiritual practices, shamanism is universally characterized by an intentional change in consciousness to engage in two-way interaction with spirits. Its most distinctive feature, which is not universal, is the out-of-body journey to other worlds. It should be noted that in some indigenous societies, there are shamans who do not journey at all, and others who journey only in the Middle World or, if they journey beyond the Middle World, may not go to both the Upper and Lower Worlds. What they all share is disciplined interaction with spirits in non-ordinary reality to help and heal others.

A core teaching of shamanism, and the defining element of near-death experiences, is that there is more than one reality.

First, there is the reality of the physical world around us, which consists of matter and extends to the end of the universe. Many who have undergone out-of-body experiences report that they traveled to the farthest reach of the cosmos, and even held the universe in the palms of their hands. But according to the shamanic experience, and NDEs as well, this is only the beginning. Shamans who report such things may have traveled far, but they still haven't left the Middle World.

The Middle World is the arena of the scientist. It consists of matter that can be measured. But even the word "far" isn't usual once we glimpse a spiritual landscape in which "near and far" don't mean anything.

According to modern scientists, what shamans call the Middle World and what Harner calls ordinary reality is bounded by the newly discovered Higgs field.

Shamans recognize that entire realities exist across the veil, on the other side of physical matter. Those are the realms Harner calls nonordinary reality or NOR. Ordinary reality is what I often refer to as our perception realm, but there are realms that cannot be perceived through our five senses, even though we walk, run, and live among and in them.

The word "reality" implies that those realms are just as real and present here as they are there. A vision of those nonordinary realities is what constitutes a near-death experience. Those are the realms that physicists only very recently have detected through the use of complex mathematics. They call it the quantum realm.

In traditional shamanism there are worlds on both sides of our perceptions.

The first consists of what is often called the Lower World. This realm is usually associated with animal spirits, and it might very well have been experienced by the ancient shamans who crawled into the great caves of Europe to render, in vivid pigments, artistic images of the animal envoys they met there.

The Upper and Lower Worlds are just as real as the Middle World, which is the one we currently exist in. Near-death experiences offer glimpses into these other worlds.

The second is the Upper World, and it is usually associated with the images of fairies and angels found in mythologies everywhere. In other words, it is associated with flight. This seems to be the predominant experience of those who experience NDEs. They often talk of being drawn upward, as in flight.

How did it all begin? When did our ancient ancestors first discover the existence of other realms that were outside of this one but still very much "real"? Probably through near-death experiences.

Confidence in sharing these experiences was given a boost in the 1960s. Mind-expanding or consciousness-raising journeys, or "trips," became common with the use of chemicals first found in plant derivatives and later synthesized. They affected areas of the brain that we seldom use in day-to-day life.

There is a reason for this. Our brains evolved to bring order to the world we live in. It doesn't mean other realities don't exist; it just means we have forgotten how to access them. It sometimes takes physical trauma to propel us outside our normal reality. That is often how people experience NDEs.

Estimates vary about how many people have brain chemistry that naturally allows them to spontaneously experience other realities and to see with what some call "sacred" eyes, but for most of us, the windows and doors that open to these realms require more dramatic stimulus. As we age, we learn to close them.

There is a reason for this. Our brains evolved to bring order to the world we live in. It doesn't mean other realities don't exist; it just means we have forgotten how to access them.

Near-death experiences, then, sometimes serve as rather violent methods of accomplishing what some shamans and their students experience through the use of ayahuasca or psychedelic mushrooms. When used correctly, these plants, and combinations of them, are ingested in a sacred manner, after careful preparation. The process is overseen by an experienced shamanic practitioner and is considered a sacred, ritualistic journey, not a recreational "trip."

There are other methods, not so dramatic, that can produce the same effect. Drumming, for instance, or meditation produce the same kind of effect in modern cultures completely divorced from shamanism. American Indian tribes were famous for inducing discomfort, and even pain, through deprivation, such as in the vision quest or, even more extreme, the Sun Dance. In those rituals, near-death experiences were often sought out and encouraged. Indeed, they were the whole point of the exercise.

Shamans are among the oldest religious practitioners known to humankind. They are familiar with the landscape of other worlds and are dedicated to service, often by healing. Thus there seems to be no question that the newly discovered world of quantum physics has been thoroughly traveled by ancient practitioners, many of whom left accurate descriptions of their journeys.

The newly discovered Higgs field has opened whole territories for scientists to explore. There, energy takes on mass. Albert Einstein discovered the central formula for what transpires: $E=mc^2$. What that means is that energy equals, or is the same as, mass times the speed of light squared. Conversely, mass equals energy. The mass of our body is composed of a physical manifestation of energy—energy that slows down as it travels through the Higgs field.

But where does that energy come from? Where does it go when the body dies?

That, in essence, is what a near-death experience is all about. On our side of the Higgs field, where matter reigns supreme, scientists can measure and describe reality to their hearts' content. Many scientists swear that unless we can measure something, it doesn't exist. Matter, according to them, is reality. They might even claim that reality begins when energy takes on mass. Until then, it's only potential. Potential becomes reality only when it collapses into their observation window.

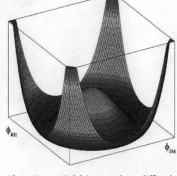

The Higgs Field is a rather difficult concept to visualize and explain to a non-scientist, but, essentially, it is a scalar field that breaks down the electroweak forces between certain particles, causing them to acquire mass.

The only way of negotiating the energy territories on the other side of the Higgs field is with math and probability studies. They can't measure energy potential, but they can estimate its "probability quotient." If they are correct, this is the only way to learn about existence outside our perception realm.

Those who have experienced NDEs, however, beg to differ. They claim they have actually gone there and seen the other side.

This leads us to a supreme irony. In order to see what's on the other side of the Higgs field, the quantum fence that separates us from other realms of existence that *don't* consist of matter and particles, we need to employ the talents and skills of a member of a fraternity consisting of perhaps the oldest spiritual practitioners known to humankind—those who are familiar with the art of the shaman. They've been journeying back and forth from this reality to other realities for thousands of years. As a matter of fact, the first shaman might very well have been contemporaneous with the first modern human.

There are now thousands of people who have willingly told their stories to trained specialists in many fields, who then study such things, each within the confines of their own specialty. It indicates that what shamans have claimed for years is, in fact, true.

Scientists use math. Shamans ingest chemicals or employ various religious exercises. Others discover the truth by going to the brink of death and beyond, and then returning to tell the tale.

They all seek to discover the same thing. It is a tale as old as the human race, and it is told all around the world.

I saw a Divine Being. I'm afraid I'm going to have to revise all my various books and opinions.

—A. J. Ayer, British logical
positivist philosopher, after surviving an NDE

Ernest Hemingway was badly injured during World War I. An exploding shell nearly took his life. He wrote a letter in which he expressed how he felt about the experience. He claimed that his soul left his body and began to fly upwards before returning back home.

> *Dying is a very simple thing. I've looked at death, and really, I know. If I should have died it would have been very easy for me. Quite the easiest thing I ever did.*

This was the genesis of one of his most famous works, "The Snows of Kilimanjaro." It tells the tale of an African safari that met with disaster. The hero, experiencing gangrene, knows he is dying. But suddenly his pain vanishes, and a bush pilot arrives to rescue him. The two fly through a storm with rain so thick "it seemed like flying through a waterfall," until the plane emerges into the light. There, before them, "unbelievably white in the sun, was the square top of Kilimanjaro. And then he knew that there was where he was going."

This story comprises the basic stages of a classic near-death experience. There is darkness, a cessation of pain, emerging into a great light, followed by a feeling of peacefulness.

Another classic NDE happened in 1900. Scottish surgeon Sir Alexander Ogston, who later went on to discover Staphylococcus, a staph bacteria known to cause many different types of infections, succumbed to a bout of typhoid fever. In his own words:

I lay, as it seemed, in a constant stupor which excluded the existence of any hopes or fears. Mind and body seemed to be dual, and to some extent separate. I was conscious of the body as an inert tumbled mass near a door; it belonged to me, but it was not I. I was conscious that my mental self regularly used to leave the body.... I was then drawn rapidly back to it, joined it with disgust, and it became I, and was fed, spoken to, and cared for.... And though I knew that death was hovering about, having no thought of religion nor dread of the end, and roamed on beneath the murky skies apathetic and contented until something again disturbed the body where it lay, when I was drawn back to it afresh.

Such vivid descriptions, found in the modern written record, go a long way to disproving the idea that NDEs found in oral history alone were the result of the superstitious tales of primitive people.

Irish hydrographer Sir Francis Beaufort—known for inventing the Beaufort Scale for wind measurement—is one of a number of scientists who have recorded having an NDE.

Take, for instance, this account written by Sir Francis Beaufort, the British rear admiral who went on to invent the Beaufort scale, which indicates wind force.

Almost thirty years after his NDE, Sir Beaufort became a hydrographer in the Royal Navy and then entered academia in the field of meteorological studies.

With all this still ahead of him, in 1791 he wrote:

A calm feeling of the most perfect tranquility succeeded the most tumultuous sensation.... Nor was I in any bodily pain. On the contrary, my sensations were now of rather a pleasurable cast.... Though the senses were thus deadened, not so the mind; its activity

*seemed to be invigorated in a ratio which defies all de-
scription; for thought rose after thought with a rapidity
of succession that is not only indescribable, but probably inconceivable, by anyone who has been himself in
a similar situation. The course of these thoughts I can
even now in a great measure retrace: the event that had
just taken place.... Thus, traveling backwards, every incident of my past life seemed to me to glance across my
recollection in retrograde procession ... the whole period
of my existence seemed to be placed before me in a kind
of panoramic view.*

His account reprises the familiar themes of peace, an out-of-
body experience, and a life review. Given his later achievements,
it is obvious he had a good reason for returning from death, but
there are sometimes other reasons for the near-death experience—
reasons that become apparent only *after* the whole episode has
played out.

Take, for instance, the case put forth by Raymond Moody in
his book *Life After Life,* and the subsequent movie by the same title.

Dr. George Rodonaia, Ph.D., was a Russian dissident while a
doctor of psychology. When he was issued an invitation to travel
to the United States in 1976, the Russian KGB decided he needed
to be assassinated before leaving the country. They didn't trust
his stated motives for the trip.

Remembering that English is his second language, read his
words:

*I was standing on the sidewalk, ready to depart to NY,
waiting for cab, when a car on the sidewalk hit me. I flew
in the air 10 meters, and then the car ran over me. My
friends and relative took me to the hospital. The hospital
staff, friends of mine, and two other professors declared
me dead. On Friday night, they put me in the morgue, in
the freezer.*

*Three days later, they took me out. So on Monday morn-
ing they began my autopsy. These three days of being out
of my body, seeing everything that was happening
around, seeing myself, my body, seeing my birth, my parents, my wife, my child, and my friends. I saw their*

thoughts. I saw what they were thinking, how their thoughts move from one dimension to another.

It was incredible experience. I was in darkness, total darkness. The darkness was pressing. This darkness existed not beyond, but it existed within. What I want say is that the darkness was pressing. And I was in the middle of this fear and I did not understand why and how this darkness existed. Where was I?

I understood that I didn't have a body because I didn't feel it. Then I saw a light. I went through a little hole into that light. But the light was so powerful, so burning. You cannot compare it to anything. No words can explain it. The light was so burning, going through flesh. I didn't have a body. That was the most interesting part. And I was scared of the light, I wanted to go into the shade to save myself from this light. What is that light? I don't know. It can be called the light of God; it can be called the light of Life. But light is light and darkness is darkness. As a psychiatrist and scientist, I did not think about that. The only thing was that I was in light.

Dr. Rodonaia was an atheist. "We were not raised in God's way. You know about the Soviet Union, we didn't go to church.... But those three days of being in the morgue, the freezer, changed all my life."

Like many who experience an NDE, Dr. Rodonaia related that he saw an incredibly bright light—the light of God? Rodonaia was an atheist, but his vision certainly made him believe in something spiritual.

It was while they were preparing for his autopsy that his eyes began to flicker. Thank goodness someone saw it, and he was revived.

His story, which so far is fairly typical for NDEs, now takes a totally unexpected twist. One of the things he most remembers is that he had great communication with children during the three days following his assassination attempt. As he told the story, "They were coming from that place I was going to."

One of the babies he could communicate with was crying. Somehow, Rodonaia understood that the child had been born with a broken hip, but none of the doctors knew about it. All they knew was that the child was crying a lot.

After regaining his body, Dr. Rodonaia was able to tell the staff at the hospital. His diagnosis was proved to be correct, surgery was performed, and the child soon recovered.

If NDEs are the result of medications or oxygen deprivation, how can stories like these possibly fit into such explanations? The fact that many experiences take place under the controlled conditions of a modern hospital surely demands study. It takes a solid disbelief in the afterlife to attempt to sweep such cases under the rug. Only people who *refuse* to believe even try to do so, but it would seem their numbers are legion. Sometimes even the most dedicated scientists and specialists, without realizing what they are doing, go to almost comical lengths to buttress their long-held opinions.

The tragedy is, however, that believing that we are *more* than our earthly bodies, that there *is* an afterlife, that actions have *eternal* consequences, and that a purposeful life *really* matters, might go a long way toward changing the conditions under which we all live. It's an important consideration.

With this in mind, we have to open ourselves to the idea that NDEs are more than the superstitions of primitive people. Such stories have been with us forever; indeed, since the dawn of our species.

But we don't have to depend on old tales. It's time to move into a new area of study, using contemporary vocabulary to describe events that might very well soon move into the arena of modern science.

PART II
SOMETHING NEW

I believe that the greatest truths of the universe don't lie outside, in the study of the stars and the planets. They lie deep within us, in the magnificence of our heart, mind, and soul. Until we understand what is within, we can't understand what is without.

—Anita Moorjani in
*Dying to Be Me: My Journey from Cancer,
to Near Death, to True Healing,* 2012

Police officers and lawyers often reference the frailty of the human mind when it comes to remembering details. That's why witnesses to an accident, for instance, need to be questioned as soon as possible after an incident takes place. It's notoriously easy to transpose details.

Sometimes at family gatherings it's fun to ask grown siblings to try and recall a particular shared scene from their long-ago childhood. It's amazing that three or four people can claim to remember vividly something from their past, only to discover that the memories don't overlap at all.

That's why the law, as is true with many aspects of our modern culture, demands facts—pictures, forensic evidence, something that can be measured beyond a reasonable doubt—anything except personal recollection, which is considered to be the flimsiest, least trusted kind of testimony.

One of the problems faced by UFO enthusiasts, Bigfoot aficionados, and those who claim to see fairies and leprechauns is that a story will probably not be accepted if only eyewitness testimony is considered. We need photographs. We need tangible evidence. Unless Sasquatch poses for the camera and offers some DNA, few will believe he's out there in the woods.

Up until recently, that's been the case with NDEs. People might claim they saw a new landscape and experienced an illuminated being, but where is the physical evidence that such a thing really happened? Unless they bring back a souvenir, few of us will believe their story. We may be convinced that *they* believe it. We don't necessarily believe they are lying. But we usually tend to secretly harbor doubts and wonder if the truth lies elsewhere. Without evidence, it could very well be nothing more than a vivid dream or flight of imagination.

The key words in that last paragraph are found at the very beginning: "Up until recently." Modern technology, for all its flaws and drawbacks, has introduced new ways to gather raw, unequivocal data. We may not be able to photograph places that are beyond the physical realm that is our current home, but, thanks to MRIs and CT scans, we can measure things that are going on in the brain, or we can determine that people are actually dead and not just dreaming in a coma.

There is now evidence from hospitals, which are beginning to take such things seriously, that the deathbed is a launch pad to realms far beyond what we can see, hear, touch, taste, and smell. Indeed, thanks to modern science, it appears that a whole new world awaits us.

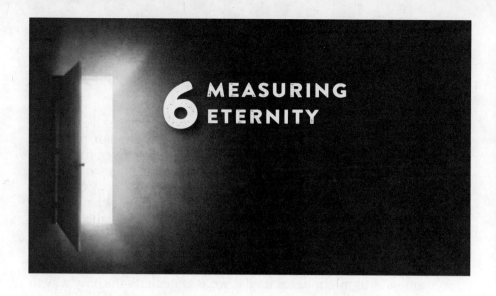

6 MEASURING ETERNITY

As interest grows in near-death experiences (NDEs), it is increasingly important to accurately identify them to facilitate empirical research and reproducibility among assessors. We aimed ... to validate the Near-Death Experience Content (NDE-C) scale that quantifies NDEs in a more complete way.

—Charlotte Martial et al. in "The Near-Death Experience Content (NDE-C) Scale: Development and Psychometric Validation," *Consciousness and Cognition Journal*, November 2020

It's hard to overemphasize how far physicists have progressed in the last hundred years when it comes to understanding the nature of material existence. For that matter, even the last 20 years' progress has been earthshaking, but before we can practically apply to our daily lives what their discoveries imply about near-death experiences, we need to at least skim over the general field of physics. We'll keep it simple. There will be no equations, but here is a general overview that will set the stage for diving into the idea of how life works and what that means for an understanding of NDEs.

The 17th century saw the beginning of a whole new way of thinking about the world and our place in it. It was the birth of the Age of Enlightenment. Old ideas about the authority of a king or a pope—and even conceptions about God—began to be replaced. Human intelligence and problem-solving began to, at great cost, overthrow the status quo.

One of the primary minds behind this progressive tide was that of Sir Isaac Newton, the English mathematician, physicist, astronomer, alchemist, theologian, and author. Even during his lifetime, he was dubbed a "natural philosopher," but what is most important to us at this point of our study is that he was the one who, for all practical purposes, codified much of what we now know as physics. Indeed, classical physics is often called Newtonian physics because of its roots in Newton's work.

Today, classical physics is so much a part of our lives that most of us might be excused if we assume that's the only way to view the world. Even scientists as illustrious as Albert Einstein thought in these terms, and with good reason. Most of the rules of Newtonian physics describe the logical way things work in the material and visible world around us.

Newton didn't *invent* these laws. He *discovered* them. Step off a cliff and you'll fall victim to the law of gravity. Everyone knows that, and we have obeyed the law for thousands upon thousands of years without the need for any authoritarian oversight. It carries its own penalties if we break it.

Sir Isaac Newton was a prime figure in the Age of Enlightenment, taking much of the mystery out of the universe with his explanations of physical principles such as his laws of motion.

Play a game of billiards and you'll be utilizing laws governing action and reaction. Live long enough and you'll discover the principles of entropy every morning when you try to get out of bed.

People were aware of these laws and had been following them forever, but the genius of Isaac Newton was to develop standard mathematical formulas that allowed them to be studied and applied in a scientific manner. In other words, he brought them into the realm of academic and systematic scientific inquiry.

Take, for example, the simple act of watering your garden. The water coming through your hose traces a parabola through the air. If you want to reach that faraway bed of flowers, you raise your hose and restrict the flow of water with your thumb, forcing the same amount of liquid to flow through a smaller opening, increasing its elevation, pressure, and speed. The result is that you gain enough height and momentum to make the water go farther. You probably didn't consider the mathematics behind what you were doing. You might not have been aware of the mathematical formula for determining the shape of a parabola, but you knew from experience that it would work.

Little did you know that you were demonstrating a Newtonian mathematical formula called a quadratic function. I promised there would be no equations, but for those inclined to reminisce about precalculus, it's

$$f(x) = ax^2 + bx + c$$

Thus, classical Newtonian physics describes conditions in which physical rules apply. It's all common sense. We learn to follow them, whether we understand them or not, because they work.

> **Way down below our perception realm … it turns out that forces that govern our visible world don't play by Newton's rules.**

But a hundred years ago something changed. We discovered the world of quantum physics—the world of the very small. Way down below our perception realm, in places too small for even the most powerful microscope to penetrate, it turns out that forces that govern our visible world don't play by Newton's rules. Tiny objects, called subatomic particles (particles smaller than an atom), simply don't pay any attention to the rules governing large objects up here in the classical world.

Isaac Newton and the scientists who followed in his wake for the next few centuries were used to objects moving in predictable patterns from place to place. But down in the quantum world, things tend to jump from here to there without moving along any observable path between two points. You're looking at something over "here," and suddenly it's over "there." Physicists had discovered what is now called a quantum leap, and no one to this day fully understands how it works. They just know it does.

This is only one aspect of quantum reality, however. There is a condition called the observer effect, for instance, that seems to indicate that unless a measurement is made, or "observed," one particle might exist in multiple places, perhaps even in an infinite amount of them. It is only when it is "observed," when its status "collapses" into the view of the observer, that its location is fixed.

This is the phenomenon made famous by Schrödinger's theoretical cat in the box. Only when you observe it will you know which condition it is in. Until you open the box, it is both dead and alive at the same time.

What all this implies is that the world in which we live and move consists of both an "inside," the world of *quantum* physics, and an "outside," the world of *classical* physics.

We come to a reconciliation of these two worlds when we move into the arena of near-death experiences. But to do so, we need to take a quick stroll through another landscape of something called consciousness.

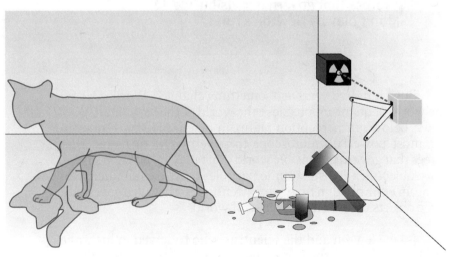

In the famous Schrödinger's cat mental experiment, a cat is placed in a box so it cannot be seen by an outside observer. Inside is a vial of radioactive poison that may or may not open at any time. Until the box is opened and the cat is observed, the cat is in a state of superposition: it can be considered to be simultaneously alive and dead.

For the bulk of our time on earth, our species tended to think that we were simply spectators in a great, impersonal game of life called "existence." Life was something that happened *to* us. We didn't have a lot of control over it.

Now that whole idea is changing. Life doesn't *happen* to us as much as it *proceeds* from us. As conscious observers, *we* are central to *its* existence, not the other way around. It sounds rather counter-intuitive. Some might even call it a bit wacky. But there it is.

Before the discovery of quantum physics, most scientists had determined that *mind* emerges from *brain*. In other words, a biological lump of tissue, matter, and chemicals—the brain—produces electrical waves that generate thoughts and ideas in what we call our mind. As René Descartes once famously said, "I think, therefore I am!"

But suddenly, with the discovery of quantum reality, we began to see that life deals with *probabilities* as much as *actualities*. We tend to observe what we *expect* to observe, and how we set up the experiments to be performed determines how those experiments will play out. If we look for a wave, we'll find a wave. If we look for a particle, we'll find a particle.

This is a much too simplistic explanation for a very complex and intriguing field of study, but it gives us something of a base on which to build a theory of near-death experiences.

Earlier, I mentioned subatomic particles that appear to "leap" from one place to another. What we learn from quantum physics is that these particles, the building blocks of all physical life, aren't just particles. They are also waves of energy.

Most of us, for instance, were taught that a subatomic particle called an electron orbits around the nucleus of an atom. If we look for it with an instrument designed to find it in that form, that's just what we discover.

Now it turns out that electrons have a secret identity. If we look for Batman, that's who we'll find. But Batman is also Bruce Wayne. If we look for him, that's who we'll see.

In the same way, electrons are also waves of energy. We can picture a single electron as a tiny particle in orbit around a nu-

> We can picture a single electron as a tiny particle in orbit around a nucleus, or we can picture it as a vague sort of cloud that inhabits a finite space.

cleus, or we can picture it as a vague sort of cloud that inhabits a finite space. Both, it turns, out, are true.

Here comes the point of this excursion. The "space" this cloud inhabits seems to consist of alternate universes that overlap each other at different "frequencies," for lack of a better word. If you were to somehow stand in a few of these parallel universes at the same time and search for the "particle" identity of the electron, you would find it. It would appear as a minuscule dot in each overlapping universe.

So when we see an electron suddenly "leap" from "here" to "there," what we are actually seeing is the electron as it appears in different places in overlapping universes. In other words, we are actually seeing, or measuring, parallel universes!

In each of these universes, different probabilities, or results, come to pass. In one universe a flipped coin appears heads up and your favorite football team elects to receive the kickoff. In another, it appears tails up, and they kick off.

Thus, in an infinite multiverse, literally everything that *can* happen, *does* happen. But you, restricted by your five senses in *this* universe, observe only one of these results, so you think that is all that happened. The other "you," in a parallel universe, sees another result and feels *that* is all that happened.

Now comes the exciting conclusion to this whole exercise. When you move outside your physical senses, as you do when you experience an NDE, you experience other realities—other universes—and observe different outcomes.

Which "you" is the real one?

Both are equally real! You inhabit all realities. It's only your five senses that create the illusion that this one is all there is. Once freed from those senses, all kinds of alternate worlds open up, including the Source from which you came, and to which you will return after physical death.

This is a concept that is very difficult to imagine even though, mathematically, it seems to be possible, perhaps even probable, whether or not we choose to believe in it. It's called the Many Worlds theory. What this theory says is that, according to some theories of quantum physics, every possible outcome of subjective reality occurs. Every possible world is created. In an infinite number of worlds and an infinite number of universes, an infinite number of people, who all think they are "you," observe the particular universe they inhabit and think it's the only physical reality possible.

When a particle like an electron "leaps" from one location to another, it might be that they have uplifted to other dimensions during the time when they seem to disappear. An NDE could be just like that, moving to other dimensions, other universes among many.

Why is there biological life in our universe that seems to be so finely tuned for it? Because we happen to inhabit one of an infinite number of universes in which life was formed as part of the wave function collapse that produced this particular environment.

In other words, everything, including the creation of life, that could possibly happen, everywhere and anywhere, has indeed happened somewhere. But because we, as observers, only see it from our small, physical perspective, we think this is the sum total of everything. We call it reality. But it is only one of an infinite number of realities. They all exist. They are all real.

The Many Worlds hypothesis was first developed by Hugh Everett back in the 1950s. Although it was never completely embraced by his colleagues during his relatively short lifetime, it is now growing in popularity because it's the only theory that ties up all the loose ends of current knowledge. Its official title is now decoherence.

The constant in all this is that consciousness, through a process called entanglement, observes all these worlds. According to this theory, consciousness is the ground of being. Our brains don't *create* it. They *channel* it. Consciousness, when it is released from

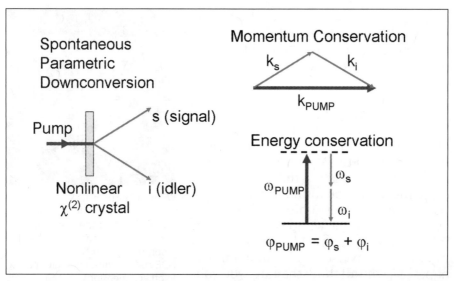

Quantum entanglement can be demonstrated in lab settings. For example, with spontaneous parametric downconversion, a high-energy photon is passed through a crystal to create two lower-energy, entangled photons whose behavior is now inextricably linked regardless of physical distance.

its physical shell, is free to observe life beyond the physical world of flesh, blood, and material existence.

- Consciousness is the ultimate "Observer."

- Consciousness is the "Source" from which we come and to which we return.

- Consciousness created life as a physical experiment to examine meaning and purpose.

- We are the cutting edge of that experiment.

At this point, it is fair to ask if we "volunteered" for this experiment, considering the amount of pain and loss that stems from physical life. Let's face it; life hurts sometimes! Who would deliberately choose this kind of existence? Who would volunteer to be a victim of the Holocaust? Who would decide to be tortured to death, spend their lives in meaningless slavery, or endure years of fighting a hideous disease?

I don't know the answer to those questions. I wish I did. But, as Dr. Raymond Moody once pointed out, we have all seen people pay a lot of money and stand in inconvenient lines for hours on end in order to take rides on a roller coaster intended to scare them half to death. There is no question that a few minutes after it begins, at least some of those who willingly go on such a ride will wish they had never signed up. Still, they do it.

For that matter, why do people pay money to be terrified out of their wits by a horror movie?

Perhaps that's what life is—a roller coaster ride of terror we willingly engage just so we can experience it.

Maybe that's the precise reason why so many report a feeling of peace, love, and acceptance during an NDE. Maybe they are meeting those who either stayed behind or who already finished. Maybe those welcoming entities are saying, in effect, "Your adventure is over! Good ride! Welcome home!"

> **It might appear as though our brains are the originator of our minds, thoughts, and ideas, but that's an illusion.**

Here in our world, brains pretty much rule. They are fantastic organs of protoplasm, cells, neural networks, chemicals, and electrical energy. It might appear as though our brains are the originator of our minds, thoughts, and ideas, but that's an illusion. According to quantum physics, mind permeates and determines the course of matter. This universe, and all universes, are the *result* of mind, not the *cause* of it. An observer brings about the collapse of a specific material result—here, there, and everywhere—in all universes, simultaneously.

I often quote Sir James Jeans, one of my favorite scientist-philosophers: "The universe begins to look more like a great *thought* than like a great *machine*." Truer words were never spoken.

At death, when our consciousness is released from the five senses of our material body—from the single reality that appears to be our only choice in this perception realm—we begin to experience quite a different landscape, inhabited by entities who

Could it be that NDEs are us separating from our physical form to gain access to other realms of existence? If we understood them better, could NDEs afford a way to actually measure and study things outside normal time and space?

appear spiritual rather than physical, and possibilities that are beyond our imagination. No wonder they often seem more *real* than our present reality. Is it any wonder that most people don't want to come back, and do so only when they are reminded that the reason they became physical beings in the first place is not yet fulfilled?

Our brains try to convince us that this life is all there is; that this is the only reality. But now we're beginning to see through that illusion. There are infinite possibilities out there, created by universal Mind, or Consciousness, or God, or whatever we choose to call it. We are here to explore because *our* minds are a part of *universal* Mind. We are already there, but only in the release of death do we realize it.

Let's try to apply all this to the subject of NDEs:

- *If* reality consists of more than our materialistic, physical environment ...

- And *if* science has come to the point where we can, at least through the use of mathematical equations, begin to measure such things ...

- And *if* consciousness is eternal ...

- And *if*, in near-death experiences, we are able to free ourselves from the illusion of our narrow understanding of time and space ...

- *Then,* we might be seeing, for the first time in the history of our species, a way to measure, or observe, eternity.

Humans have seen glimpses of this reality for as long as there have been people around to glimpse it. Countless folks over the centuries plainly saw the other side and reported on their experiences. We may finally have arrived at the point where our science is catching up with our vision. That means it's not just a spiritual, pie-in-the-sky, metaphysical or paranormal dream. There's a "real" reality out there, waiting to be explored. Before now, we lacked the physical tool kit to do so. We had to rely on first-person accounts described with inadequate language skills.

No more! Our left-brained, intellectual, and scientific methods may be on the verge of breaking through, not to a visionary world, a religious world, or even a spiritual world, but to a reality that so far has eluded all but the most otherworldly of us.

"Seeing is believing" we often say, while ignoring the fact that seeing is no longer sufficient for those who don't believe in anything that can't be proven in a court of law or scientific laboratory. It might be that we are finally going beyond mere sight. Where are these sightings taking place? That's where we'll go next.

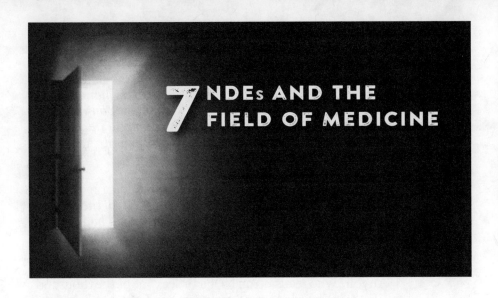

7 NDEs AND THE FIELD OF MEDICINE

At 18 hospitals in Britain and the United States there are pictures hanging in Emergency Rooms. But they're facing up. Only visible from near the ceiling. The reason? To see if out of body, near-death experiences actually happen.

—J. J. Sutherland in "Are Near-Death Experiences Real?" National Public Radio. October 26, 2010

Psychiatrist Brian Weiss once told a fascinating story that has since gone on to be peer reviewed and published by the Magis Center in August 2022:

> [She] suffered a cardiac arrest during her stay in the hospital where I was the chairman of the psychiatry department. She was unconscious as the resuscitation team tried to revive her. According to her later report, she floated out of her body and stood near the window, watching [the resuscitation]. She observed, without any pain whatsoever, as they thumped on her chest and pumped air into her lungs. During the resuscitation, a pen fell out of her doctor's pocket and rolled near the same window where her out-of-body spirit was standing and watching. The doctor eventually walked over, picked up the pen, and put it back in his pocket. He then rejoined the frantic effort to save her. They succeeded.

A few days later, she told her doctor that she had observed the resuscitation team at work during her cardiac arrest. "No," he soothingly reassured her. "You were probably hallucinating because of the anoxia [lack of oxygen to the brain]. This can happen when the heart stops beating."

"But I saw your pen roll over to the window," she replied. Then she described the pen and other details of the resuscitation. The doctor was shocked. His patient had not only been comatose during the resuscitation, but she had also been blind for many years.

Anyone who reads up on NDEs, or sees one of the thousands of testimonies recorded for posterity on YouTube, has heard this before: "I was pronounced clinically dead...."

That seems to be the standard opening line of almost all NDE recitations. But what does it mean to be "clinically dead"?

There is a death pronouncement protocol that medical people follow:

- A patient must be what laypeople call "flatlined." That means that their electroencephalogram (EEG) registers a flat line on a monitor. It indicates a complete absence of electrical activity in their cerebral cortex. That's the part of the brain that registers any kind of higher cerebral functioning.

- They must demonstrate a complete absence of a gag reflex.

- The pupils of their eyes must be fixed and dilated, which indicates a significant reduction of lower brain functioning.

- Their organs are now considered to be totally nonfunctional. What this means is that their brain can no longer process any sensory signals.

- Thinking, processing memories, and any sort of speaking functions are, of course, completely absent.

- There might be some brain activity in what is sometimes called the "lower brain." But, at best, these electrical signals are minimal.

When all these measurements are noted, the patient is pronounced clinically dead, and the exact time is noted, or "pronounced" by whoever is in charge, for the death certificate.

What happens when all this takes place and a patient is somehow revived, complete with memories that indicate the ability to see and perceive despite the absence of any kind of brain activity after his or her death was pronounced by a team of highly specialized professionals? In some cases, even patients who had been born blind, never having seen anything in their lives, reported that they saw what was going on around them.

For a patient to be declared dead takes more than just the heart stopping. Brain activity and all organ function should also cease completely before someone is declared dead.

That's what is called a near-death experience. Despite a lack of brain function, patients sometimes describe what they saw, heard, felt, and otherwise experienced. According to most medical professionals, that's not supposed to happen. It should be impossible. But it happens anyway, and the medical establishment is mystified about how and why a person is able to have a sensory experience with only limited brain function, and without full use of his or her physical senses.

As far back as 1982, data gathered by polls such as those of the well-respected Gallup organization reported that some eight million adults in the United States have experienced an NDE. The poll associated nine characteristics reported by those who were contacted:

- An out-of-body experience

- Accurate visual perception

- Accurate auditory perception

- A feeling of peace and painlessness

- An encounter with loving white light

- A life review

- Meeting entities from outside our normal perception realm who were obviously interested in and supportive of the patient

- The experience of some kind of tunnel or portal

- Some sort of precognition

Since then, many other polls confirm the data. There are now thousands of such studies based on actual case studies. Even if we throw out many of them for lack of supporting evidence, faulty reporting, or insufficient objectivity, or because they are merely anecdotal examples, there remains a huge amount of fully substantiated claims, and the number grows every year. We can now depend on accepted clinical, cross-cultural, and long-term studies, firmly established in peer-reviewed papers, that demonstrate a complete lack of manipulative agendas. It's easy to discount someone who makes a private claim. It's much harder to negate the testimony of highly trained, completely objective doctors and nurses who have at their disposal the very latest scientific equipment.

When someone is pronounced dead in a regulated environment but is able to relate conversations that took place in a nonadjacent waiting room, convey impressions of his or her surroundings in highly technical medical vocabulary with which they were not previously familiar, or even describe the color of clothes family members were wearing, simple answers involving lack of oxygen to the brain, the presence of pain-relieving drugs, or intermittent electrical pulses in the brain just don't hold up to scrutiny.

Many who have had NDEs have been able to report activities and describe things that happened while they were dead.

The confounding evidence of experiencing consciousness while hooked up to machines that were built to determine exactly when there was no consciousness present, the ability to see and hear while other machines built to measure such things say that that ability has ceased, and all this in the presence of highly trained, experienced witnesses, simply defies belief.

How can a person think, reason, communicate, and describe the reality of things such as lights, tunnels, and even other people when the very machines that were designed and built to record the absence of such sensations are working properly and efficiently?

No one knows, but the medical establishment has coined a term that describes such an environment. They now call it "transphysical." That just means it's not limited by the physical senses. When professionals make up their own specialty vocabulary, it usually means they want to separate themselves from what they consider to be the "hysterical" ideas of the general public. But there is no doubt that if the medical establishment is now inventing their own language and accepting criteria to determine near-death experiences, they are beginning, for the first time, to bring NDEs into the realm of real science.

It didn't happen overnight. As usual, the field of science tends to move slowly and carefully. This is probably a good thing, as long as those who are slow to move don't attack the character or personality of those who want to push ahead, instead of giving their work serious consideration. Sad to say, such personal attacks are a frequent response.

As I mentioned briefly, those who doubt the gathering data tend to argue that NDEs are merely hallucinations. They base their opinions on three main arguments:

- *Anoxia*: This is the theory that says lack of oxygen to the brain could lead to the firing of neurons that are responsible for visual perception. That might be why patients report a white light at the end of a tunnel. Here's the problem, though. If this were the case, *everyone* should report a similar phenomenon of leaving their bodies or seeing a bright light. In truth, only about 18% experience it.

- *Narcotics*: This idea involves the fact that most patients who die in the operating room have been administered painkilling drugs of some kind. But such narcotics tend to *exaggerate* visions. Instead, just the opposite happens. NDEs usually consist of very lucid and accurate descriptions.

- *Post-death electrical surges*: Experiments have been conducted that produce out-of-body experiences. But they are usually accompanied by a false sense of reality. Sometimes they produce epileptic seizures, but these seizures don't compare with the NDE experience. Further, that's what EEGs are supposed to measure. A flat line indicates lack of electrical surges in the brain.

We can conclude these explanations are offered because those who insist they are reasonable have already formed a negative opinion about the possibility of anything existing outside of material explanations. That is not science. It is rank speculation based on preconceived ideologies.

What kind of stories pass the medical, peer-reviewed studies of what is called veridical data? This is a term used to describe evidence that is verifiable—that can be confirmed or disproved when a patient has returned to his or her body.

In one study, for instance, a man who was revived from a deep coma later confided to his nurse that he recognized her even though she had not taken her station until after he was unconscious. When she asked how he knew it was her, he said he had seen where she had placed his dentures during the struggle to revive him. He was able to accurately pinpoint the location of the cart she had used and described it to her. She checked out the cart and found the dentures, exactly as he had recalled.

Other studies tell stories of patients who could accurately describe the motions of the doctors and anesthetists, even when their actions were out of the ordinary. One patient described the nontraditional multicolor shoelaces one nurse was wearing.

> In many of these cases the patient seemed to hover close to his or her body, sometimes never leaving the operating room, but observing what went on from a viewpoint near the ceiling.

These accounts are unique in several ways. First, they don't follow the usual pattern. There are no tunnels, lights, or bright entities. There is no life review. In many of these cases the patient seemed to hover close to his or her body, sometimes never leaving the operating room, but observing what went on from a viewpoint near the ceiling. They were out-of-body but had not traveled on.

When we start to consider the cases of people who undergo a trans-physical experience, however, we move away from veridical data and enter the world of subjective evidence. Here is where things start to get interesting in terms of traditional concepts of afterlife as recorded in most religions.

We're talking now about the concepts of heaven and hell.

There is good evidence that whether a person has a heavenly experience or a hellish one depends to a great deal on their state of mind when they died. In other words, there is a possibility that our first impression of another reality depends on what we *expect* to find.

The vast majority of NDEs are reported as being full of joy, peace, acceptance, and love. They are pleasant experiences from which people often do not want to return.

There are, of course, exceptions to the rule. Let's examine those reports, beginning with the validity of the experiences.

When hospitals gather information about NDEs from revived patients, they are not attempting to prove or disprove the doctrines of a particular religion. They are simply gathering evidence to study the possibility that a component of a person, sometimes identified as "soul," exists after physical death and returns to transmit information about an afterlife. They will follow the evidence wherever it leads, even if it means questioning or sometimes disproving the patient's testimony.

In one case, for instance, I was called by a person representing a New England hospital and asked about the religious beliefs of one of my congregants who had reported a near-death experience. The psychiatrist who questioned me was curious to compare the patient's experience with any doctrinal teachings that might have influenced her to perceive things the way she did.

Her story was typical of most Christian teachings, involving descriptions of biblical passages as commonly interpreted by most people who attend church every Sunday. The being of light who was encountered was called "Jesus," for instance. The psy-

Some Christians will have visions of Jesus or Mary during their NDEs, with one theory being this is the result of their being indoctrinated with religious teachings that lead them to expect such a holy experience.

chiatrist who called me happened to be Jewish and understandably was prone to slough this off as religious indoctrination.

I assured him that I was in full agreement with him. Just because I was a clergyman active in a particular faith didn't mean I ever preached, at least during that point in my career, any dogma that insisted Jesus was the "only way" to heaven, although I could understand why many Christians believed that to be the case.

At the end of our discussion, we agreed that there was a very good possibility that his patient, my parishioner, could very well have "seen Jesus" because she *expected* to do so. There were other typical Christian-type examples involving a heavenly choir, clouds, and a generally spiritual atmosphere, that could also have been conjured up in the expectations of someone who had been, dare I say it, brainwashed by teachings, texts, and pictures, going back to Sunday school days.

Nevertheless, I was troubled when I hung up the phone. What I had just participated in was a typical, liberal, intellectual exercise. Two academically trained "experts" had just agreed to patronize a person who didn't possess our educational experience. We had decided that what she saw was one thing, while the patient herself was convinced it was something quite different.

Without ever telling the patient herself, her story was quietly, and probably correctly, filed under "Subjective Accounts." Even though I still agree with that determination, I am troubled. After all, who are we to say whether or not the patient had actually seen Jesus? We weren't there, and it is only our precon-

> There are many NDE testimonies that describe traditional religious conceptions of heaven and hell, bardo, paradise, a "happy" hunting ground, or whatever ... but there are just as many that don't.

ceived religious notions, one of us a Christian and the other a Jew, who questioned her.

This anecdote leads us into some difficult terrain that needs to be traversed. There are many NDE testimonies that describe traditional religious conceptions of heaven and hell, bardo, paradise, a "happy" hunting ground, or whatever the culture might be that surrounded the one who died and came back, but there are just as many that don't. In some cases, the after-death experience was totally unexpected by the person who died. Often, they change their entire lives around afterward and spend the rest of their days convinced they know what awaits them.

Do we who question the validity of their report have the right to assume we somehow know better that those who have actually experienced death and resuscitation? It's a real problem, and one that I don't feel comfortable answering.

When I tune in to YouTube these days and watch one of the thousands of accounts of those who tell their stories, once in a while I find that I can't listen through to the end because the person telling the story is convinced that their experience was the "right" one, even if it disagreed with those of others who are

Regardless of religious (or nonreligious) background, a common vision of many NDE experiencers is entering some kind of beautiful, peaceful, heavenly realm.

equally convinced in the validity of what *they* saw and heard. It's not that I think some people are lying. It's just that I have come to suspect any human being who is so sure they know "the TRUTH" that they claim sole knowledge of it. I'm much more comfortable with someone saying "this is what it seemed like" than I am with the one who says, "this is the way it is!"

There are, however, some characteristics that stand out after we have eliminated any obvious religious lookalikes.

Those who say they have experienced a "heaven," whatever their religious convictions, tend to emphasize phrases such as "freedom from physical limitations," "transcendence," "unconditional love," and "total acceptance." They talk about having familiar abilities involving seeing and hearing, but they are at the same time able to move through walls, ascend upward, and travel beyond familiar physical terrain.

One would expect this from religious Christians, for instance, because since childhood they have been taught that Jesus had those freedoms in his resurrected body. Thus, they look forward to the same thing for themselves. They *expect* to experience a dimension of beauty, joy, and paradise. They *expect* their lives to finally know ultimate fulfillment.

But this doesn't explain atheists having the same experiences, even though they reject such teachings.

Most religions teach that love is central to the realm of God. NDE patients regularly describe overwhelming love as the dominant environment in the dimension of light. But so do those who come from unloving environments and who have completely lost hope in the goodness of humankind.

Some patients are greeted by deceased family members whom they might not even recognize at first because the family member died before the patient was born. They often introduce themselves and reveal facts about themselves that the patient's relatives or friends are subsequently able to verify.

But so do patients who have never, ever, believed that there is any sort of life after death.

Besides these heaven-like visions, there are also a few rare but still statistically relevant stories about environments that more closely resemble hell than heaven.

Patients come back with testimonies of being in a dark void, or even a place of consuming fires, accompanied by screams of those who are experiencing what can only be called eternal torture.

One patient, for instance, reports:

When I reached the bottom, it resembled the entrance to a cave, with what looked like webs hanging. I heard cries, wails, moans, and the gnashing of teeth. I saw these beings that resembled humans, with the shape of a head and body, but they were ugly and grotesque. They were frightening and sounded like they were tormented, in agony.

This kind of evidence, both positive and negative, is not usually considered veridical. It can't be corroborated as occurring during a patient's clinical death by an independent source. But it is valuable just the same, if only because it is so universal. There are many similar accounts. We can't just assume they don't count for anything.

We also must take into account the notion that some patients reveal, probably without meaning to, information about meeting deceased relatives whom they never met or, in some cases, never even heard about. These experiences *can* be checked out and verified. They cannot be simply swept under the rug.

A minority of experiencers remember visions not of heaven but of hell, complete with monstrous beings and dark, depressing scenes of death and decay.

In short, many medical specialists want to move forward in a scientific manner when it comes to studying NDEs. They gather data, make comparisons, and see where the facts lead. Some stories must be thrown out of the mix because they are strictly subjective and cannot be verified. This is not to say that those who share these stories are lying. It's just that they offer no tangible proof that can be objectively studied.

But that leaves many, many stories that *do* offer such proof. Checking out NDEs is a relatively new medical endeavor. The science of NDE studies is really in its infancy. It is only to be expected that many in the field don't want to believe something before it can be scientifically verified. That is probably a good thing. It offers objectivity to a subject that is notorious for being a bit flighty, to say the least.

While an NDE is a subjective experience, tens of thousands of people report having had one. Similar characteristics are reported across the range of individual experiences. They offer up lots of interesting questions to study:

- Why do blind subjects universally report that they were able to see, and deaf subjects that they could hear?

- How can people recognize distant relatives whom they never met, including dead siblings who they never knew

In an unusual and unexpected phenomenon, some families have related stories in which the mourners surrounding a loved one's deathbed all experience a moment of transcendent joy, love, and peace as if sharing what the dying person's experiences.

existed, and learn details about their lives that were, up to then, family secrets, unknown to almost everybody else?

- How is it that when family are gathered around the deathbed of a patient, the whole group sometimes experiences what are called "shared NDEs"? In other words, the living loved ones also experience a brief time of transcendence, love, and peace. They seem, for a single moment of time, to be carried away to another realm; when they eventually share the experience, they discover that they all witnessed the same thing.

These are the kinds of questions hospital staffs are beginning to ask. They gather information that is, more and more frequently, being compared and cross-referenced so as to put together long-term data that can be examined by independent groups of academics.

It will take years, no doubt, but when the evidence becomes peer reviewed, as is now starting to happen, it is very possible that NDE research will rise to a peak in a culture that has, up to now, tended to ignore such stories. For NDEs to ascend those heights, they will need to stand up to the tests of science. What better way to gather that kind of evidence than in the very culture that is set up to record, measure, test, and evaluate it—the medical establishment?

8 NDEs AND THE MILITARY

It was through (Skip Atwater's) efforts that I would be recruited into the army's secret, psychic-spy unit, Stargate, as Remote Viewer #001.

—Joseph McMoneagle in Skip Atwater's *Captain of My Ship, Master of My Soul: Living with Guidance*, 2001

The fact is that not long ago, when the scientific mainstream was busy ridiculing the mere possibility of remote viewing, Captain Atwater and others were actively using it in highly classified intelligence gathering programs. I was one of the few scientists who were quietly working on the research side of those secret programs ... It was an enormously stimulating job.

—Dean Radin, Ph.D., in Skip Atwater's *Captain of My Ship, Master of My Soul: Living with Guidance*, 2001

I often hear variations on the question "If we can perceive things that happen outside our perception realm, why haven't we heard about it? After all, someone in a position of importance must believe in this stuff!"

Let's take the second point first. How about the U.S. military? Are they important enough?

The first question is answered just as easily. It's because they haven't told you about it.

This is not conspiracy theory. Everything you are about to read is now public information. But it took many years to be able to learn about it, and only after the reports were declassified.

What we are about to cover is not, strictly speaking, material about near-death experiences. Instead, it is called remote viewing. But it is so closely related to both NDEs and OBEs (out-of-body experiences) that it makes what came to be known as Stargate Project extremely relevant to our research.

NDEs, OBEs, and remote viewing all involve the same basic principle: We are not limited to our physical bodies.

That being said, we have to point out that those who have undergone both out-of-body experiences and successful remote viewing emphasize a basic difference between the two. In remote viewing, the subject has the impression of remaining "here" while observing something "there." In both OBEs and NDEs, the subject has the impression of traveling somewhere in some type of spiritual or astral body.

Whether this "body" actually exists or is merely a memory, or habit left over from physical life in the body, remains to be

seen, but a person undergoing a near-death experience often looks back and sees the body he or she left behind. The same thing sometimes happens in an out-of-body experience, but the fact that something in us—call it a soul or something similar—does not seem to be confined to our physical selves is the common denominator of OBEs, NDEs, and remote viewing, so it is helpful to study all three.

Fort Meade in Maryland serves as the headquarters for the National Security Agency, the Central Security Service, and the U.S. Cyber Command. It was also the center of Stargate Project, a research project into psychic remote viewing to spy on U.S. enemies.

Certain individuals, whether living or recently dead, seem to have discovered the ability to move outside their bodies and make verifiable observations. For most people, caught up as they are in the press, noise, and confusion of daily life, only the peace of death and release from physical senses allows this fact to be made known. This is the basis of near-death experiences. Some of us, however, seem to be born with an innate gift to achieve the same thing while still living.

Just as the music world occasionally produces a Mozart or the field of art a Rembrandt, the ability to bypass the senses in an out-of-body experience is a raw talent some people come by naturally. Others have to work at it, but like all skills, practice leads to improvement.

Many who could become very talented musicians never excel at their craft. They are interested in other things that consume their time, so they don't get around to acquiring the specific skills that are needed to allow their abilities to rise to the surface. The basic skill is there. But, like all skills, it needs to be developed in order to flourish.

One aspect of seeing what is going on outside our sphere of perception is called remote viewing. In 1978, the Defense Intelligence Agency (DIA) and a government-funded private California company then called the Stanford Research Institute (now SRI International) came together at Fort Meade in Maryland. Their purpose was to study the potential of remote viewing primarily for military use, but also for domestic intelligence.

> In 1978, the Defense Intelligence Agency (DIA) and ... the Stanford Research Institute (now SRI International) came together ... to study the potential of remote viewing primarily for military use, but also for domestic intelligence.

In other words, they wanted to study the possibility of spying without having to send actual people out into the field.

In true military fashion, all sorts of projects were begun, each with its own top-secret (civilians might even say silly) name. "Grill Flame," "Sun Streak," "Center Lane," and "Project CF" were just a few. But in 1991 they were consolidated into one program called Stargate Project.

Until 1987, the man in charge of the project was Lt. Frederick Holmes Atwater. Lt. Atwater, known as "Skip," went on to become the president of the Monroe Institute. He would later write an influential, highly enjoyable, and very readable book called *Captain of My Ship, Master of My Soul*, which, partially because of the classified content it dealt with, was not published until 2001.

In his book, Atwater reveals the fascinating story of an upbringing that he considered normal, not realizing that it was anything but that. He was blessed to have parents who were entirely comfortable with the idea of moving outside the physical body, and brave enough to recount his very first experience as a young boy who endured the embarrassment of dealing with the problem of bedwetting. His family never made an issue of it, except for the occasional reminder to use the bathroom before he went to bed at night. The last time this happened to him, he broke into tears when his mother responded to his cries after waking up, having wet the bed yet again.

"I went to the bathroom, I went to the bathroom!" he insisted, having a clear memory of getting up, using the bathroom, and then coming back to bed.

"Perhaps you forgot to take your body with you," she said. She then explained that he only spent part of his day in his body, and that he had just forgotten to take it with him when he went.

This was said in all seriousness. Would that we all had such intuitive parents! His mother really believed it, so young "Skippy" did, too. He began to pay attention to what happened to him at night when he was either sleeping or very close to it. He began to realize that he was attending, in his words, some sort of "night school." If he didn't concentrate too much on it, he found himself free to travel out-of-body.

Frederick Atwater grew up in an unusual family in which the parents saw out-of-body experiences as something that was normal. Skip, as he was called, discovered that being out of his body was a natural ability.

His nighttime travels gradually expanded to trips around the neighborhood, even entering the homes of neighbors from time to time. It was only later that he came to understand that what happened to him was not the norm outside his own family. It may have happened to many children, but the difference is that most children are weaned away from such activity by parents who don't understand it or think it is fantasy. Skip's parents not only believed it; they encouraged it.

As he writes in his book:

Poor folks don't think of themselves as poor. They see themselves as normal. Children in horrible dysfunctional families establish a comfort zone of normalcy in such situations and strive to recreate similar family units for themselves in adulthood. Heterosexuals think of themselves as normal and measure others' lifestyles by their own reference frame. Until some authority from outside tells us there is something wrong, or different, or strange about our family or us, we grow up under the illusion that we are normal.

With these words, he put his finger exactly on why NDEs and OBEs so often fall outside the purview of so many "normal" people in society. They have been taught, or at least encouraged, to think it is abnormal for people to experience them, because influential adults never did.

This is the principal obstacle to overcome when we try to experience an out-of-body trip for ourselves. Without realizing it, we have been brainwashed to believe they are fantasies.

As I pointed out in my book *The Quantum Akashic Field*, which is aptly subtitled *A Guide to Out-of-Body Experiences for the Astral Traveler*, this is a difficult problem to overcome. In my case, it took more than 60 years.

Atwater was much more fortunate than I was. He was raised to believe that "this voyage, this journey through earthly life, is a real trip. So if what we are experiencing—electromagnetic physical reality, earthly life—is actually a trip of sorts, then who, what, where, and when are we?" He goes on to declare that "the illusion of time and space simply provides for a sea of experience."

With such a background, the army seems to have picked the perfect person to head up Stargate Project. They didn't know all about this, of course, but if Atwater is correct in believing we have help from unseen sources, those sources undoubtedly helped secure his assignment.

He was again aided, seemingly by accident, to meet with Bob Monroe, founder of the Monroe Institute. It was Monroe who introduced Skip to Hemi-Sync® technology (see page 92) and its ability to aid in OBEs through meditation, which we will cover in detail in the next chapter. Monroe's techniques were a tremendous help, even providing some of the basis for the government's work.

The unit Atwater put together was small. There were fewer than 20 individuals involved in its working core, although many more scientists and specialists worked in the wings, supporting them. They worked, in Skip's words, in "an old, leaky wooden barracks," but their objective was to see what was happening worldwide and gather pertinent information.

As it turned out, the CIA was less than impressed with the results. The project was terminated in 1995, and information about it was finally declassified. But for almost 20 years, the insiders were convinced they were on to something that their political and governmental overseers simply refused to acknowledge, probably because those who controlled the purse strings were short-sighted business-types who had their eyes only on the profitability column. When they didn't receive the type of information they were after, they nixed the whole operation.

British author, journalist, and film-maker Jon Ronson penned *The Men Who Stare at Goats,* which is about the U.S. Army's First Earth Battalion that aimed to use psychic powers for the military.

This is, according to many of those who have worked for the government, a common symptom. Ever since Christopher Columbus, it appears, explorers and visionaries have had trouble finding financing for projects that were beyond the scope of the wealthy. But any new undertaking takes time to develop. Twenty years is hardly enough time to develop the kind of talents needed for this kind of work. The material gathered in these fledgling decades was often vague, sometimes erroneous, and often irrelevant. Patience, however, is not usually a virtue to those who want economic or even practical results.

In 2004, British journalist and filmmaker Jon Ronson wrote a book about those early days of psychic research. It was called *The Men Who Stare at Goats.* In 2009 it was made into a highly entertaining movie starring George Clooney and a number of well-known actors. Because habits are hard to break, neither the book nor the movie mentioned the Stargate Project by name, even though by then it was legal to do so.

The first man Atwater recruited, after passing a highly scrutinized performance test, was Joseph McMoneagle. His official title became Remote Viewer #001.

McMoneagle, born in 1946, would grow up to be awarded the Legion of Merit for providing information on 150 targets that were unavailable from other sources, and to write books such as *Remote Viewing Secrets: A Handbook* and *The Stargate Chronicles: Memoirs of a Psychic Spy*, but he grew up surrounded by alcoholism, child abuse, and general poverty. These conditions forced him to turn inward and, without realizing it, to develop the skills that would later serve him so well. At night, in the dark and all alone, he began to have visions. Only later would he come to realize he was a very talented psychic. Like Atwater, he, too, would eventually be drawn to work with the Monroe Institute.

The reason Atwater, McMoneagle, and the rest of the team were drawn together in this work was that in 1970, U.S. intelligence sources came to believe that the Soviet Union was intensely involved with what they called "psycho-tronic" research. Because of the large budget the KGB had appropriated, more than $21 million per year, it was thought that their program had produced significant results. Otherwise, why the generous funding, spread out over 20 separate institutions?

Of course, the CIA responded by launching something similar. They soon installed their own program to study remote spying, or, as it came to be called, remote viewing.

The initial tests had been conducted by SRI, located in California. Russell Targ, cofounder of the Institute, had been investigating psychic abilities, specifically remote viewing, and eventually wrote about it in journals such as *Nature, The Proceed-*

Parapsychologist and physicist Russell Targ worked for SRI's remote viewing program and, later, for the Stargate Project.

ings of the Institute of Electrical and Electronics Engineers (IEEE), and the *Proceedings of the American Association for the Advancement of Science* (AAAS). He would go on to write books dealing with the scientific investigation of psychic abilities, specializing in Buddhist ideas concerning the transformation of consciousness. One of his most well-received books is *The Reality of ESP: A Physicist's Proof of Psychic Abilities.* In his retirement he would go on to teach remote viewing.

His colleague, Harold Puthoff, was instrumental in developing biofeedback and biofield measurements, but he became well known after his remote viewing research at SRI. Some of his experiments consisted of a simple test for ESP in which one person would go to a specified location while another attempted to describe what the first person was seeing.

Targ and Puthoff reported remarkable success and published their findings in their 1977 book, *Mind-Reach.* Others, following their lead, were able to replicate the experiments.

Critics, however, claimed to have found a flaw in their research. They claimed subjects had been given subtle clues prior to the results being declared. This prompted new research that prevented the cueing. Robert Jahn, physicist and founder of Princeton Engineering Anomalies Research (PEAR) lab, reported positive results with the new format.

Uri Geller, shown here performing his famous spoon bending trick in front of a crowd, is a magician who passed his prestidigitation off as a form of psychic skill.

One of the subjects Targ and Puthoff studied was Uri Geller, an Israeli-British illusionist, magician, television personality, and self-proclaimed psychic. His most famous claim to fame was that he could bend spoons with his mind, but he was later found to have used typical conjuring tricks known to many stage illusionists. When he was investigated by Dr. Ray Hyman, professor of psychology at the University of Oregon, Hyman pronounced Geller a "complete fraud." Partly because of this, the SRI had trouble maintaining their government contract.

They did, however, manage to score one significant point. In 1976, they located a lost Soviet spy plane. This was enough to launch Stargate Project under Lt. Atwater in 1977.

The SRI team worked clandestinely until 1984, when the existence of the program was finally discovered. When it became public, however, the National Academy of Sciences National Research Council didn't approve. Army funding was cut off. By 1995 a defense appropriations bill transferred the program to the CIA. A subsequent report found that remote viewing had not been proved to work by psychic mechanisms and assured the public that the program had not been used operationally. Eventually, it was canceled and declassified. In 2017, the CIA finally published online records of Stargate Project.

The people who worked on the project, however, now freed from the constraints of classification, have, in many cases, a different story to tell. Joseph McMoneagle, for instance, believes that "the Army never had a truly open attitude toward psychic functioning." He said the criticism was obvious in terms such as "giggle factor" and an "in" saying at the time, "I wouldn't want to be found dead next to a psychic."

According to others who participated, they had produced some reliable intelligence that the army didn't want to publicize because they were afraid it might be discounted simply because it came from Stargate Project.

Still, questions continue to follow the project. There are some who see only a red herring in the announcement that the program was canceled. After all, the same was said about UFOs after the Roswell incident, but it is now acknowledged that Project Blue Book continued until December 1969.

The best theory is probably one of expediency, however. The simple fact is that remote viewing, at its best, is subject to human error. The advanced intelligence-gathering ability of electronic surveillance and spy satellites developed since 1995 offers a much more sophisticated, reliable system, but it's hard to ignore some pretty obvious examples of success.

President Jimmy Carter, for instance, made a campaign promise to check out and make public secret government information about UFOs. After he was elected and questioned by the media, he pivoted away from a direct question, and in doing so he revealed the government's involvement with remote viewing:

> *We had a plane go down in the Central African Republic—a twin-engine plane, small plane. And we couldn't find it. And so we oriented satellites that were going around the earth every ninety minutes to fly over that spot where we thought it might be and take photographs. We couldn't find it. So the director of the CIA came and told me that he had contacted a woman in California who claimed to have supernatural capabilities. And she went in a trance, and she wrote down latitudes and longitudes, and we sent our satellites over that latitude and longitude, and there was the plane.*

The program was set up to include two separate, segregated units, each with its own specialty. The first was operational. Its mission was to train remote viewers to specifically perform intelligence gathering.

The second consisted of a research program to study the activity itself. What they learned was that if remote viewing was a reality, there were three different things that might be going on.

· The first was that remote viewing is an example of clairvoyance. This consists of the viewer in effect hovering over a target and describing it or, usually, drawing a picture of what he or she saw.

· The second involved telepathy, or reading the mind of the subject involved in the study.

· The third was precognition, or reading the future after the information was later discovered through other means.

Let's consider an example. Suppose you are on the West Coast of the United States and decide to remote-view a friend who is on vacation on the East Coast, visiting a national park. You tune in and get a clear reading of a seashore and lighthouse. Later, this turns out to be accurate. Three things might have happened:

1. You saw the same landscape your friend was seeing (clairvoyance).

2. You read your friend's mind (telepathy).

3. Your friend would soon send you a postcard, but you already saw what that postcard would contain (precognition).

It would be very easy, at this point, to wander far afield of NDEs and delve deeply into the government's remote viewing program. It's a fascinating subject. Remote viewing and NDEs are not the same thing, however. They may be close cousins, in the sense that both illustrate the idea that we are more than our physical bodies

Clairvoyance, telepathy, and precognition are three types of psychic abilities that would allow a sensitive person to perform remote viewing.

and consist of something above and beyond biology that can separate and exist independent of material cells and organs. But our purpose in this book is to specifically study NDEs, so we will resist the temptation to delve too far into remote viewing.

Still, a few examples might prove interesting. By 1995, at its conclusion, the program had produced a number of what they called "eight martini" results. The name comes from the fact that some of the data they collected was so mind-blowing that the participants felt that at the close of day they all wanted to go out and share some drinks to come down from the high they had experienced. Joe McMoneagle alone claims to have provided information for at least 150 separate targets.

In 1974, a remote viewer appeared to have correctly described a Soviet nuclear testing area at Semipalatinsk. He correctly reported an airfield consisting of a gantry and crane at one end of a field. This indicated the possibility of an underground nuclear testing site. There was sufficient corroboration to obtain map coordinates, which later verified the possibility of just such a facility.

In September 1979, the National Security Council staff asked about a Soviet submarine they believed to be under construction. A remote viewer reported that a very large, new submarine, with 18 to 20 missile launch tubes and a "large flat area," would be launched in 100 days. One hundred twenty days later, two submarines, one with 24 launch tubes and the other with 20 launch tubes and a large flat area on the aft deck, were sighted.

One of the targets of Stargate Project was Libyan revolutionary and tyrant Muammar al-Qaddafi. A bombing raid based on remote viewing was executed, but Qaddafi escaped unharmed.

There are, as of now, unconfirmed reports that remote viewers tried to locate and target Muammar al-Qaddafi in 1986. Their results led to a bombing raid, but Qaddafi was not harmed.

A similar result, in that it was unsuccessful, was obtained by attempts to locate Osama bin Laden in late 2001. The same thing had happened during the Gulf War. Remote viewers were reported to have suggested the whereabouts of Iraq's Saddam Hussein. There was never an independent verification of this finding.

In 1988 a remote viewer claimed that Marine Corps Col. William Higgins was being held in a specific South Lebanon village. Later, a released hostage was said to have claimed that Higgins had probably been in that building at that time.

Many other examples could be examined. Numerous anecdotal stories about finding Scud missiles and secret biological and chemical warfare projects circulate from time to time, along with reports about tunnels and extensive underground facilities in various countries. They were so persistent that Sen. Claiborne Pell and Rep. Charles Rose were convinced of the effectiveness of the program. But by the early 1990s, the program was plagued by uneven management, poor unit morale, divisiveness within the organization, poor performance, and few accurate results. In 1995 the defense appropriations bill directed that the program be transferred to the CIA, with instructions to conduct a retrospective review. In September of that year their report was released to the public.

Despite a statistically significant effect under laboratory conditions (psychics were said to be accurate about 15% of the time), the final recommendation was to terminate Stargate Project. The CIA had concluded that there was no case in which ESP had provided data used to guide intelligence operations.

More than 20 psychics had been employed over the years. Some ended up in psychiatric hospitals. Others seemed to get sidetracked, obsessing over things such as alien intervention and crop circles. Some $20 million had been invested, which, however, is not very much compared to other military projects. But the suspicion is widely held that the real reason the project was shelved did not involve money. It was just that the Defense Department was embarrassed by the whole thing.

In short, anyone who involves themselves with psychic abilities, or their close cousins, NDEs, needs to be careful of public backlash.

9 RESEARCH FROM THE INSTITUTE OF NOETIC SCIENCES (IONS)

We need to make the world safe for creativity and intuition, for it is creativity and intuition that will make the world safe for us.

—Attributed to Dr. Edgar Mitchell, source unknown

In 1971, Edgar Mitchell was on his way home from work. His commute was longer than most folks are accustomed to: more than 239,000 miles (382,500 kilometers). But it gave him time to think.

He had just become the sixth person in the history of the planet—or, for that matter, the 13.8-billion-year history of the universe—to walk on the surface of the moon. As a member of the Apollo 14 space mission, he had been trained to conduct research on the lunar surface. Little did he know that the actual thing that would transform his life would happen on the way home. He would gain an entirely new purpose in life that would define him for decades to come and probably forever change life on his home planet.

Looking out the window, contemplating the darkness and vastness of space, he remained fixated on the small blue sphere that he called home. In that moment of meditation and reflection he was enveloped by a profound sense of connectedness. Gazing out at the place where everyone he ever knew and everything he read about had happened:

> *I realized that the story of ourselves as told by science—our cosmology, our religion—was incomplete and likely flawed. I recognized that the Newtonian idea of separate, independent, discrete things in the universe wasn't a fully accurate description. What was needed was a new story of who we are and what we are capable of becoming.*

A year later, in 1972, he retired from both the navy and the space program. A year after that he founded the Institute of Noetic Sciences (IONS) in California. In his 1996 book, *The Way of the Explorer*, he wrote about his experience as an astronaut and the depths of the spiritual journey that began way out in space. His goal for the institute was to apply the scientifically exact tools he had been part of in the exploration of *outer* space to a new frontier: the mysteries of *inner* space. To this end he dedicated the rest of his life, until his passing in 2016.

He never experienced an NDE himself, but his work informs the experience of everyone who ever has. According to the mission statement of the Institute of Noetic Sciences:

> *We use the power of science to explore our inner space, understanding that both objective knowledge and subjective knowing are necessary for a more complete understanding…. The mission of the Institute of Noetic Sciences is to reveal the interconnected nature of reality through scientific exploration and personal discovery. We trust that individuals who have had their own transformative experiences will learn from our research—both our scientific experiments and our opportunities for personal discovery—and gain a deeper sense of their own purpose. We believe that by accessing that same sense of interconnectedness Dr. Mitchell felt on his return from the moon, we can all contribute to enhancing the quality of life on Earth.*

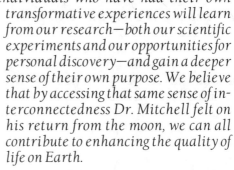

Aeronautical engineer, retired test pilot, and NASA astronaut Edgar Mitchell is the founder of the Institute of Noetic Sciences in California.

The chief scientist at the institute is Dr. Dean Radin. His original career path involved studying to become a concert violinist, but after earning a bachelor of science degree with honors in electrical engineering from the University of Massachusetts, a master's degree in electrical engineering from the University of Illinois, followed by a Ph.D. in educational psychology, that path took a turn. Among other appointments, he found himself working with SRI International, eventually conducting top-secret research in conjunction with the military's Stargate Project. Eventually this led him to IONS.

The author of numerous popular books on the subject, including *The Conscious Universe: The Scientific Truth of Psychic Phenomena*; *Entangled Minds: Extrasensory Experiences in a Quantum Reality*; *Supernormal: Science, Yoga, and the Evidence for Extraordinary Psychic Abilities*; and the best-selling *Real Magic: Ancient Wisdom, Modern Science, and a Guide to the Secret Power of the Universe*, he has also authored and coauthored many scientific papers.

One of his most recent papers, "Rating the Persuasiveness of Empirical Evidence for the Survival of Consciousness after Bodily Death," coauthored with Helané Wahbeh and Arnaud Delorme and published in April 2023, is about the science of NDEs.

The objective of the study is straightforward:

Throughout history and across all cultures, many people have believed in some form of afterlife. Recent surveys show that most people worldwide believe they will survive after bodily death. Those who do not believe would require substantial empirical evidence to influence their skepticism. This study's objective was to evaluate what types of evidence might persuade academic professionals that some aspect of consciousness survives after bodily death.

In their research, they write:

We surveyed academic professionals and collected demographic and professional background data, personal confidence in survival, and paranormal belief ratings. Respondents also rated the persuasiveness of 10 relevant experiments and the likelihood of their success. These data were analyzed over all participants and partitioned by confidence in survival.

Taking into account such factors as gender bias, paranormal belief, and age, they concluded that although prior belief heavily

The majority of people in most cultures believe there is some kind of existence after bodily death. For example, Dia de los Muertos (the Day of the Dead) is a Mexican tradition combining All Souls' Day from the Spanish with Aztec traditions that acknowledge the deceased are still with us and can be honored and even presented with gifts.

influenced whether people accepted many subjective studies in the field, "successful experiments designed to test for survival may influence skeptics' prior beliefs."

In earlier chapters of this book, we suggest that when it comes to accepting the reality of NDEs, many people first form an opinion, based primarily on their cultural experience, and then go on to buttress that opinion with cherry-picked facts that bolster what they already believed.

This seems to agree with the findings of Dr. Radin's study, but if this is the case, it simply offers more reason to conduct detailed, carefully controlled research that can be used to at least keep channels of communication and mutual respect open between those who seek truth within the confines of their various spiritual "tribes" and scientific "denominations."

It sounds rather easy. All we have to do is conduct scientific research into a universal human experience. It's rather straightforward, isn't it?

Well, no it isn't! Given the loaded emotional and cultural climate that surrounds this subject, it sometimes seems all but impossible to finance such endeavors, publish them in peer-reviewed journals, and then find qualified and accepted panelists who will agree to examine and debate the subject. Fear of ridicule reigns almost supreme on one side. A history of deceit and simplistic faith statements infect the other.

Consider this now-famous example.

> Given the loaded emotional and cultural climate that surrounds this subject, it sometimes seems all but impossible to finance such endeavors....

In 2014, a movie came out called *Heaven Is for Real* (see also page 26). It was based on the book *The Boy Who Came Back from Heaven,* published in 2010. The book sold more than 10 million copies and spent 206 weeks on the *New York Times* Best Sellers list. The movie went on to earn some $91 million. It told the story of a young boy who revealed to his parents that he had experienced an NDE during emergency surgery, and had visited heaven.

The road to such success had been paved by countless thousands of NDE narrations, but two recent books, *Proof of Heaven* by Eben Alexander and *To Heaven and Back* by Mary C. Neal, M.D., certainly have contributed to the mix. Alexander is a well-respected neurosurgeon who experienced an NDE during a medically induced, week-long coma brought on by meningitis. Neal's had occurred during a kayaking accident. Both had primed the *New York Times* best-seller pump, one spending 94 weeks on the list, and the other 36.

Those who accepted NDEs were elated. Their time in the sun seemed to have finally arrived.

Those who rejected NDEs were less than enthusiastic and spent their time hoping the subject would eventually die away when public consciousness moved on to something more palatable.

Then the positions reversed. The young boy at the center of the controversy admitted he had made the whole thing up.

"See?" crowed the naysayers. "We told you so!"

The believers weren't convinced. Had the boy really "made the whole thing up," or had a young, impressionable kid succumbed to the intense pressure put on him by friends and, even worse, sarcastic and unfeeling reporters who were looking for publicity? In other words, was he finally won over by those who insisted his highly subjective experience was simply a product of his imagination?

(This experience is not limited to impressionistic children. Hamish Miller was a dowsing mentor of mine, even though we never met in person and probably were never on the same continent at the same time. Called by some the "grandfather" of British dowsers, his books and films are quite famous. He has taught thousands of people how to dowse for earth energy. Although he died before I got to the UK, I had tea one day in his home in Cornwall with his wife, Ba Miller, a wonderful, gracious lady who told me that sometimes even Hamish, the chief dowser himself, would come home, throw his dowsing rods in the corner, and say, "I'm making up the whole thing in my head!" Then, next day, he would be out doing it again. Such is our tendency to doubt ourselves, especially when we are experiencing something that tends to elude the ability of material science to prove.)

This whole episode ignited a firestorm of passionate arguments on both sides of the issue. It must have been much worse for the youngster, in the throes of what we all had to deal with while growing up yet caught in the middle of a tempest and ridiculed by both sides. As is often the case in these terribly divided days, during which a standard means of argument is to attack a person's character rather than their facts, it led to a further rift between opposing camps.

IONS tends to be a beacon for truth in these divided times. They strive to make their research methods impeccable enough to satisfy even a highly critical scientific community that is steeped in the scientific method and hedged in with strict checks and balances, but the subjects they take on are often rejected out of hand by those who claim objectivity while often holding biased positions.

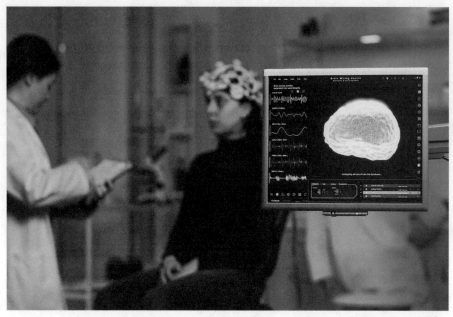

Neurologists and other medical professionals have been studying brain activity as it is related to consciousness, sleep, and death for years. There is still no consensus on issues such as "what is consciousness?" and "is consciousness and identity linked to certain parts of the brain?"

A recent study at IONS, for instance, was described online. Its objectives were simply stated:

> *While research evidence is strong that some aspect of our consciousness may exist beyond physical death, the ideas about exactly what persists are varied. Do our personalities—with memories, thoughts, and emotions—remain intact indefinitely, or does our consciousness merge with something larger, or something else entirely? World religions certainly have much to say about this topic, but what do people believe? IONS is conducting a study to assess people's beliefs on what survives physical death.*

Results from this longitudinal study are still forthcoming.

An April 2015 article in *The Atlantic*, written by Gideon Lichfield, is called "The Science of Near-Death Experiences: Empirically Investigating Brushes with the Afterlife." In it, he begins with the familiar litany of universal instances that outline the typical stages of an NDE. He then offers the usual arguments of the disclaimers about stresses on a dying brain. He admits that a respected neurosurgeon such as Eben Alexander must be taken seriously by the scientific community, even though the NDE led to a spiritual transformation that is probably not very scientific. But, in Lichfield's words:

> Alexander has not published his medical findings about himself in any peer-reviewed journal, and a 2013 investigative article in Esquire questioned several details of his account, among them the crucial claim that his experience took place while his brain was incapable of any activity. To the skeptics, his story and the recent recanting of The Boy Who Came Back from Heaven are just further evidence that NDEs rank right up there with alien abductions, psychic powers, and poltergeists, as fodder for charlatans looking to gull the ignorant and suggestible.

On the other hand:

> Even skeptics rarely accuse experiencers of inventing their stories from whole cloth. Though some of these stories may be fabrications, and more no doubt become embellished in the retelling, they're too numerous and well documented to be dismissed altogether. It's also hard to ignore the accounts by respected physicians with professional reputations to protect. Even if the afterlife isn't real, the sensations of having been there certainly are.

And so the debate, some might call it a war, continues to this day. Neither side trusts the other. Neither, it seems, will even listen to the other. That's what makes the work of IONS so valuable. Though sometimes scorned by believers and unbelievers alike, they continue to study what is undeniably a scientifically intriguing subject as well as a paranormalist's dream.

There is something compelling about wanting to know what happens when we die. As medical technology continues to improve, it's bringing people back from the very brink of death. Are those people pioneers, or are they just deceived by biology?

Maybe that's what makes real scientific research more important than ever.

10 STORIES FROM THE MONROE INSTITUTE (TMI)

We are more than our physical bodies.

—Robert A. Monroe

Just as is the case with the Institute of Noetic Sciences (IONS), to tell the story of, let alone analyze, the work done at the Monroe Institute would take more than a chapter in a book. Indeed, many books have been written, and continue to be written, about the humble, provocative, farseeing, and insightful Bob Monroe, who, probably more than any other, put science into the study of out-of-body experiences. The work there goes on uninterrupted long after his death in 1995, and no book about NDEs would be complete without at least mentioning his name and legacy. Earlier we talked about his work with Skip Atwater and the military's Stargate Program. In effect, we brought Monroe into Atwater's story. Now it's time to complete the picture by bringing Atwater into Monroe's. But first, some background.

When Bob Monroe entered this earthly sphere, he found himself in a tiny body that weighed all of two pounds. His life took on much greater stature with the passing of time, of course. Physically and mentally, it wasn't an easy path. He found himself, at one point, riding the rails as a hobo, looking for work. But he eventually graduated from Ohio State University, studying pre-med, English, engineering, and journalism. His interests ran from flying, to music, to mechanics. With this varied background, it is probably not surprising that he went on to pioneer

Sleep learning is the theory that a person can absorb information while asleep by hearing recordings played. Researchers eventually concluded that, no, this doesn't work at all.

a totally different field, and it would seem even that happened by accident.

In 1953, Monroe formed RAM Enterprises. It was a corporation that specialized in network radio programing. But three years into his work he created an R&D division designed to study the effects of various sound frequencies on human consciousness. Included in this research was a project that studied something in which he was increasingly interested. He wanted to study sleep-learning.

This fit right into his life journey at the time, because during an early experiment he had his first out-of-body experience. In his book *Journeys Out of the Body*, he described it as a "sensation of paralysis and vibration accompanied by a bright light that appeared to be shining on him from a shallow angle." This happened nine times over a period of six weeks, culminating in his first OBE, a term he either coined or rescued from obscurity.

When his company later moved to Virginia, changing its name to Monroe Industries, he became active in radio, cable television, and the production of audio cassettes. The cassettes soon became a vehicle for the discoveries that eventually led to Hemi-Sync®, about which we shall soon have more to say.

In 1985, the company name was changed again, this time to Interstate Industries, Inc. Eventually this move would be used as a handy metaphor Monroe would employ when describing Hemi-Sync® as "a ramp from the local road to the interstate which allowed people to go full steam ahead in the exploration of consciousness, avoiding all of the stops and starts."

Eventually, as OBE research took on more and more importance, the Monroe Institute would be founded as an independent, nonprofit, privately held company. Even after his death, his daughter, Laurie Monroe, continued his research into universal consciousness and the mind's potential, until her death in 2006. Tens of thousands of people have attended the institute's programs and courses at its locations around the world.

In 1978 the U.S. military evaluated TMI and arranged to send officers there for OBE training. The one who arranged all this was, of course, Lt. Frederick Holmes (Skip) Atwater.

Hemi-Sync® is short for hemispheric synchronization. It is a highly sophisticated process that is probably too technical to go into in great detail in a book such as this, but the basic concept, taken from the Monroe Institute's website, is this:

> Hemi-Sync® is an audio-guidance process that works through the generation of complex, multilayered audio signals, which act together to create a resonance that is reflected in unique brain wave forms characteristic of specific states of consciousness. The result is a focused, whole-brain state known as hemispheric synchroniza-tion, or "Hemi-Sync®," where the left and right hemi-spheres are working together in a state of coherence. As an analogy, lasers produce focused, coherent light. Hemi-Sync® produces a focused, coherent mind, which is an op-timal condition for improving human performance.

How it works is not as important as the fact that thousands upon thousands of people, including me, have used it with great success and swear by its efficacy when it comes to aiding the achievement of out-of-body experiences.

Take, for example, one of the first OBEs I had after I began to use Hemi-Sync®. I wrote about it in my book *The Quantum Akashic Field*:

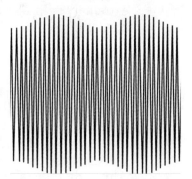

> Suddenly I found myself, completely unexpectedly, on Martha's Vineyard in Massachusetts, trying to talk to the President of the United States. He seemed as close to me as if we were both in the same room. My wife used to live on Martha's Vineyard, and I've visited a few times. When she later asked me if I recognized any buildings, I drew a complete blank. I have no idea why I "knew" I was there. Later, as a matter of fact, I remember thinking that I must have been mistaken. I assumed that

Hemi-Sync® uses binaural sound beats to synchronize the brain's two hemispheres. A binaural sound (il-lustrated here as two sine waves) is employed with a different tone in each ear. The variance in Herz frequencies will result in a beat paced according to the difference be-tween the two tones' frequencies.

with all the current tension in the Middle East, President Obama must be in Washington. But, as it turned out, he was there on the Vineyard at the time, doing whatever passes for a presidential vacation, assuming that there is such a thing. I seem to remember that I had a message that needed to be delivered to him. The message was, "faith, trust, and belief." That's all. But I said it a few times and he seemed to nod, as if hearing the words.

When I returned to my body I wondered if someone had given him a copy of the book I had written with that title. My ego thus reared its ugly head. But at the time, I wasn't interested in him thinking of me at all. I just felt that in the midst of all the turmoil he was experiencing the need to be grounded in faith, trust, and belief. That's all.

(Later: It turns out someone did eventually send him a copy of my book, *Faith, Trust, & Belief*. I did! He and Michelle sent me a nice thank you letter. It was a form letter, of course, but I really appreciated it.)

The Monroe Institute's Gateway program, the primary introductory course offered at TMI's facility, introduces participants, step by careful step, to explorations of inner consciousness. It is thoughtfully conceived and carried out, perfectly safe, and extremely helpful when it comes to dealing with the emotional response such an endeavor is bound to create in each individual.

Programs have grown at the institute, which now offers, among others, a course in contacting and guiding to new realities those who have died but somehow have become "stuck" in a condition they don't fully understand.

Traditionally, this has been the task of the psychopomp, or guide, whose primary function is to escort souls to the afterlife. Although stories of these beings are found throughout mythology in virtually every culture on earth, the folks at TMI have brought a new dimension to the role.

In many cases, when students return from an OBE with reports of having found or even escorted people onward and upward, they go to the trouble of consulting public records to find and identify the deceased.

The results have been surprising. It's tough to argue that the student made the whole thing up when confronting the death certificate of a person never known to any of the participants of the course.

To cite another personal example, this is one of the experiences I had, which occurred completely unexpectedly. Indeed, I had never even heard of such a thing before it happened to me. But this is the account I recorded in my dream journal right after it happened:

Many cultures have stories of spirits who help to escort the dead to their new place in the afterlife.

She always enjoyed that time of the year when her family traveled to this hilltop to gather the stone blanks they needed to make tools for the coming year. Folks would come from far away each spring. It was a time of celebration and companionship—a time for sharing food and the closeness of the fire circle. The old people told stories and the young caught up with news from all over. It was a time for weddings and dancing.

For many years now she had felt a kinship with the stones they found here. They were bright and beautiful—good material for working into tools, but also somewhat mystical. It was as if stones contained a hidden magic, a message they would reveal if only she held them long enough and listened carefully.

Once she had found, right here on this hill, a small rock that, with only a few well-placed strokes of her small hammer stone, she shaped into the image of a hawk, a bird she especially respected. Hawk was her spirit messenger.

She kept the hawk/stone with her at all times while they visited this quarry, and then hid it carefully in a special place above the shore line where she could easily find it when they returned during the next season.

But this year was a time of rains and storm. On the eve of the day they had decided to leave they experienced the biggest storm yet. Water rose to the place where they often played and fished. She felt compelled to go and see that her hiding place for hawk was safe.

No one saw what happened next. They only knew she disappeared during the flood. Had the bank collapsed? Had she stood too close to the edge?

Her family called and called, searching in the storm for any sign of her, but they never saw her again. They finally placed a small mound of stones high on the bank of the river where they thought she had last stood. Maybe it would serve as a beacon to guide her spirit home. Eventually they gave up, and departed in sorrow.

The effigy of the hawk remained hidden in its secret place. It would not be found for many years. The mound of stones eventually collapsed as the river became a stream, and then a mere seasonal trickle of water. Once every few years the trickle would swell to a flood as if remembering what it once had been, but it was a parody of its former self. Men came and went—strange men who had forgotten the important things that had once happened here. The world became a different place. But the hawk effigy knew and remembered. Years passed, and times changed, but hawk kept vigil.

> **The little girl was not conscious of the passing of time, but she was somehow troubled. She didn't quite know what had happened to her, and she had many questions.**

The little girl was not conscious of the passing of time, but she was somehow troubled. She didn't quite know what had happened to her, and she had many questions. She felt the same, but somehow different. Her surroundings seemed somewhat gray, as if the sun was hidden from her view. It was not unpleasant, but she didn't know what to do next.

She thought it best to stay where she was and wait for help—for guidance. This place was familiar, somehow, but seemed different than she remembered.

Then one day she felt a calling, a tugging, that guided her to the last place she remembered on Earth. Although the mound of stones up on the hill had long since disappeared, there was a new circle of stones placed below, ringing in the place of power that had beckoned her long ago and caused her to walk too close to the edge of the river. She was fascinated by the wheel of stones, and approached it with pent-up anticipation.

It was here that she saw the spirit guide. He was a kindly man with a white beard, who recognized her immediately and called her "ancestor." He held out his hands and invited her to dance. At first, they just held hands and twirled around with no pattern and no ritual. But it was joyous. Then he asked her to teach him to dance the way she was accustomed. She backed off and began to show him the dance steps used by her family on special occasions—celebrations of good things. Together they danced round and round the circle.

As they danced the gray began to lift. She began to awaken as if from a long sleep. She looked up toward the side of the stream where she had last stood, where the mound of stones marking her passing had been placed. A strange structure now stood there, rising up far above her.

And there stood her family! They greeted her as if she had returned from a journey! She was reunited with those whom she loved. The skies cleared above her and all was bright, and blue, and gold.

Below her the spirit guide ceased his dance and slowly faded away. For a moment it was as if she had been contained within an immense universe of love. And then that universe in turn filled her to overflowing.

Far above, hawk looked down and smiled. All that had been needed was time. And time meant nothing, really. It was all an illusion. But a very pleasant one.

What does all this mean? I've had years now to consider the possibilities. Did I imagine the whole thing? Did I string together thoughts and images, dreams and daydreams, to weave a com-

The hawk stone I discovered.

pletely imaginary fabric of illusion that, for some reason, I want to believe?

My problem with this simple but obvious explanation is that on many levels I don't want to believe it really happened, in this or any other universe. If it did, and if I accept it, that means much of my life has been spent living a lie, or at least being misguided by a powerful illusion.

For most of my professional life I simply did not believe in such things. I even privately looked askance at those who did. In fact, there is a very big part of me that still refuses to believe it is possible for everyday people like me to see into hidden dimensions and time zones, all of which must be real if this story is true. It would be much easier to retire and die a peaceful death, after a successful life well spent.

But I can't. The images are too real, the experience too vivid. My study of metaphysics, although certainly not academically certified, has produced too many questions to doubt the validity of the possibility of such things.

And there's one more thing. It might sound silly, but I can't ignore it.

A few years ago, my wife, Barbara, was looking for stones to build a fence. She was searching along a natural shoreline that once would have been part of an ancient tributary of the Savannah River. This would have been the beach of that ancient lake that covered the ground where our Medicine Wheel is now located. We built our gazebo right at the high-water mark. It's a good place to look for material that would make a dandy stone wall.

One of the stones she found was palm-sized, obviously worked by an ancient hand, and felt warm to the touch. It appeared to have been shaped into the image of a hawk.

Perhaps the best way to get a handle on the work of TMI is to examine their initial Gateway program. What is it, how does it work, and what is the science behind it?

Our Medicine Wheel is located where there was once a lake beach.

In 1983, the U.S. Army Operational Group ordered an analysis and assessment of the Gateway process. The mission was spearheaded by Wayne M. McDonnell, and the mission objective was to thoroughly examine the program to, in effect, answer the very questions we just asked.

Skip Atwater, a former director of TMI, was kind enough to send me the letter McDonnell wrote after the committee finished its work:

9 June 1983

SUBJECT: Analysis and Assessment of Gateway Process
TO: Commander
US Army Operational Group
Fort Meade, MD 20755

You tasked me to provide an assessment of the Gateway Experience in terms of its mechanics and ultimate practicality. As I set out to fulfill that tasking it soon became clear that in order to assess the validity and practicality of the process, I needed to do enough supporting research and analysis to fully understand how and why the process works. Frankly, sir, that proved to be an extremely involved and difficult business.

The committee went on to study such things as hypnosis, biofeedback, and transcendental meditation. They soon learned that more than intellectual logic was required. They needed to employ, in their words, "a touch of right-brain intuitive insight" if they were going to grasp the concepts.

> **Their first obstacle involved the problem of religion, because any study of what is often called a "spiritual" subject involves individual religious experience....**

Their first obstacle involved the problem of religion, because any study of what is often called a "spiritual" subject involves individual religious experience:

I felt that it was necessary, after having completed the analysis, to point out that the resulting conclusions do not do any violence to the fundamental mainstream of either eastern or western belief systems.

After pages and pages of very dense prose, some final conclusions were reached:

There is a sound, rational basis in terms of physical science parameters for considering Gateway to be plausible in terms of its essential objectives.

They then recommended a twelve-step process and concluded that:

If these experiments are carried through, it is to be hoped that we will truly find a gateway to Gateway and to the realm of practical application for the whole system of techniques that comprise it.

The entire analysis is available free of charge through TMI. It is informative, very detailed, and incredibly boring unless you are accustomed to military-speak mixed in with science and philosophical mumbo-jumbo. It never uses one word when ten will serve just as well.

To put Gateway into a simple context, a group of 24 interested participants gathers at the Institute's facility on a Saturday afternoon. They stay through the next Friday morning, each day alternating informal lectures with hands-on participation. Each participant is assigned what amounts to a sleep/cubicle area that is equipped with headphones connected to a central broadcasting booth. After each gathering, specific Hemi-Sync music is played through the earphones and a guided meditation begins, designed to help listeners through various stages of environments labeled with such names as Focus 10, Focus 12, Focus 15, and Focus 21. These levels describe various states of consciousness.

The success rate of participants is high enough that many come back for advanced courses, featuring the same type of methodology but focusing in on a specific area of the OBE experience.

It's easy to disparage TMI's courses, given that they are outside the mainstream and practical experience of most people. But the subject matter is, by definition, outside the mainstream. That's exactly the point. To study these subjects is to move outside the mainstream, but the experiences are so widespread, and they consist of such universally similar examples, that aside from the few agencies we're looking at in this section, no one is even *attempting* to bring them into a field of formal academic study that is so necessary if we want to understand the complete nature of humanity.

That brings us to the final agency we will examine.

11 IANDS AND THE CURRENT SCENE

NDEs are perhaps the only spiritual experience that we have a chance of investigating in a truly thorough, scientific way. It makes them a vehicle for exploring the ancient human belief that we are more than meat. And it makes them a lens through which to peer at the workings of consciousness—one of the great mysteries of human existence, even for the most resolute materialist.

—Gideon Lichfield in "The Science of Near-Death Experiences: Empirically Investigating Brushes with the Afterlife." *The Atlantic*, April 2015

If there is one central storehouse for NDE research, it is probably the International Association for Near-Death Studies (IANDS), a nonprofit organization now based in Durham, North Carolina.

Originally called the Association for the Scientific Study of Near-Death Phenomena, founded in 1978 by John Audette, Bruce Greyson, Kenneth Ring, and Michael Sabom, the association changed its name in 1981 and established headquarters in Connecticut. In the late 1980s, IANDS moved its base to Philadelphia and opened branches across the country. Consisting of some 50 local groups and worldwide membership of more than 1,200, its purpose is to "study and provide information on the phenomena of the near-death experience ... and to build a global understanding of near-death and near-death-like experiences through research, education, and support."

Kenneth Ring is an American psychologist who cofounded the International Association for Near-Death Studies. He also served as the organization's president and is founding editor of the *Journal of Near-Death Studies*.

If you attend one of its yearly conventions, you will find panel discussions reporting on such varied topics as "What Medical Neuroscience Can Learn from NDEs," "Sacred Geometry Dance: Creating a Vortex to Open to the Divine," and "Group Past-Life Regression."

One of the most valuable contributions accomplished by IANDS is a byproduct of its research. By collecting data from all over, they have become a clearinghouse for information. Kept under one roof, so to speak, is an immense quantity of firsthand accounts, historical papers, and results of the latest studies. From what is considered to be the oldest known medical description of an NDE, written by 18th-century French military doctor Pierre-Jean du Monchaux (see also page 17), to the latest medical research since the publication of Raymond Moody's famous *Life after Life* in 1975, thrust NDEs into the public eye, there have been thousands of testimonies that might never have seen the light of day. Thanks to IANDS, many of those stories are now readily available for study and research. As a result, a small but growing community of psychiatrists, psychologists, cardiologists, and specialists of various kinds now have access to research that greatly speeds up the process of longitudinal studies that once took years to accomplish. Besides that, these medical specialists now feel free to give talks and lectures that spread the word even faster.

They all share a common belief: the mind, or perhaps soul, exists in some nonmaterial form, independent of but closely connected to the brain. NDEs seem to indicate evidence for their belief. Where once the field was nearly forgotten, or at least shoved under the proverbial rug, a recent database maintained by the United States National Library of Medicine now lists some 240 specific papers on the subject. Countless more can be found in mainstream medical publications.

This isn't totally good news. Many of the accounts occurred years ago, the ones telling the stories having kept quiet until it became socially acceptable to bring their memories into the light of day. Recollection is a tricky thing. Perhaps, some say, the stories

The United States National Library of Medicine in Bethesda, Maryland, is the largest medical library in the world. The extensive collection includes some 240 papers on NDEs.

were embellished over time. This doesn't imply deception on the part of the one telling the story, but it's only natural for the intellect to try to connect dots and make the story more uniform.

For this reason, researchers now try to arrange an interview of consenting patients at a hospital as soon as possible after the experience. Patients are usually asked open-ended questions about what, if anything, they experienced while doctors were trying to revive them. If something unusual pops up, medical records are compared and analyzed. So far, more than 300 personal NDEs are on record.

IANDS is a central clearinghouse for all these accounts. A researcher could spend days getting lost in the online material they have amassed.

This is not to say that all is bright, beautiful, and rosy in the land of modern NDE research. The principal argument against so-called scientific research is that there is, and probably always has been, a distrust of science within the NDE community. When something happens that is deep, emotional, and life-changing, it is disconcerting to have some "expert" try to debunk your dream.

Gideon Lichfield attended an IANDS conference in which he interviewed psychiatrist and professor Mitch Liester, who ad-

British journalist Gideon Lichfield often reports on science and technology reviews for such publications as the *Economist* and *MIT Technology Review*.

mitted to a "near-death-like experience" even though he wasn't near death at all. Neither was he under the influence of any hallucinogens. When asked what he thought about NDEs, Liester answered, "Many people who've had near-death experiences aren't that interested in the science. My rational brain doesn't quite believe it but, having experienced it, I know it's true. So it's an ongoing discussion I'm having with myself."

Lichfield went on to ask if there was a middle ground somewhere between spiritualists and materialists.

Liester's answer was telling. "A lot of materialist scientists don't seem to think it's a serious field of scientific inquiry.... Meanwhile, many people who've had near-death experiences aren't that interested in the science."

Once a week, Liester said, he has breakfast with a group that includes a physicist, a scientist, an artist, a chaplain with a philosophy degree, and a hospice counselor who is also a Native American sun dancer. They talk about how to take NDE research forward with a rigorous scientific attitude but an open mind. "I think there is a way to bridge the gap," he said.

In his opinion, research could be pushed forward by imaging the brains of people such as shamans while in a mystical state or trance. They could "try to probe the nature of the memories formed during NDEs, and how they differ from ordinary memories. They could devise experimentally sound ways to test the claims of people who say they have become sensitive to electromagnetic fields or can interfere with electronic devices. They could do more research into the death spike that University of Michigan researchers found in rats, and perhaps even attempt to isolate it in human patients. And so on."

One of the principal speakers Lichfield heard at the conference was Jeff Olsen. According to his message, which has been recounted in both books and YouTube interviews:

His car crashed after he fell asleep at the wheel while driving his family back from vacation. Lying in the wreckage with his back broken, one arm nearly torn off, and one leg destroyed, he was for a while conscious enough to register that his 7-year-old son was crying but his wife and infant son were silent. In I Knew Their Hearts, one of his books, he writes, "What do you say to a man who feels responsible for the death of half his family?"

The answer—at least if you are a spiritual being—is, "You are perfect; you are my son as much as anyone ever was; and you are divine." That is what Olsen recounts hearing—or feeling, or having somehow transmitted to him—as part of a "brain dump" during his near-death experience. He seemed to find himself in a room with a crib, holding the son who had been killed. When he picked him up, he in turn felt himself being enveloped by a loving presence that he understood to be his "divine creator."

Lichfield beautifully sums up his reaction to a tear-jerking story such as this:

This is key to what makes near-death experiences so powerful, and why people cling so strongly to them regardless of the scientific evidence. Whether you actually saw a divine being or your brain was merely pumping out chemicals like never before, the experience is so intense and new that it forces you to rethink your place on Earth. If the NDE happened during a tragedy, it provides a way to make sense of that tragedy and rebuild your life. If your life has been a struggle with illness or doubt, an NDE sets you in a different direction: you nearly died, so something has to change.

As the conference entered its third day, science journalist Lichfield began to notice that there seemed to be almost an aversion to materialistic ideology. He gently confronted Diane Corcoran, who was the leader of the event.

Whether or not NDEs are real or just your brain chemistry fooling you, they can be so intense as to be life-changing, especially those that occur after a traumatic event such as a car accident.

"Over the years," she said, "and with the research that's been done, we've moved past that. There's always a skeptic or two, but we don't bring them into this environment, because this is meant to be a supportive environment, not a questioning one. We put out a call for papers, but we've never had a skeptic put in a paper."

"They probably feel that they wouldn't be welcomed," said Lichfield.

"That's probably true!" Corcoran replied. "But we're trying to expand the field, and there's a lot of work in consciousness existing outside the brain." One prominent researcher, she said, argues that "when someone publishes a paper saying 'This is the explanation,' it's not even worth responding to. Most people who do that have not investigated the field in any serious way."

She is probably correct in her assessment. As we've said in previous chapters, those who question the near-death experience often do so by ridiculing the one telling the story. It seems to be a product of our age that in many cases we've gone from attacking an opponent's facts to attacking their intelligence. It's true in many, many fields, and you only need listen to the talking heads on the morning news discussing political viewpoints to verify this.

It's also true that many non-scientists resort to simplistic explanations couched as scientific knowledge. Scientists are often frustrated when their highly technical work is reduced to the size of a bumper sticker and presented as scientific "fact" to buttress what is really an emotional argument.

The purpose of IANDS, just like TMI and IONS, is to shed some light in the darkness of the no-man's-land between believers and nonbelievers. The field of study involving the nature of consciousness is shaping up to be one of the defining conflicts of the 21st century.

Take the explosion of artificial intelligence (AI), for instance. We are almost to the point when we might be able to create machines as complex as the human brain. Will they be conscious?

For that matter, many reputable scientists are now speculating that we, ourselves, are the product of a future computer's programming. What are the implications for near-death studies? What do we see when we die?

No one knows ... yet.

But somehow it is comforting that there are at least some organizations that exist to seek answers to these kinds of questions.

PART III
SOMETHING BORROWED

We can't imagine our own deaths.

—Sigmund Freud

Somewhere in the 17th century the church and the scientific community reached an unspoken, unofficial agreement. Science would no longer be under the thumb of theology. Galileo, although still very much feeling the inescapable power of the Inquisition, proved too big an opponent for ecclesiastical hierarchy. Gradually, without ever signing any official treaty, science no longer had to consult scripture when it came to conclusions about whether the earth revolved around the sun or vice versa.

But then a strange thing happened. Just like the new Protestant church, science found itself splitting into denominations. Specialties arose. Cosmologists grouped together and stayed out of the field of archaeology. Physicists studied different things than historians. Astronomers kept their eyes on the heavens while geologists dug in the earth.

That is an oversimplification, obviously, but gradually we found ourselves in the position we're in today. We entered, step by careful step, into the age of the specialist. There is now a huge difference between traditional physicists and quantum theorists, and even theoretical physics is divided into denominations such as Copenhagenists and Everettians.

Werner Heisenberg, one of the developers of the Copenhagen interpretation of quantum physics, is famous for his uncertainty principle in which either the location or the momentum of a particle can be measured at any point but not both at the same time.

American physicist Hugh Everett III (1930–1982) came up with the "many worlds" explanation for quantum physics, which holds that there is no wave function collapse, which, in turn, necessitates that all outcomes are not only possible but actually *happen* in limitless other realities. On the other hand, the Copenhagen interpretation developed by Niels Bohr, Werner Heisenberg, and Max Born asserts there is an objective reality and measurement collapses the wave function so that one can interpret the complementary properties of location or the motion of a particle but not both simultaneously (i.e., the uncertainty principle).

Practitioners of these differing points of view all study the nature of reality, but they raise interesting questions. During an NDE, people see a different reality than the one we experience in day-to-day life. What are they seeing? What is its nature? Presumably, we come from somewhere and go somewhere. But where? And what? And when?

Can after-death reality be understood at all, given the nature of all our specialization? Can those who study consciousness get anywhere without understanding the nature of atomic particles, or dream theory, or biology, or electrical processes of the brain, or the subjective nature of universal mythology, or, dare we say it, the religious experience of our ancestors? Can we understand the whole by studying just the parts?

Pretend, for a moment, that some distant ancestor someday discovers an old Chrysler carburetor rusting away in the dirt. Maybe he even examines it in detail and comes to understand how it once worked. Does that automatically lead to understanding the reality of an automobile?

Of course not! He would have to discover pistons and wheels and driveshafts and steering wheels and windshield wipers and cup holders and many different categories of things. If those who study each part refuse to talk to each other, or simply don't bother because they think those who study wheels have nothing in common with those who specialize in ignition switches, they will never come to understand what an automobile was.

That, sad to say, is the situation we find ourselves in today. We are choking on minutiae.

Maybe it's time to end the rat race of specialization and begin to focus on generalization. We can't do that, of course, if specialists continue to look down their noses at generalists, and universities don't offer courses in the science of generalization.

In other words, to understand the whole we may have to stop analyzing the parts and look at the big picture.

Quite frankly, there is very little interest these days in getting to that point. When a person devotes years of study to finally arrive at the point of earning a Ph.D. in a minuscule area of study, it's hard for them to think some generalist is going to understand their expertise enough to apply it a meaningful way. Academic jealousy is a real thing.

Cross-academic study works to a point. Highly trained specialists sometimes work together in peace. Computer engineers, for instance, cooperate with electricians, astronomers, and others to send a rocket to a particular point in space. They really don't understand each other's work, but they must tolerate and even respect each other if they want to achieve a common goal.

And there's the answer! *A common goal!* Until recently there has been no common goal concerning NDEs. But maybe times are beginning to change.

As we have seen in previous chapters, the last few decades have seen people borrowing from the work of various specialists and sharing information while working together to understand the nature of where we go when we die, if we indeed "go" anywhere. The field is still in its infancy, but medical specialists are consulting with psychologists, physicists are opening their research results to philosophers, and mythologists are again being recognized by those in the "hard" sciences.

Swiss geologist Albert Heim was noted for his studies of the Alps culminating in his three-volume work, *Geologie der Schweiz* (*The Geology of Switzerland*).

Often it takes a personal experience to open the eyes of those who had never been willing to even consider the possibility of a conscious life after death. Take, for example, the experience of Albert Heim, a 19th-century Zurich geology professor and alpinist. He interviewed mountain climbers, masons, and roofers who survived potentially fatal falls from high places. His reports are very similar to modern accounts of near-death experiences. He heard about a sense of euphoria and calm, a past-life review, and a vision of bright light.

His interest stemmed from the fact that he himself had fallen from an Alpine glacier while climbing at an altitude of 5,900 feet. "I saw my whole past life take place in many images, as though on a stage at some distance from me," he recalled. "I saw myself as the chief character in the performance. Everything was transfigured as though by a heavenly light and everything was beautiful, without grief, without anxiety and without pain. There was no anxiety, no trace of despair, no pain, but rather calm seriousness, profound acceptance, and a dominant mental quickness and sense of surety."

He felt a sense of connectedness when the people he interviewed found "reconcilement and redeeming peace. They were the last feelings with which they had taken leave of the world and they had, so to speak, fallen into Heaven."

Despite testimonies such as these, which certainly grab our attention when recorded with great style and intellect, it might be that we don't have the intelligence to understand the underlying nature of reality. Consciousness, if it proves to be the ground of our being, is, by its very nature, eternal and omnipresent. Intelligence is mostly the result of evolution over time through the gathering of experience. Maybe it will never prove adequate to understand, let alone explain, what lies beyond our perception realm. Maybe we will never be able to say, "This is what things *are*." Maybe the best we will ever be able to accomplish is to say, "This is what things are *like*."

But we don't know that for sure. Shouldn't we at least try?

We're about to study the work of those who are trying to do just that. But strap yourselves in. This is going to be quite a ride!

12 MYSTERIES OF THE QUANTUM WORLD

Not only is the Universe stranger than we imagine, it is stranger than we can imagine.

—Werner Heisenberg in *Across the Frontiers*, 1974

Sir Alfred Jules Ayer, known to his friends as "Freddie," died in 1989 after establishing an enviable reputation as an English philosopher. In books such as *Language, Truth, and Logic* and *The Problem of Knowledge*, he championed a rather esoteric academic philosophy called "logical positivism." Then, during an episode of pneumonia, his heart stopped beating for four minutes. Those four minutes changed the rest of his life. He encountered a foreign landscape and discovered, in his words, that

> [t]he representatives of the government of the universe had left space slightly out of joint. A further consequence was that the laws of nature had ceased to function as they should. I felt that it was up to me to put things right. It then occurred to me that whereas, until the present century, physicists accepted the Newtonian severance of space and time, it had become customary, since the vindication of Einstein's general theory of relativity, to treat space-time as a single whole. Accordingly, I thought I could cure space by operating upon time.

He proceeded to spend the rest of his life doing just that.

Sir Alfred Jules Ayer was a logical positivist, which is a philosophy of science that asserts truth can only be revealed in the observable world, but an NDE had a deep impact on his beliefs.

His experience raises a fascinating question. Ayer seemed, in those four fateful minutes, to view the universe in a radically different way. Does an NDE offer, as it were, a different platform with which to see reality beyond our perception realm? Does such an experience allow us to step outside the fence of our five senses and see, for the first time, what reality is?

If so, then glimpsing how the universe works might help us understand what we see when we depart our material bodies, but it might also help us to explain basic questions in physics, cosmology, philosophy, and other related disciplines. In short, we might be able to start stitching together threads from many different scientific spindles in order to weave a whole new cloth of understanding that is not visible from the perspective of our familiar five senses.

Parallel universes, string theory, quantum entanglement, alternative consciousness, wormholes, "M" theory, warp drive, "God" particles—these are words that have come to be part of 21st-century vocabulary, even if most folks don't really understand the mathematics and theory behind them. Whatever the phrases mean in a technical sense, they have come to represent a central truth: the universe is a strange place, and it doesn't behave in the way our senses seem to perceive.

Ever since the Renaissance, thoughts about how the cosmos is structured have pretty much followed a single premise. There have been variations on this theme, of course, but lately a whole new song has made its way into the repertoire of the scientific chorus.

The standard model proposes that the universe is a vibrant but lifeless stage onto which consciousness has evolved to take its place in a great drama. At the forefront of that drama, we somehow became the first sentient species on planet Earth, and possibly in the whole universe, to evolve to a point where we can begin to ask questions such as "Where did we come from?" and "What is our purpose?" For billions of years, according to this script, random particles just collided with each other with no real purpose, until we somehow appeared to contemplate the process.

In many academic forums, couched in much more convoluted language, of course, this is still the dominant script.

But critics in the audience aren't quite satisfied with this plot any more. The question of "how?" has popped out of the equation into the light of day, and no one is really satisfied with any explanations put forth so far. That's not to mention the question "why?"

Darwinian mechanisms raised a smoke screen for a long time, but winds of change have started to blow them away. The biggest problem seems to be this: Consciousness has now taken its place in the center of the stage, and the problem of understanding what it is and how it developed refuses to be swept under the rug, as it was for so many years. No number of smooth-talking biologists, who claim it springs from electrical impulses and a spoonful of chemicals in the brain, can cloud the issue any more.

Just when it seemed the whole thing was never going to be resolved—that Newtonian physics was all that counted in the great scheme of things and was sufficient to solve all problems—along came a brand new, counterintuitive theory that beckoned followers into the strange world of the very, very small.

Hindu rishis had postulated this world thousands of years ago, but now it appeared in the formulas of mathematicians and theoreticians. Even the most jaded scientists must listen to mathematicians and theoreticians. It is metaphorically written into the small print of their contracts. To make matters even worse, a hundred years of experimentation has made it one of the most unapologetically proven, and thus accepted, scientific theories in history. We know the quantum world exists and is the basis for all things, but we don't understand it.

The ancient Indian natural philosopher Maharishi Kanāda speculated that matter is composed of increasingly divisible particles that express certain properties that unite them all, eliminating the observer/observed problem of the uncertainty principle.

Consciousness is no longer just an issue for biologists. Physicists must now deal with it, along with philosophers, religionists, and, it seems, everyone else.

Put simply, it is not sufficient to say *how* a piece of music, or a rainbow, or a star-filled sky is the way it is. We now want to know *why* it's beautiful, and there is nothing in modern physics that explains how a group of molecules in a brain decides how it *feels* about that. The worst thing is, most physicists don't seem to *want* to consider such questions. They insist the problem of "why" and how something "feels" is not their problem, so they ignore it, even though every other person on earth cares, and cares a lot.

And there are other such problems. Putting aside, for the moment, issues about life and consciousness, we still don't know why the universe seems to have sprung into existence some 13.8 billion years ago, in a huge event that was labeled the Big Bang, even though Fred Hoyle, the one who first coined that label, used it to denigrate the idea when the theory was first proposed. Now, given the latest findings from the James Webb Space Telescope, even *that* hypothesis is being threatened.

The state-of-the-art James Webb Space Telescope has peered deeper into the cosmos than we have ever seen before, and the observations have called into question some accepted theories such as the Big Bang theory. What else might we discover about space, time, and the nature of matter and energy that might lead to mind-blowing conclusions regarding the nature of our reality?

The simple truth of the matter is that there are more questions being raised every day, and fewer answers. Some scientists tend to get a little patronizing when people express their belief that you simply can't get something from nothing, and that the Big Bang is insufficient to explain the origins of everything. At best, they say, it's only a partial description of a single event in a timeless continuum. But there are so many details to consider, making the whole field so complex, that many experts just don't want to take the time to explain it all, especially to people who usually want a simplistic answer.

Make no mistake about it, science has done a magnificent job when it comes to understanding things, and it continues to do so. But maybe, just maybe, even science is not sufficiently geared to explain something that goes beyond the complexities of narrow specializations.

Here's the bottom line. Today's science is amazing when it comes to figuring out how the individual parts work. What is missing is the big picture. Although a theory of everything may emerge someday, ultimately combining classical relativity and quantum mechanics, it is elusive right now.

"There is no way to obtain observations," we are told. How can we possibly reproduce something like the Big Bang? Science depends on replicating experiments.

Well, maybe we have those observations right at hand, and have had them for thousands of years. Maybe they are to be found in the testimonies of people who have had near-death experiences. Have we been looking in the wrong place? The simple truth might be that there is no universe "out there" to observe. Maybe it's "in here."

Enter the presence of quantum reality. The answers might not be too *big* to observe. They might be too *small.* Or, even better,

It might be that NDEs will prove to be the very observations we say are not possible, given our perception limitations.

they might not be there at all, until we begin to observe them. It might be that NDEs will prove to be the very observations we say are not possible, given our perception limitations.

This is hard. Admittedly, quantum physics is pretty much impervious to visualization and descriptive language, but let's try anyway, using the language of metaphor.

Quantum physics demands the presence of an observer. Schrödinger's cat in the box sums up the problem. Is the cat dead or alive? No one knows until they open the box. Until then, for all practical purposes, it is both dead *and* alive until it is observed.

In the same way, light is both a particle and a wave at the same time. Until you look, it remains elusive. But when you observe it, you find either one or the other, depending on which it is you have decided to see. If you want to know its velocity, it's a wave. If you want to narrow down its location, it's a particle. Until you do one or the other, it is merely amorphous potential.

Let me tell you about my workshop. It's filled with lots of specific tools, just like science is filled with specialty fields. I know how to mix and match them to produce some quality work.

But I'm not always working there. Sometimes I turn off the lights and go upstairs.

Now, is my workshop still there, even when the lights are off and no one is looking at it?

"Of course it is," you say. "That's obvious!"

But just like Schrödinger's cat in the box, the answer is not that simple. You see, in quantum reality, those tools are not as they seem to be at first glance. My wrench may feel solid and heavy in my hand, and according to standard physics, it is. It has a specific density, size, and weight. But the more I look, the less it really is that way. At the quantum level it is a shivering, quiver-

"If a tree falls in the woods and no one is there to hear it, does it make a sound?" is a classic question in philosophy. The answer might be "yes and no," for the tree will emit sound waves but if there are no eardrums to receive them then no sound is perceived.

ing cloud of atoms and even smaller particles that collapse into my reality when I observe it. If we look even closer, even the particles eventually disintegrate into waves of energy. It appears, at my level of perception, to be one thing. But that's only because I perceive it to be that way.

So, which is it: a cloud of subatomic energy or a solid piece of steel? The answer is: both! And at the same time. It exists in one form when it's off by itself, but morphs into another when a conscious observer, me, comes along and picks it up.

When Albert Einstein was confronted with this truth, for many years he refused to believe it. "Does the moon only appear when I'm looking at it?" he once famously asked.

Well, yes! At least from the standpoint of quantum reality. This has been known ever since Max Born, the German physicist, demonstrated it, way back in 1926, eventually winning over a skeptical Albert Einstein.

Essentially, my wrench exists as a statistical prediction. The particles that make it up are really probability waves. They exist only as likely outcomes of my intentions and perspective. They are nothing but a likely outcome. Outside of that, there is nothing actually "there." At least, nothing of actual material substance.

You can carry this idea all the way up in size to the physical universe.

Now, take this idea into the study of NDEs. When we "leave," for lack of a better word, our bodies, we are leaving behind sense perceptions that evolved within the framework of that body. For our whole life we have perceived the world through this network of sense perceptions. What we see doesn't take on shape and substance until it reaches our brains. Only then does it become reality.

We perceive a tree, for instance, and agree with one another that a tree looks like it does. We label it and it takes on an agreed-upon, consensus reality. But to ants and birds and mice and termites and, who knows, dogs, it appears to be something quite different.

Why is our label the "correct" one? Because we have created the parameters and commandeered the labeling process. If a

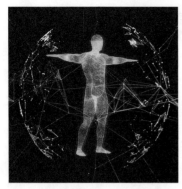

Once released from your body and all the sensory-input mechanisms it uses to perceive "reality," your out-of-body consciousness will experience a world completely different from that with which you are familiar.

bigger, more important species comes along and decides to ignore our description, there's nothing much we can do about it.

It is no wonder that this is a difficult concept for us to appreciate. But apparently, we still perceive reality after death. We simply see it in a different way, with differing kinds of sense perceptions. There might even be "bigger and more important" species out there who pay no more attention to our parameters than we pay attention to the "ants and birds and mice and termites and, who knows, dogs."

Consider, for example, this story taken from the archives of IANDS. I've edited it for length, but the background is that Alice Morrison-Mays nearly died at the Marine Hospital in New Orleans, Louisiana, after being rushed into intensive care while in a coma, two weeks after the birth of her baby:

> I found myself in a place of such beauty and peace. It was timeless and spaceless.... Then I became aware of other loving, caring beings hovering near me. Their presence was so welcoming and nurturing.... They said they were my guides and helpers as well as being God's Messengers.... Then I was aware of an Immense Presence coming toward me, bathed in white, shimmering light that glowed and at times sparkled like diamonds.... Even though I felt unworthy, I was being lifted into that which I could embrace.... The Joy and Ecstasy were intoxicating. It was "explained" that I could remain there if I wanted; it was a choice I could make.... Part of me wanted to remain forever, but I finally realized I didn't want to leave a new baby motherless. I left with sadness and reluctance.

People who view reality in such a way tend to return, calling it more "real" than the reality some of us insist is all there is.

Think of it this way. Where is the universe located? Our standard way of viewing the world is to say that it is "out there" somewhere, separate from us. It would be the same whether or not we were here to look at it.

But is that really the case?

Nothing can be perceived that is not somehow interacting with our consciousness, and since such things are said to be real and not imaginary, what we see must exist somewhere, in some location.

Scientists know that light is both a wave and a particle. When they look for its location, it becomes a particle. When they measure its speed, it is a wave.

The ethereal beauty described by many afterlife experiencers could, perhaps, be the result of their being freed of their mortal senses to experience a world behind the veil.

In other words, light takes on form depending on the measuring device we use to look at it.

Our eyes are measuring devices. They contain retinas that transform light, by means of electromagnetic currents, to the back of our brains, where we perceive shape and form. Then we flip through a Rolodex of previous experiences and say, "That's a (this) or (that)."

Now, where does the perceived image take shape? It's not "out there," separate from us. It takes shape within our brains.

That means things really exist in the brain of the observer, not some place with coordinates in space. Only custom demands that such a position is out in space and time somewhere.

By now, you might be thinking that two realities exist, one "out there" and one "in here." One is expressed in standard, Newtonian physics, the other in terms of quantum reality. But, as physicist John Archibald Wheeler once said, "No phenomenon is a real phenomenon until it is an observed phenomenon."

In this case, the instrument used to observe is a human eye, and because we are so accustomed to it, it is easy to assume there are no other instruments to employ that could render quite a different phenomenon. We might be only one tool in the workshop of scientists who inhabit quite a different realm than us, and NDEs might be the process whereby we step outside of customary, agreed-upon parameters and view the world through different eyes.

If you're not used to thinking along these lines, you may have already decided the whole thing sounds like semantic poppycock. I don't blame you. It takes us down winding pathways that are very difficult to negotiate.

At the risk of being overly simplistic, let's try to dumb it down just a bit. Here's the bottom line. We live in the material world and relate to that world through the only process we have ever been trained to use. We call it objective reality. It is a trusty process and works very well, and there's nothing wrong with it.

But NDEs expose us to a different reality. We are forced to abandon perceptions that have served us well for our whole lives. Is it any wonder people can't find words to express what they have experienced when they return to this material world? Our language is a human invention designed to describe things in *this* world. It doesn't work over *there*.

Even our method of communication is different. On this side of the material fence, I talk, you listen, you talk, I listen, and we arrive at a mutual understanding. Over there, however, it is not uncommon at all for people to receive what they sometimes call "blocks of teaching" that communicate in whole paragraphs or ideas, all at once. Being creatures with ears, eyes, and brains doesn't work over there.

When people come back from an NDE it is not uncommon at all for them to describe not facts, but feelings. "Love," "acceptance," and "security" are very common words. Those aren't descriptions of what you *saw*. They refer to what you *felt*. There's a big difference.

If that simpler explanation gave you some comfort, take a deep breath while we plunge back into another aspect of quantum reality. This one might be even harder to understand. It's a principle called entanglement, and it's very weird (see also pages 49–50, 116, and 206). Albert Einstein called it "spooky action at a distance."

In 1964, Irish physicist John Stewart Bell postulated an experiment that, when conducted over and over again, always with the same results, turned the whole world of logical process on its head.

To put it simply, it appears as though two particles, once they are "entangled" and then separated, communicate instantly for the rest of their lives. If one spins to the right, the other will spin to the left, no matter how far apart they are. And they do it instantly, not at the speed of light, which Einstein had insisted was a kind of universal speed limit. One particle might be in the Milky Way galaxy, and the other way out past Andromeda somewhere, but they are joined at the proverbial hip forever. They don't *send* a communication between them. They just *instantly* know what the other is doing.

Physicist John Stewart Bell is remembered for his Bell's theorem, which argues that quantum theory conflicts with classical theory as to how physics works locally—that is, with regard to particle interactions in a local environment.

That's weird. But here's the point. For centuries, ever since the time of the ancient Hindu rishis some 6,000 years ago, philosophers have speculated that everything is connected—that "all is one." Now it seems as though quantum physicists have proved it.

Think about it in relation to the standard NDE. Maybe we don't "go" anywhere. Maybe we are already there. Maybe our *experience* of separateness here in this material realm is simply illusion, created by our senses. Maybe we are not separate beings after all. Maybe that's just the way we *feel*. And during an NDE, when we "take leave of our senses," we return to understanding the truth that all *is* one. Maybe that's why people come back with such a sense of acceptance and love. They no longer feel the separateness of individuality and ego. Maybe that's why so many don't want to come back. (Honestly—would you?)

Does entanglement prove that the universe really is one whole, unified presence? If we could live with that realization forever in our minds and hearts, it would change the way we live.

According to the testimony of the great majority of near-death experiencers, that's exactly what happens.

Isn't that a comforting thought?

In this chapter we have merely scratched the surface of quantum reality. But it seems as though that reality can go a long way toward explaining why NDEs have a basis in science as well as in spirituality, and help us understand what people say about their experience when they come back from one.

It would seem to be a mistake, then, for some to claim that NDE research is an esoteric, or nonscientific, branch of study. When we step out of our individual "tribes" of specialization, it might yet prove to be the particular source of knowledge that will finally lead us to the promised land of understanding. The answers to question such as "Who are we?" and "Why are we here?" might finally be within our reach.

13 FROM PHYSICS TO THE CENTURY OF BIOLOGY

The 21st century is predicted to be the Century of Biology, a shift from the previous century dominated by physics. It seems fitting, then, to begin the century by turning the universe outside-in and unifying the foundations of science, not with imaginary strings that occupy equally imaginary unseen dimensions, but with a much simpler idea that is rife with so many shocking new perspectives that we are unlikely ever to see reality the same way again.

—Robert Lanza in *Biocentrism*, 2009

According to astrophysicists, we live in a Goldilocks world. In other words, it's not too hot or too cold, too much this or not enough that. Even when we consider the microscopic scale of the atom and the macroscopic scale of the universe itself, there is a whole list of traits that indicate everything is tailored to produce life. If the Big Bang had been even one degree in a million more powerful, it would have expanded too fast for galaxies to develop, to say nothing of human life. If the strong nuclear force were downgraded by only 2%, atoms would never have formed. If gravity decreased by a just a fraction, our sun would not have been able to ignite.

In short, every force in the universe seems perfectly calibrated to form atoms, elements, planets, liquid water, and eventually, biological life. Change any of them, even a minuscule amount, and we would never have existed to experience NDEs.

How could this be? Are we so important that the whole universe is geared to sustain us?

There are currently four explanations to this mystery:

- God did it that way: This is a popular idea that has been hijacked by a religious group who used to call it "creation science" but now label it "intelligent design." It depends entirely on faith and the acceptance of one religious concept out of many.

- It's an incredible coincidence: Maybe so, but that seems to be a bit of a cop-out.

- The anthropic principle: This idea says that conditions favor us because if they didn't, we wouldn't be here to speculate about such things.

- Biocentrism: It's a bit of a complicated conjecture, and the newest hypothesis of the four, but its bottom line says that the universe is created by life and that without life no material universe would exist at all.

The first three are obvious and have been around for a while. Each of them has something positive going for it. The fourth will take some explanation, and a form of it might be supported by NDE testimonies as well as philosophical speculation.

The brilliant physicist John Archibald Wheeler, who theorized that all electrons are actually one electron traveling on a world line through space time, believed that existence depends upon observers.

Theoretical physicist John Archibald Wheeler was a major player in the field of nuclear fission. He worked extensively with Niels Bohr and helped bring Einstein's theory of general relativity, on which we will have something more to say in a few chapters, into the popular American mindset. He was convinced that we live in what he called a "participatory universe," in which there could be no cosmos without observers to observe it. In other words, life is required to bring the universe into existence. He saw only two possible ways to explain why there is something rather than nothing:

- *Either* the universe came to be by a coincidence of immense improbability

- *Or* what we see came about because the cosmos is biocentric in its very nature.

In other words, in his view, biology joins physics at the center of everything.

That seems pretty egocentric at first glance. Who do we think we are that life is at the center of something as cosmic, distant, cold, huge, and seemingly impersonal as the universe?

Before you go too far and too quickly down the path of rejecting something that sounds too much like human-biased philosophy, though, consider a number of NDE stories, of which this is just one:

> *There were some presences there. There were some ladies. I didn't know them at the time. They were so loving and so wonderful, and I just didn't want to come back. I didn't see any pictures of them until I was an adult, but then I said, "Oh, yeah. They were my great-grandmothers who had died years before I was born."*

Over and over again, those who experience NDEs come back with the same story. On the other side of death, they meet people who were either known or unknown ancestors, relatives, or, at the very least, entities who were once people. These deceased people, ghosts, spiritual beings, or whatever you want to call them seem to be waiting for us, and in many cases want to help us. The experience is so common we seem to take it for granted. But if we accept, for the moment, that people who have gone on before might be real, what are they doing? Where are they located? What is their purpose?

Consider this example, taken from Matthew 17:1–9:

> *After six days Jesus took with him Peter, James, and John the brother of James, and led them up a high mountain by themselves. There he was transfigured before them. His face shone like the sun, and his clothes became as white as the light. Just then there appeared before them Moses and Elijah, talking with Jesus.*

> *Peter said to Jesus, "Lord, it is good for us to be here. If you wish, I will put up three shelters—one for you, one for Moses, and one for Elijah."*

While he was still speaking, a bright cloud covered them, and a voice from the cloud said, "This is my son, whom I love; with him I am well pleased. Listen to him!"

When the disciples heard this, they fell facedown to the ground, terrified. But Jesus came and touched them. "Get up," he said. "Don't be afraid." When they looked up, they saw no one except Jesus.

As they were coming down the mountain, Jesus instructed them, "Don't tell anyone what you have seen, until the Son of Man has been raised from the dead.

This is not an account of an NDE, but millions of people accept it as a true story. Moses and Elijah step out of the pages of an Old Testament past and seem to be counseling Jesus about death. At least we can assume that is what they talked about, because according to the Gospel account, right after it happened, Jesus set his face toward Jerusalem where he was to die.

But where had the two Old Testament characters been all the time since their death, centuries earlier? Where did they come from? What had they been doing? Why did they show up right at that moment? Why were they hanging around earth rather than enjoying heaven?

Even if we accept the fact that this might be metaphor rather than history, those who wrote the story seem to believe it was true. And millions of believers since then have accepted it as well. This wouldn't happen if there were not some place in the human psyche that somehow agreed there is life after death.

A painting of the transfiguration of Jesus at Saint John the Baptist Cathedral, Trnava, Slovakia, shows Jesus with Moses and Elijah while Peter, James, and John fall to their knees in astonishment.

In the story, the long-dead prophets came, in the tradition of spirit guides, to counsel Jesus. (At least, we assume they were "long-dead." The truth is that both met suspicious ends. Moses wandered alone up into the mountains where his burial place was never discovered. Much later,

In 2 Kings 2, the prophet Elijah ascended into Heaven while riding a fiery chariot. Hey, if you're going to Heaven, do it in style! (Fresco by Natale Attanasio, Santuario della Madonna del Carmine in Catania, Italy.)

in the New Testament book of Jude, we are told that the devil disputed with the archangel Michael over the body. This seems a bit irregular. As for Elijah, he was transported to heaven in a fiery chariot—not a usual method of departure by any means.)

Countless stories report that those who experienced NDEs were told they must go back, even though they wanted to stay in their newfound environment. They had a mission of some kind to fulfill back on earth. Usually, it involved caring for loved ones.

But why should spirit guides care about life on the planet they no longer inhabited?

In an earlier chapter, I mentioned having tea with the late Hamish Miller's widow while I was on a trip to Cornwall. Hamish was a matter-of-fact, blue-collar worker during the first part of his life. He once wrote, "I was dedicated to the rat race because I believed that the work ethic is the most important thing."

In his books *It's Not Too Late* and *A Life Divined*, as well as in many videos about his later work as a practitioner and teacher of the art of dowsing, he recalled the time he had a near-death experience that changed his life, and subsequently the lives of countless others, as a result of what he went on to do with his remaining time. He had a typical experience of going through a tunnel (he called it a "tube") toward a light, whereupon he met a group of mirth-filled counselors who introduced him to a whole new world.

"These are our precepts," they told him. "If you understand even some of them, you are welcome to stay. Otherwise, you must return."

Hamish recounted that he didn't understand *any* of those precepts.

"Maybe I'd better go back," he said.

He was convinced that the cosmos has a sense of humor when they responded with laughter, "Maybe you'd better!"

Hamish went on to fame and fulfillment when, after his experience, he completely changed his way of thinking and subsequently lived a life of deep spiritual insight as a dowser and explorer of earth energies.

His experience is only one of countless stories in which people journey to the other side but are sent back with a mission. Their lives are forever changed. Taken together, the sheer number of such experiences indicate that beings on the "other side" of our perception realm are not only present, they *care* about us.

If the cosmos is vast, cold, and impersonal, why does it seem to be so teeming with life on the other side of human perception? Why all the ghost stories, spiritual myths, and tales of concerned, caring, long-dead relatives? Could it be that the universe itself might be nothing more than a stage in the minds of biological actors, who play out their parts in a never-ending drama performed before an unseen audience?

To understand what this might imply, we need to briefly consider a rather new theory called biocentrism, which is the brainchild of Robert Lanza, who the *New York Times* recently called one of the top three scientists in today's world. To put it mildly, it is already causing quite a stir.

In the last few decades, major puzzles found in mainstream science have demanded that we re-evaluate the nature of the universe and our ideas about its conception. Even the new James Webb Space Telescope has upended traditional views concerning the nature of the Big Bang. Its developers thought it would reinforce and prove the current understanding of how the universe was formed, but the implications stemming from new snapshots of the very early universe go far beyond anything we could have imagined. Indeed, the cosmos might be of a far different age than we thought, and maybe it never "banged" at all! If that proves to be true, the old question rears its persistent head: How did it get here in the first place?

Medical doctor, professor, and chief scientific officer at the Astellas Institute for Regenerative Medicine, Robert Lanza proposed the theory of biocentrism, which fundamentally asserts that consciousness generates life.

In a nutshell, biocentrism says that there is nothing "out there" separate from us. Consciousness didn't somehow evolve into existence, eventually arriving at the point where it could contemplate the vast arena in which it found itself. It didn't emerge into a lifeless universe. Instead, the opposite is true. Consciousness created, and is creating, the universe. Biology is its most evolved host. Physics alone can't explain the workings of the cosmos. Only biology can do that. A Theory of Everything will never be found unless biology is included.

If you've never considered this, I'll be the first to admit it is tough to grasp. It flies directly in the face of everything we have been taught, so let's try to simplify it.

Think about everything that exists around you right at this moment. Consider, for instance, the sky above your head. It's "up there," isn't it? It's something you must fly into if you want to travel there. It's separate and distinct from you—a big, blue presence that fills your day.

But is it "up there," really? Is it even blue?

No! It *appears* that way, because electrons fired off in your brain when acting upon light particles that entered your mind through your eyes, at which point your brain assigned colors and perceived substance, and finally concocted an image that subtly said to your intellect, "That's a blue sky up there." You perceived it as something separate from yourself, but it really took shape inside your mind. Until then, it could best be described as a kind of uncollapsed quantum foam.

Some other kind of consciousness, say one belonging to your dog, or a cricket, or a bird, probably sees something quite different than you do. Maybe it's red, or green. Maybe it takes on a totally different image.

So, who's right—you, or your dog, or the cricket, or the bird? Or, for that matter, any of you? And where *is* the sky? If it didn't take shape until it was formed in your brain, technically speaking, it exists only in your mind.

> **That act of observation, just like Schrödinger's famous cat in the box, didn't take on form until you looked at it, or "measured" it, as physicists say.**

In other words, as quantum theory suggests, you became an observer and created what you are looking at. That act of observation, just like Schrödinger's famous cat in the box, didn't take on form until you looked at it, or "measured" it, as physicists say. And it looks the way it does because you *expected* it to look that way. That's how your optical equipment was trained to work from the time you were born. If you had used a different measuring device, such as the eyes of a dog, cricket, or bird, it would appear different. And (here's the hard part) until you, or somebody, observes it, it doesn't exist at all. (This was the part Einstein couldn't accept until Bohr finally convinced him. So don't feel bad if it seems a bit unreal.)

As for its location, if it didn't appear until your brain concocted it, it doesn't exist "out there," it exists in your head. You created it. Thus, biology—the consciousness currently permeating material life—creates the universe, not the other way around. That, in a simplified nutshell, is biocentrism.

Way before I ever heard of this theory, back in 2012, I had an experience during an OBE that may have been my introduction to the field. After about an hour of meditation, I had one brief, terrible, wonderful vision that probably changed my life. It certainly left me with a profound unease.

Here is how I wrote about it later. This is a passage from my dream journal:

> *I felt myself inside a great vortex of swirling energy. I thought I was at peace, but knew somehow that I wasn't quite there. Then it occurred to me that my mind was in constant motion, trying to shape my experience and keep myself in the vision. For an instant I was suddenly able to let go and surrender completely to what was happening. My mind cut loose and drifted off into the void, and I was suddenly aware of the whole universe being inside of me. I had expanded, somehow. I could see planet Earth, hanging in space and surrounded by stars, and I was the Cosmos. I didn't just experience it. I was the whole universe. It was inside me. I felt like God. Not "one with God." I was God, and the universe was my creation.*

Having recently read *Observer*, a novel written by Robert Lanza and Nancy Kress to bring the concept of biocentrism to a wider public, I am amazed at how much my experience from years ago echoed exactly what they sought to portray.

According to quantum physics, the universe, beginning with the Big Bang of 13.8 billion years ago, couldn't have come into existence without a conscious observer, so consciousness *must* have come first. Consciousness didn't pop into existence out of nowhere, finding itself in lifeless space. It *preceded* creation. It must have. And then evolved itself into it.

Nancy Kress, the winner of numerous sci-fi awards such as the Hugo and Nebula Awards, cowrote the novel *Observer* with Robert Lanza to create a narrative that would explain concepts of biocentrism in a memorable manner for readers.

In the famous double slit physics experiment, which has by now been proven beyond the shadow of a doubt, if you look at light and see it as a particle, it goes through either one slit or the other. If you're looking for a wave, it goes through both slits.

The reason for this is that light is both a wave *and* a particle at the same time. It doesn't become a particle until you decide you want to see a particle. Until then, it is more like an amorphous quantum wave of energy. It only takes on the form of a particle when you decide to determine its location.

You decide! That's the important thing. You, in effect, create either a wave or a particle depending on what you're looking for. You are the observer. You are in control. And until you decide to look, light doesn't even exist.

But if you are an incarnation of consciousness that has taken on physical, biological form, then you are at the center of it all.

Hence—biocentrism.

But be careful. Biocentrism doesn't mean human-centrism. There is a difference. Humans aren't the only beings, or maybe even the most important ones, to possess consciousness. But according to this view, cold, hard physics alone can't produce a universe. The Big Bang theory of theoretical physics is a human construct, invented because of our human desire for completeness and totality.

However, like many comprehensive theories, physics fails to account for one crucial factor: *We* create the theories. A biological creature has fashioned all the stories. It is a biological creature who makes the observations and gives everything a name.

That explains why most other theories fall short. They don't take consciousness into account.

Ralph Waldo Emerson wrote in his 1844 essay, "Experience":

We have learned that we do not see directly, but mediately, and that we have no means of correcting these colored and distorting lenses which we are, or of computing the amount of their errors. Perhaps these subject-lenses have a creative power; perhaps there are no objects.

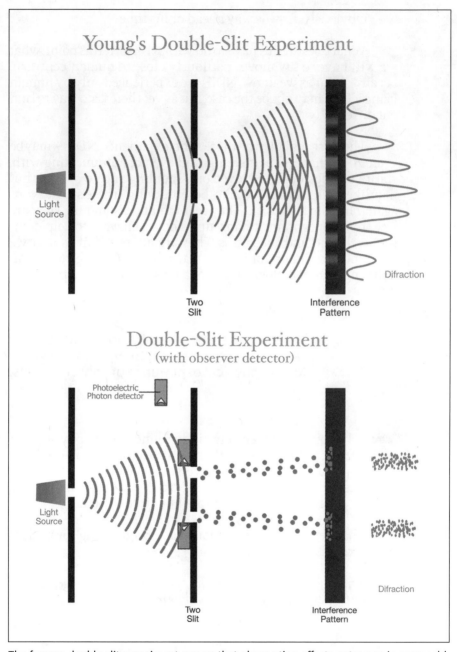

Young's Double-Slit Experiment

Light Source

Two Slit

Interference Pattern

Diffraction

Double-Slit Experiment
(with observer detector)

Photoelectric Photon detector

Light Source

Two Slit

Interference Pattern

Diffraction

The famous double-slit experiment proves that observation affects outcomes in our world. When light is shined through two slits in a barrier it behaves as a wave when unobserved, forming an interference pattern on the wall at right (top image). But when the experiment *is* observed, light behaves like particles, choosing one or the other slit and shining only two bars of light on the wall (bottom).

Obviously, he was way ahead of his time.

What does all this have to do with NDEs? At this point, what we will have to say moves perilously close to human-centrism, because as far as we know, NDEs are experienced only by human beings. That may not be the case, but as yet there is no way to find out differently.

The vast majority of those who experience NDEs—maybe even *all* of them—report seeing, and even communicating with, spirits, entities, departed loved ones, guiding angels, or other humanlike beings who seem to be observing (there's that word again!) life here on earth. They seem to understand us. They are free from our egocentric hang-ups. They even want to help, comfort, welcome, and console us. They are interested in us, as if we are somehow important in the great scheme of things. We seem to be engaged in biological life for a reason. We have a purpose.

> We seem to be engaged in biological life for a reason.... Is life on earth, then, a testing ground for the physical experience of consciousness?

Is life on earth, then, a testing ground for the physical experience of consciousness? Is that life's purpose? Are *we* being observed, just as we create the universe as *we* observe *it*? In other words, is the consciousness that created the universe, and biological life, observing *us*, having brought *us* into existence?

That's exactly what religions have been saying for millennia. Take this famous example:

> *And God said, "Let us make humankind in our image, in our likeness...." And God saw that it was good!*
>
> —Genesis 1: 26, 31

Notice the emphasis on the word "saw." Without understanding that this very same idea would someday be expressed in scientific language, the early writers seemed to think that God, or perhaps "consciousness" would be a better word, pictured consciousness as an observer, who created a world by looking at it. And consciousness even selected the form the creation would take: "Let us make humankind *in our image, in our likeness.*"

This passage, written at least 3,000 years ago and expressed, of course, in the language of *that* day, captured exactly what biocentrism and quantum physics says in *ours*. Those who experience NDEs report that it was a true statement back then, and it is a true statement now.

If we accept this idea, then we might say that biocentrism is a *material* expression of an *eternal* reality. It is not *ego*-centric, but rather a key to understanding who we are and how the universe came into being. In other words, biocentrism expresses the idea that what is "out there" is really "in here."

Hinduism embraces the concept that *Brahman*, a universal expression of all that is, sometimes called "God" in the West even though "consciousness" is probably closer to the truth, cannot be defined. Brahman is beyond words and cannot be contained in a box of language. But *atman*, sometimes called "soul" in the West, dwells within us all. And the great realization of the rishis more than 6,000 years ago was that *Brahman* and *atman* are one: *Thou art That.* Consciousness and the soul are a single unity. Consciousness is "out there," but the soul is its manifested host "in here."

Keep that concept in mind when you consider this story about Dave Bennett, who, in 1983, was a chief engineer of an underwater research vessel. One night he was thrown into the ocean. He'd been taught to recognize the signs of oxygen deprivation, but as he drowned, those lessons took on quite a different form than anything he had read about. He felt as though there was an omnipresence keeping him from being alone. Darkness slowly faded into light, and he started to move toward it.

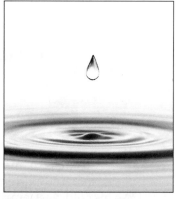

One can visualize *atman* as being like a drop of water that then merges into an ocean that is *Brahman,* becoming one with it.

In a speech he later gave to a conference held at the International Association for Near-Death Studies, he recounted:

As I got closer, there were waves and waves of love that were just wrapping me in this warm embrace. It was the most amazing feeling I ever had, and it felt as if this love was actually permeating my being, and it transformed me into this being of life. And as I got closer to the light, the light appeared to me like it was millions upon millions of fragments of light. [I saw] what seemed to be my family—not the ones I'd had on Earth, but a second "soul family," who relived my life through different viewpoints. I was told to go back to life to fulfill my purpose, and after 18 minutes underwater, I popped back to the surface.

In his experience, *atman* within communicated with *Brahman* without. They were one and the same. He was not alone. A "soul family," each an expression of Brahman, joined together to reassure and sustain him.

This is just one of many examples, some of which we have previously shared, that indicate the presence of some kind of supporting cast that is very concerned with what happens to us. In this case, it consisted of a soul family, but often it is composed of actual family members who have passed on.

The question then becomes: What is it about biological life on earth that is so important to those who have either previously lived such lives or are extremely interested in how things are going?

> **If life is so important that it is observed by beings from outside material existence, it must have some kind of eternal purpose.**

If life is so important that it is observed by beings from outside material existence, it must have some kind of eternal purpose. This cold, vast, empty thing we call the cosmos might really be a theater designed for the purpose of being experienced by biological life. Indeed, perhaps it was created and is being sustained for that very purpose.

Science reporter Dennis Overbye wrote something very chilling in a May 2, 2023, article for the *New York Times*. It's entitled "Who Will Have the Last Word on the Universe?"

> *At some point in the future there will be somewhere in the universe where there will be a last sentient being. And a last thought. And that last word, no matter how profound or mundane, will vanish into silence. Will that last thought be a profound pearl of wisdom? An expletive? It's hard not to want to scream at our own insignificance in all of this.*

He went on to speculate about the science behind it all:

> *If that worries you, here is an encouraging metaphor straight from Einstein's equations: When you are inside a black hole, light pours in from the outside universe, which seems to speed up while you appear to be frozen. In principle, you could see the whole future history of the galaxy or even the whole universe speed past you as you fall toward the center, the singularity where space and time stop.*

> *Maybe death could be like that, a revelation of all the past and future.*

Is this, in essence, what an NDE is? Is it a glimpse from within the "black hole" beyond the curtain? Is it consciousness released from its material host? If so, how can we possibly find words to express a vision that is so outside our normal perception?

Perhaps Overbye sums it up best in his closing paragraph:

> *A whiff of eternity can illuminate an entire lifetime, perhaps even mine.*

This seems to be the testimony of almost all those who have experienced an NDE. They come back changed people, because they have stepped outside biology and glimpsed reality. They feel as though they were, for a little while at least, back home.

14 DREAM RESEARCH AND THE NEAR-DEATH EXPERIENCE

Lucid dreaming does appear to be an interesting new research tool for exploring the dreamworld and better understanding the abilities of the mind, which consistently seem greater than we could ever have expected.

—John Cline, Ph.D., in "New Frontiers in Lucid Dreaming," *Psychology Today*, March 2021

Have you ever had a dream when you were aware that you were asleep and dreaming, yet were somehow able to control the events? It probably felt something like being the author and director of a movie—vivid and real, and you were in charge.

If so, you've experienced a lucid dream. They've been the subject of research for years now, but during the COVID-19 pandemic, perhaps because people either had more time, dozed more, or spent more time communicating about interesting things on their computers, they became a kind of craze among post-millennials. Social media became packed with conversations about lucid dreams and something called "reality shifting."

People who practiced reality shifting came to believe they could intentionally alter their current reality by shifting their consciousness in order to transcend to alternate universes and realities through focused visualization.

But those engaged in professional dream studies came out quite strongly against the idea of reality shifting being equated

In a lucid dream, not only does your environment feel very real, but you are also aware that you are dreaming and are able to manipulate that dream according to your will.

with lucid dreaming. Lucid dreaming, they insisted, is a scientifically verified state of consciousness that has been subjected to academic, peer-reviewed papers based on clinically controlled experiments. Reality shifting, on the other hand, was a subjective, New Age belief that only spread because it became popular on TikTok. They had a point, to be sure. TikTok does not qualify for the peer-review process common to scientific inquiry.

Lurking in the wings of the whole fad, however, was the subject of NDEs. Could NDEs be explained by the results of lucid dreaming research?

Science reporter Natalie Wolchover decided to explore the process for NBC News. She interviewed participants of a Los Angeles–based organization called the Out-Of-Body Experience Research Center. Under the leadership of Michael Raduga, they studied lucid dreaming by training four groups of 10 to 20 volunteers to perform a series of mental exercises to be undertaken when they woke up during the night. They were taught to mimic intentional near-death experiences in which they flew toward a light at the end of a tunnel. The researchers came to believe that their experiments demonstrated NDEs, which were products of the human mind rather than metaphysical experiences. Eighteen of the volunteers reported that they were successful in separating from their bodies and flying toward a tunnel and a bright light.

One of them had this to say:

I was able to leave my body after a couple of tries. Now that I was out of my body, I wanted to see the tunnel and it immediately appeared in front of me. Once I flew to the end of that tunnel, I saw my deceased husband there in the spirit. We spoke for several minutes. His words, touch, bearing, and feelings were real, just like during his life. Later, when I felt it was time to leave, I went up to the tunnel, jumped and gently landed in my body.

Because upwards of eight million Americans report having had a near-death experience, many of them while under the influence of medically monitored, anesthesia-induced sleep, it's good that someone is paying attention and doing some solid research. But we have to question whether research bias entered the picture. In other words, do those who produce the studies find what they find because that's what they *expect*, or maybe even *want*, to find?

A doctor, for instance, can give someone medicine that mimics the symptoms of a heart attack, but that doesn't mean the patient is really having a heart attack. He or she is merely showing the symptoms of one.

In the same way, mimicking NDEs by training people to experience the results of one doesn't mean they died and traveled over to the other side, so we have to be a little suspicious of a researcher who successfully trains volunteers to experience the stages of an NDE and then announces that, in the words of Michael Raduga:

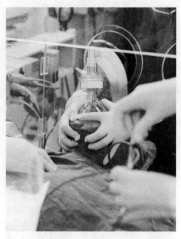

Many NDEs occur while someone is under anesthesia, which has led some to ponder whether it might be just some kind of side effect of the drugs used during surgical procedures or as a result of brain damage if the patient is dying.

> *NDEs, as the most trusted reason for belief in life after life, may be just the result of spontaneous and hyper-realistic lucid dreams, induced by narcosis or brain damage during dying. This means that NDEs aren't evidence of life after life.*

In her piece for NBC, Wolchover reported on the work of Kevin Nelson of the University of Kentucky, who suggested that NDEs are generated by the same brain mechanisms that cause lucid dreams. She suggested that Nelson's research shows that

> *[b]oth types of experiences arise when part of the brain called the dorsolateral prefrontal region—our "logical center," which is usually active only when we're awake—becomes active during REM sleep, allowing extremely vivid dreams that seem to be happening in real life. He calls the transitional state between dreaming and wakefulness a "borderland of consciousness" and believes it is in this mixed state that lucid dreams and NDEs occur.*

REM sleep refers to the period of "rapid eye movement" sleep in which the sleeper's eyes are moving about, and their brain is actively in a dream phase.

Although Nelson said conclusions from the research should be "cautiously drawn" until the findings pass the peer-review process, they are nonetheless "well-aligned with prior research on NDEs."

He was quoted in an interview with *Life* magazine as saying, "Lucid dreaming can be conditioned and bears an uncanny similarity to near-death."

Maybe so, but where is the monitor that demonstrates the flat line of physical death? In other words, where is the veridical data? All they did was mimic the stages of a typical near-death experience. You can do the same thing through hypnotism. And since all we have to go on is the word of the volunteers, how do we prove they weren't simply capable of great feats of imagination?

As of this writing, the group has not published their findings for peer review. I suspect that when they do, they might run into some pushback.

That being said, however, any study of NDEs has to consider the close relationship between dreams, visions, and near-death experiences. They all seem to be connected at some level, in that they at least begin in the mind.

But this is easier said than done, because once you broach the subject to experts, a startling truth emerges. No one—that's right, *no one*—really knows what dreams are. Many say they do, and they present their case in well-written papers and books. But there is honest disagreement that sometimes becomes very heated. Consider just a few alternative theories:

· Ancient shamanism: When released from the normal bounds of restraints of the waking, analytical hemisphere in our brains, our true nature, our consciousness, returns to the Source. With practice we can follow along while fully conscious, perceiving parallel dimensions in which we learn truths that guide our waking activities.

· Therapeutic psychotherapy: Your brain tries to make sense out of things while you sleep in the safe environment of your bed. Events of the day are analyzed for meaning and projected on the wall of your conscious mind when you wake up and remember. Your emotions then attempt to make sense of the symbols.

- Modern technology: When your home computer is at rest, programs automatically kick in to clean up and organize clutter, defragmenting and systematizing things so the computer will work more efficiently. The brain operates in the same way. While you sleep, your brain organizes all the thoughts and external stimuli you encountered during the day.

- Robert Moss in *Dreamgates*: "Our physical reality is surrounded and permeated by the vigorous, thrumming life of the realms of spirit and imagination to which we return, night after night, in dream. There is no distance between the Otherworld and its inhabitants and our familiar, sensory reality; there is only a difference in frequency."

- Sigmund Freud in *The Interpretation of Dreams*: "Dreams are disguised fulfillments of repressed wishes."

- J. Allan Hobson and Robert McCarley: "Dreams are a symbolic interpretation of signals generated by the brain during sleep. The symbols, if interpreted correctly by a trained analyst, can reveal clues to understanding what is going on in our subjective unconscious."

We may not understand what sleep and dreaming are all about, but we know that the physical body ceases to function without them. When we are tired and deprived of sleep, the first thing we lose is creativity. Then we start to forget things. Modern dream-deprivation studies indicate that without dreams, we die.

Dreaming might seem "normal" to us, but in actuality it is no less mysterious than NDEs. There is considerable speculation as to how we dream and why, but no one knows the answer for certain.

In introducing this book, I admitted my prejudice that when it comes to the debate about whether NDEs are real or a final spasm of a brain on the verge of death, I'm on the side of the former rather than the latter, but it seems to me that a fair analysis must consider all options. It might be that NDEs will someday prove to be a final dream. But I think it equally possible, maybe even *probable*, that just the opposite is true. NDEs are not dreams. They are the reality that awaits when we *wake up* from a dream.

Someday we may be able to develop a technology to prove that the old song is correct when it declares, "Life is but a dream." Perhaps NDEs put us in a state we have all experienced when we wake from sleep and need a minute to figure out which reality is upon us—the vivid dream or the awakened reality. Maybe the day will even come when dream research goes to the next level: that of realizing that we must sleep and dream to recharge our physical batteries by connecting with the reality that is our real home. If we die because we are denied the opportunity to reconnect with the source of our being through the dream state, it could be that we resemble a toy that ceases to function when its batteries run out.

If so, that makes dreams extremely important to our physical existence. When we are told we must stop "wasting time" because we are "sleeping away" much of our lives, that's probably very bad advice. The purpose of sleep and dreams might be to restore our connection with who we really are. It is only when our waking consciousness is stilled enough in sleep to remember who we *really* are and where we *really* live that we can access the knowledge of why we came here in the first place.

Is it any wonder that those who return from the other side often comment that their near-death experience seemed more *real* than their normal life?

We feel connected to Source in every fiber of our being. That feeling is deep inside each and every one of us. But in the hectic activity of our busy lives, we forget, so we need to be reminded. Sleep calms down the physical energy that often consumes us. Dreams take us home for a while to regroup.

That could very well prove to be the answer to what NDEs are: They are our awakening from the dream of physical existence that we call life.

15 THE PHENOMENON OF SHARED DEATH EXPERIENCES

The term shared-death experience may be new, but it went by different names centuries ago. The Society for Psychical Research in London documented shared-death experiences in the late 1800s, dubbing them "death-bed visions" or "death-bed coincidences."

—John Blake in "Beyond Goodbye."
CNN.com, December 2014

After a career with the Merchant Marine, Ron was now in hospice, dying from stomach cancer. Few relatives or friends visited him, so William Peters, one of the volunteers who helped care for him, spent hours every day reading to him from books such as Jack London's *Call of the Wild*. Ron grew more and more frail every day. He seemed to be struggling to hold on to life.

There came a day when Peters found Ron only semiconscious. He tried to read to him, but it was obvious Ron didn't have long to live. What happened next surprised the caregiver in a way he never forgot. He felt a force jerk his spirit upward, out of his body, and found himself floating above Ron's bed, looking down at the dying man. Glancing next to him, he saw Ron floating alongside, looking at the same scene below.

Peters later recalled, "He looked at me and he gave me this happy, contented look as if he was telling me, 'Check this out. Here we are.'"

Peters then felt himself drop back into his body. The whole experience was over in an instant, and Ron died, but Peters' questions about that day lingered on. Those questions led him to research what had happened, and he discovered his experience was not unique. What he came to learn was that he had undergone a shared-death experience.

Raymond Moody coined the term near-death experience (NDE) in his book *Life After Life*. In a later book, *Glimpses of Eternity*, he labeled what is now called the shared-death experience (SDE). For 20 years he collected stories from patients and eventually published them, despite the fact that as an established medical doctor and psychiatrist he had to endure the metaphorical slings and arrows of those in his chosen profession who didn't approve of colleagues mixing, in their eyes at least, "serious" medicine with "frivolous" metaphysics.

But Moody soldiered on. He had been intrigued by such stories ever since he was in medical school, had collected hundreds of them, and wasn't about to quit examining what he thought was solid evidence of life after death.

> His [Moody's] skeptics tried to explain away these experiences as hallucinations triggered by anesthesia or anoxia, a loss of oxygen to the brain.

His skeptics tried to explain away these experiences as hallucinations triggered by anesthesia or anoxia, a loss of oxygen to the brain. That *might* explain near-death experiences, although Moody doubted even that, but it certainly couldn't explain shared-death experiences, when perfectly healthy bystanders, who were under no such extraneous effects, saw the same things.

"We don't have the option of anoxia in shared-death experiences because the bystanders aren't ill or injured, and yet they experience the same kind of things," Moody said.

In his book *Parting Visions*, Melvin Morse described what happened to Karl Skala, a World War I German soldier who barely escaped injury when an artillery shell exploded near a foxhole where he huddled with another frightened comrade. His friend died in his arms, but Skala said he

> *felt himself being drawn up with his friend, above their bodies and then above the battlefield. He could look down and see himself holding his friend. Then he looked up and saw a bright light and felt himself going toward it with his friend. Then he stopped and returned to his body. He was uninjured except for a hearing loss that resulted from the artillery blast.*

In another account, Dr. Penny Sartori, had also been a nurse for 21 years, recounts what she called a deathbed vision that left her shaken. While preparing to bathe a dying patient as part of her night-shift duties, she later recounted that "everything around us stopped." The patient was hooked up to a ventilator and the usual life-prolonging equipment found in the hospital. When she touched the man's bed, she said, "It was almost like I swapped places with him." In a report for CNN, John Blake recounts:

> *She says she could suddenly understand everything the man was going through, including feeling his pain. He couldn't talk but she says she could somehow hear him convey a heart-wrenching message: "Leave me alone. Let me die in peace ... let me die."*

She had previously heard about such experiences, shared by medical colleagues she trusted, and was thus moved to spend the next five years researching similar stories, eventually publishing them in her book, *The Wisdom of Near-Death Experiences: How Understanding NDEs Can Help Us Live More Fully.*

In the same book, she wrote:

> *There would be a sudden drop in temperature at the bedside of a dying patient, or a light would surround the body just before death. It's very common for a clock to stop at the moment of death.... I've seen light bulbs flicker or blow at the moment of death.*

A song written by Henry Clay Work in 1876 and popularized by Johnny Cash in 1959 now takes on new meaning. It's called "My Grandfather's Clock":

At the moment of death, according to Dr. Penny Sartori, it is not uncommon to see that a clock has stopped, or a light flickers, or that there is a sudden drop in the room's temperature.

*My grandfather's clock was too large for the shelf
So it stood ninety years on the floor.
It was taller by half than the old man himself
Though it weighed not a pennyweight more.
It was bought on the morn of the day that he was born
And was always his treasure and pride.
But it stopped short, never to go again,
When the old man died.*

Apparently, the phenomenon is real and not just poetic. It resonated with a lot of people and made the song a success.

Other such effects have been noted by those who work with dying patients. Some health care workers report seeing a light exit from the top of a person's body at the moment of death. "Others," in the words of Raymond Moody, "say it's like the room changes dimensions. It's like a port opens up to some other framework of reality."

Anecdotes abound that some people who have participated in a dying person's transition experience profound psychological/spiritual/emotional effects. These events are often ignored in hospice and palliative medicine because of their subjective nature, but when reported and taken seriously they seem to fall into four categories:

· Remotely sensing a death

· Witnessing unusual phenomena

· Feelings of accompanying the dying

· Feelings of somehow assisting the dying

There also seem to be three distinctive aftereffects:

· Changes in belief

· Reconciliation of grief

· Perceptions of continued relational bonds with the deceased

These accounts indicate that something is going on, but it seems so out of the ordinary that few people have followed up on it. Obviously, a lot more verified research needs to be done.

The Monroe Institute, as we have previously seen, is doing some of that work. A study specifically aimed at SDEs reports that individuals present with a dying person sometimes "mentally join him or her in the preliminary journey to the next world."

In some accounts, an NDE is like opening a door to another world, another reality.

Scott M. Taylor, a former president and executive director of the Monroe Institute, provided a written account of the near-death experience he shared with a loved one.

> A study specifically aimed at SDEs reports that individuals present with a dying person sometimes "mentally join him or her in the preliminary journey to the next world."

Mary Fran and her son were killed in a car crash. Mary died instantly. Her son succumbed in a hospital a few days later. When it happened, his grieving family surrounded his hospital bed, and what they saw shocked them to the core:

When he departed his physical body for the last time, Mary Fran crossed the divide between the nonphysical world and the physical, and scooped Nolan out of his body. As Nolan's heartbeat patterns flattened and the monitor beside his bed sounded the constant, unwavering tone of organ failure, every member of his extended family wept....

Except for Dr. Taylor. He continued his story:

Their reunion embrace was exquisite. Then, to my surprise, Mary Fran and Nolan turned and included me in

*their embrace. Together, the three of us went to the light.
I know of no English words for the combination of joy, ecstasy, love, and requited longing that burned within me.
It carried me to a dimension I never knew existed. In
that moment, there was no pain of loss, only unity, rap-
ture, and reunion.*

In the closing words of the report, Taylor struggled to find
words to describe what he had experienced:

*I was fully conscious, fully present in the hospital room
with the grieving gathering. Yet simultaneously I was
lifted to a place beyond description. I experienced bi-lo-
cation: two fully conscious vantage points, one on the
window sill and a second, somewhere in another dimension, embraced by Mary Fran and Nolan as she guided
her son farther into the Light.*

Stories such as this make us wonder if we are somehow connected in our individual minds to a universal mind, and to a much
greater world than our physical senses can embrace.

Kaylin Kaupish, after editing a story found in an article for
Guideposts magazine entitled "The Divine Power behind Shared
Death Experiences," relates that:

*Jeff Olsen arrived at the hospital after a car accident. His
wife and child both died in the accident and doctors
were working to revive him. Dr. Jeff O'Driscoll, another
doctor at the hospital who had never met Olsen, went to
his room in the ER. There he saw a woman floating above
Olsen's gurney. She looked at Dr. O'Driscoll intently,
then disappeared. He innately knew this was Jeff Olsen's
wife, expressing her gratitude to the medical staff for
saving her husband.*

The story profoundly moved her. She decided to investigate
and contacted William Peters. When we met Peters in the first
paragraph of this chapter, he was a hospice volunteer. By now,
after being moved by his initial experience, he had gone on to become a psychotherapist and founder of the Shared Crossing Project, an organization dedicated to educating people about the
profound experience of death and the healing opportunities in
end-of-life phenomena.

Dr. Peters started the project in 2013, based on the idea that some people have "experienced the initial stages of the after-life. It can happen to caregivers, loved ones, or even just bystanders."

He believes that although every SDE is different, they share a few common factors:

- Visions of the dying appearing healthy and happy

- Seeing a mystical light

- Entering a heavenly realm with the dying person

In shared-death experiences there have been several commonalities among those reporting what happened to them, and those experiences have always had positive qualities such as a sense of happiness, light, and heavenliness.

They can seem like waking visions, out-of-body experiences, or dreams.

"It's a dynamic experience," he says. "We are being allowed to witness a journey from this human life into what lies beyond."

According to research conducted by the Shared Crossing Project, there are four types of participation:

- *Sensing:* The experiencer has a feeling or intuitive know-ing that a loved one is dying. This type of participation occurs when the experiencer is located apart from the dying loved one, or not at the bedside of the loved one. It is often accompanied by a profound sense of the dying person's presence.

- *Witnessing:* The experiencer sees part of the dying process that's often reported by those who've had NDEs—a glimpse of the dying person's life review or of the dying person being greeted by a deceased loved one in heaven.

- *Accompanying:* The experiencer goes with the loved one toward a heavenly light or through a tunnel. Peters shared the profound and beautiful story of this type of SDE ex-perienced by a woman who was her dying husband's caregiver: "When he passed, she joined him as he as-cended. She felt the euphoric bliss of heaven, and saw her husband's mother, who had already passed. She handed him over to her. Then it was over. She was left feeling like she'd gotten reassurance and closure. It was an affirmation that her husband was at peace, and with his beloved mother."

· *Guiding*: This is a type of SDE that can help loved ones to let go. "One of our experiencers had his while he was flying in a plane," Peters said. "He was relaxing in his seat when a vision came to him. His father was there and confused and didn't know where to go. Inherently, the son knew his dad needed to go toward a light. He helped him and watched his father go through a portal. When the son landed, he learned his father had died."

According to Peters:

Some dismiss NDEs as just the body's biological response to physical trauma, but for SDEs, this is a mystical experience happening to a healthy person. And there are so many commonalities in firsthand accounts of NDEs and SDEs, it has to be more than a coincidence.... They still feel the loss of their loved one, but now this loss is held in a larger context imbued with greater meaning and a knowing that everything is fine just as is. [It is] a natural part of the human experience and there is some kind of benevolent power behind it that allows them to see it so they can heal.

SDEs are almost as common as stories of those who underwent NDEs. There is no reason to dismiss them as separate events. They need to be compiled and studied if only because they undercut the argument that NDEs are nothing more than hallucinations triggered by anesthesia or anoxia. Any phenomenon that involves eyewitnesses is important. The field of SDE research offers precisely that experience.

16 SOME WHO MADE A DIFFERENCE

I finally came to the point where I realized that to maintain my atheism, I would have to believe that nothing produces everything, that nonlife produces life, that randomness produces fine tuning, that chaos produces information, that unconsciousness produces consciousness and that non-reason produces reason. Frankly I just didn't have enough faith to continue to believe that.

—Lee Strobel, Twitter (X) post dated December 24, 2017

In Part III of this book, we have been considering the fact that one field of scientific study must often "borrow" from others so as to arrive at the overall "big picture" that explores the truth of NDEs. Studies in quantum physics must borrow from biology. Those who do dream research must sometimes share insights with those who study shared-death experiences. The world of medicine must take its findings into the laboratory. The way NDE research has exploded on to the scene of public media is yet another example. Those who write for a living seem to have discovered that they now have something exciting to write about that strikes a popular chord while grounding itself firmly in the academic world of the scientist.

You can't dig very deeply into this explosion of material without coming into the presence of a few giants who appear again and again—telling their stories, relating their research, revealing the fact that they overlap and borrow from different tra-

Quite a few celebrities—such as rocker Ozzy Osbourne (pictured)—have reported experiencing their own NDEs.

ditions, speaking at cross-academic conferences, writing books and articles, appearing on television talk shows, and generally spreading the news. There are too many to include everybody here, but these few captured the public eye in a special way over the last few decades.

I'm not talking about celebrities, necessarily. Elizabeth Taylor, Tony Bennett, Sharon Stone, Ozzy Osbourne, and Donald Sutherland, to name just a few, have all shared their near-death experiences, all of which are valid and important. But the stories that follow are about people who were not famous until they wrote influential books and advanced NDE research in an important way. They stepped out of their own field of academic and professional specialization, borrowing from various disciplines to cross over into the arena of media attention. Indeed, because of their cross-discipline efforts they may have changed the whole process of how NDEs came to be studied.

In roughly chronological order of their popular presence, here are their stories.

DEEPAK CHOPRA

I first became aware of the work and wisdom of Deepak Chopra more than 35 years ago. Someone had given me a series of cassette tapes he recorded, and I was immediately struck by his clarity of thought and depth of intellect. This was a man I could respect! He immediately joined those few people in my life whom I called "mentors I would never meet." He seemed to be a wise elder I could look up to and learn from, taking advantage of his years spent gaining spiritual growth. I started buying and reading all his books. It's safe to say that he cost me a pretty penny over the decades, given his prolific output. I wanted to model my life after his. I looked up to him as someone who had gathered a wealth of wisdom.

Then I sat down a few minutes ago, before writing this, to gather some biographical facts from the plethora of material the internet has to say about him, and discovered that I'm six months older than he is!

Needless to say, it was a humbling experience. When I see what he has accomplished in his 77 years, and what I've accomplished in mine, it certainly helps keep my ego in check.

Chopra was born in India, surrounded by a culture rich in both spirituality and scientific rationalism. He eventually grew to be fluent in the thought patterns of both Vedanta philosophy and modern Western medicine. Described by some as a philosophical idealist, he became convinced that consciousness preceded matter—that "dynamically active consciousness" is a fundamental feature of the universe. It is no wonder that when he became a prominent figure in what soon began to be called "New Age" thinking, many of his

New Age figure and alternative medicine advocate Dr. Deepak Chopra, who, in his books and lectures, talks about "quantum healing" as a means of achieving perfect health.

colleagues accused him of technobabble—"incoherent babbling strewn with scientific terms"—which drove many theoretical physicists nuts.

In other words, they simply couldn't understand what he was saying because in many cases they had never even heard of Vedanta, let alone understood what it meant.

But he was more than up to the task of defending his views. He had studied medicine in India before coming to the United States in 1970. After finishing his residence in internal medicine and earning a degree in endocrinology, he went on to become chief of staff at the New England Memorial Hospital near Boston. With credentials like these, it was hard to claim that he wasn't an established medical professional.

But 15 years into his new life as an American citizen, his Indian roots surfaced. He met Maharishi Mahesh Yogi, whom the Beatles later popularized, and became involved in the Transcendental Meditation (TM) movement. Soon after, he resigned his prestigious position to found the Maharishi Ayurveda Health Center.

The late Maharishi Mahesh Yogi, who taught and inspired both the Beatles and Deepak Chopra, founded the Transcendental Meditation (TM) movement in 1955.

His books caught the attention of Oprah Winfrey in the early 1990s, and as with many others she brought to public attention, the rest, as they say, is history. When it came time for him to leave the burgeoning TM movement, partly because of his fear that a cult-like atmosphere was developing around Maharishi Mahesh Yogi, he became the executive director of Sharp HealthCare's Center for Mind-Body Medicine and eventually, when he was 50 years old, co-founded the Chopra Center for Wellbeing.

Chopra, to the best of my knowledge, never experienced an NDE himself, but his insights into the nature of consciousness, and his tremendous popular appeal when it came time to express the nature of non-duality in a way that caught the ear of the public, paved the way for others to follow.

In his book *The Future of God*, he directly confronted a reality that many were experiencing:

Our old model of God is being dismantled before our eyes. Instead of trying to pick up the pieces, a deeper shift must take place. Reason, personal experience, and the wisdom of many cultures are coming together already. This new synthesis is like God 2.0, where human evolution takes a leap in matters of the spirit.

God 1.0 reflected human needs, which are many and varied, and these needs took on divine personification. The needs came first. Because humans need security and safety, we projected God as our divine protector. Because life needs to be orderly, we made God the supreme lawgiver. Reversing the Book of Genesis, we created God in our own image. He did what we wanted him to do.

In his view, consciousness is both subject and object. Consciousness creates reality. Evolution is consciousness seeking expression. Through our brains, the universe experiences itself: "We are the eyes of the universe looking at itself." We are not "physical machines that have somehow learned to think, but thoughts that have learned to create a physical machine."

He opposes reductionism and argues that borrowing from many disciplines is the key to understanding the nature of reality that many try to express after having a near-death experience.

Of course, this kind of thinking draws criticism. He has been called a pseudoscientist, but his education and credentials make that a laughable proposition.

Richard Dawkins, the voice of skepticism who wrote the 2006 best-seller *The God Delusion*, claims Chopra uses "quantum jargon as plausible-sounding hocus pocus."

To this, Chopra responded, "With Dawkins, I am just pissed off. I am pissed off by his arrogance and his pretense of being a really good scientist. He is not, and he is using his scientific credentials to literally go on a rampage."

When Chopra is accused of having made a lot of money from his writing, he responds, "I put everything I earn into good use. How can I apologize for that? Does Tom Clancy apologize for his books? I have always done well, yeah. In America, you should never apologize for being financially successful."

True, he makes a lot of money from his public lectures. His speaking fee can reach as high as thousands of dollars. To this he offers a frank response: "Should I say, 'I'll do it for you for free?' To a corporation? No."

What he usually doesn't add is that he contributes much of his money to worthy foundations and often does pro bono lectures for nonprofits. He also rarely mentions the fact that he spent his early days as a doctor working in rural India in a village where the lights went out whenever it rained.

British evolutionary biologist Richard Dawkins is an atheist who has been highly critical of those who believe in intelligent design, creationism, and biocentrism.

One of the reasons he began intense meditation was to kick a habit of "drinking black coffee by the hour and smoking at least a pack of cigarettes a day." The spiritual practice was so beneficial that he continues to meditate for two hours every morning and half an hour in the evening.

His work in alternative medicine included clients such as Elizabeth Taylor, who once had an NDE and consented to talk about it various interviews. He also worked with and began a friendship with Michael Jackson that lasted for 20 years. After Jackson's death in 2009, a death that some believe was hastened by heavy doses of prescription drugs, Chopra said he hoped it would be a call to action against the "cult of drug-pushing doctors, with their co-dependent relationships with addicted celebrities."

It is when Chopra talks about the nature of the cosmos that he seems to connect with the experiences of those who try to describe what they saw during their NDEs. He pictures the universe as a "reality sandwich" that has three layers: the material world of our primary experience, a quantum zone of matter and energy, and a virtual zone outside of time and space. This last is the zone both Albert Einstein and Stephen Hawking called "the mind of God." Human beings are "hardwired to know God," he says, and the functions of the human nervous system mirror divine experience.

In 2012 Chopra took on the establishment in a debate that became a best-selling book. *War of the Worldviews* consists of contrasting arguments between Chopra and theoretical physicist Leonard Mlodinow. In it, they debated the big questions that cause

cross-discipline arguments. They dealt with cosmology, life, evolution, the mind and brain, and even divinity. The two authors, although deliberately presenting opposing views, became friends. Chopra even taught Mlodinow how to meditate.

One of Chopra's arguments about the continued existence of life after death draws not from metaphysics but from biology. The cells of our body replace themselves every six months. In some cases, even less. So how do they remember the experience their "ancestor" cells had with certain bacteria? How do they program themselves to fight disease?

American physicist Leonard Mlodinow is known for his work in the quantum theory of light and infinite-dimensional expression of atoms.

The answer, he claims, is that DNA "programs" memory into each cell. DNA is a tool of consciousness. The cells constantly come and go, but their host continues. Because consciousness is the creator of the host, it would seem logical to believe that eventually it will migrate away from biological life altogether. Consciousness is eternal. It dwells within a host—us. When the time comes for the host to finally return its material cells to the elements, consciousness will move on. The host will have outlived its usefulness. That, in essence, is what happens at death, and the transition is sometimes experienced through NDEs.

With this as a background, given the popularity of Chopra's teaching, is it any wonder that the public was ready for Raymond Moody when he introduced the term "near-death experience" to the world?

RAYMOND MOODY

If we need to mark the exact beginning of the birth of a popular phenomenon such as the current explosion of public interest in NDEs, we can safely pinpoint the year 1975 and the publication of Raymond Moody's book *Life After Life*. That was the book in which Moody coined the term "near-death experience."

Before 1975, NDEs were considered to be generally interesting, but certainly not something to be discussed around the office water cooler. They were life-changing to the people who had experienced them, but simply a metaphysical oddity to most folks, somewhat akin to a discussion about ghosts, fairies, and leprechauns.

After 1975, it is safe to say that they became a legitimate field of study. For that reason, Moody is now called "the father of near-death experiences." Since then, he coined the term "shared-death experience" as well, so any discussion of either of these experiences must begin with Dr. Raymond A. Moody Jr., physician, psychiatrist, philosopher, author, and much-sought-after public speaker.

His interest in the subject that became his passion was probably sparked by an encounter with Dr. George Ritchie in 1965. Moody was an undergraduate at the University of Virginia when Ritchie told him about an incident in which he believed he experienced what Moody would later label an NDE, during which, at the age of 20, he died for nine minutes and crossed over into the afterlife.

If you're wondering who coined the term "near-death experience," it was physician, psychiatrist, philosopher, and author Raymond Moody.

Ritchie would write about the incident in his 1978 book, *Return from Tomorrow*, but Moody began collecting similar accounts by people who had experienced clinical death and come back to tell the tale. He soon discovered common features, such as having an out-of-body experience, experiencing a sensation of traveling through a tunnel, encountering dead relatives, and seeing a bright light. These accounts led to his writing *Life After Life*, and to the birth of what has become a legitimate field of research.

In an interview with Jeffrey Mishlove, Moody reveals what has become his signature contribution to the field and the impact it has had on him:

I don't mind saying that after talking with over a thousand people who have had these experiences, and having experienced many times some of the really baffling and unusual features of these experiences, it has given me great confidence that there is a life after death. As a matter of fact, I must confess to you in all honesty, I have absolutely no doubt, on the basis of what my patients have told me, that they did get a glimpse of the beyond.

Then, in 1991, his academic interest became personal. An undiagnosed thyroid condition severely affected his mental state, and he attempted suicide. In *Paranormal*, the book that describes his ordeal, he reveals that during this time he experienced his own NDE.

Since *Life After Life*, he has gone on to write many books, the total of which now surpasses 20 million copies sold. Any Google search for NDEs will invariably begin with a Raymond Moody interview.

Of course, his work was criticized, sometimes vehemently, by a few colleagues.

Psychologist James Alcock, for instance, says that Moody "appears to ignore a great deal of the scientific literature dealing with hallucinatory experiences in general, just as he quickly glosses over the very real limitations of his research method."

Barry Beyerstein, a professor of psychology, declared Moody's alleged evidence for an afterlife flawed, both logically and empirically.

Philosopher Paul Kurtz, writing in his book *Toward a New Enlightenment: The Philosophy of Paul Kurtz,* thinks "Moody's evidence for the NDE is based on personal interviews and anecdotal accounts and there has been no statistical analysis of his data. There is no reliable evidence that people who report such experiences have died and returned, or that consciousness exists separate from the brain or body."

Secular humanist and skeptic Paul Kurtz (pictured) criticized Moody for merely gathering anecdotal evidence for NDEs without any hard scientific research to back up his ideas.

But many reliable and accredited specialists disagree with these opinions. Once again, it seems as though preconceived notions dominate any discussion about NDEs. Materialists who don't believe in life after physical death have a knee-jerk reaction to criticize anyone who does, and Moody has spent his life countering his detractors point by point, in a style that is laid-back, scientifically accurate, and almost chatty in nature. To listen to him talk about this subject is akin to a meeting with a trusted neighbor on your front porch. He is conversational, nonconfrontational, and always interested in the person he is talking to at the moment. If there is a metaphorical God somewhere who wants to spread the word and defend NDEs, she could not have chosen a better spokesperson.

BETTY EADIE

In 1992, the book *Embraced by the Light* was published and went right to the top of the *New York Times* best-sellers list. Betty Eadie, its author, followed it up with another best-seller in *The Awakening Heart* in 1996. Clearly, she had found a market that was ready to read about NDEs, because her near-death experience was at the heart of both books, as well as *The Ripple Effect* in 1999 and a daily devotional booklet called *Embraced by the Light: Prayers and Devotions for Daily Living* in 2001.

Born and raised on the Rosebud Indian Reservation in South Dakota, Eadie was placed in St. Francis Indian School, an American Indian boarding school, along with six of her siblings, after her parents separated. She was forced to drop out of school to care for a younger sister, but she eventually received her college degree.

What motivated her to write her book was an NDE that she experienced in 1973. She was 31 years old and recovering from an operation when it happened. She tells how she felt herself fading to lifelessness before feeling a sudden surge of energy followed by a "pop" and feeling of release. There followed a feeling of immense freedom and unhindered movement. It seemed as though gravity didn't exist in the new landscape in which she found herself.

Three "angelic beings" spoke with her, reminding her of the previous existence she had known before she was born into a physical body. Her memory, she was told, was suppressed in order to fully participate in her earthly experience of material life.

She was able to visit familiar locations, such as her home, merely by thinking about them. After she returned to the hospital, however, where her body lay in death, she passed through a dark tunnel where she saw, or rather sensed, other beings. They appeared to be in some sort of transition stage.

Her doctor later verified her clinical death, attributing it to a hemorrhage during a nurses' shift change. Although time didn't exist in her new environment, she speculated she was gone for about four hours. Independent verification of the length of her death was not recorded.

Eadie related how after she crossed through the tunnel she encountered Jesus Christ, who greeted her with a comforting hug.

After traversing a dark tunnel, Eadie found herself in the presence of an intense white light, where she was embraced by Jesus Christ—hence the title of her book. She remembers a strong sense of love.

Obviously, she had many questions, which were all answered via a type of high-speed transfer.

Finding herself in some kind of spiritual body, she visited places such as natural parks and gardens far more beautiful than any that exist on earth. She was accompanied on a sort of tour, where she instantly learned things that would have taken months to absorb in her physical life.

She was taught what she called the key lesson of her NDE. Her life's purpose involved learning how to grow in love. This process could only be achieved through her free will, and it included the common human propensity to make mistakes.

There were other lessons as well. One of them was that our lives were chosen, prepared for, and agreed upon by each of us before our birth. Out of necessity, our memories of all this are suppressed because to remember where we came from and why we are here would deprive us of opportunities to learn and grow. But life contains hope, which is, in itself, a kind of memory.

For this reason, she learned, suicide is wrong because it interferes with the whole experience of a previously agreed-upon life path. What was yet to happen was kept from her so as not to tip her off as to her life's purpose, but upon learning this, she protested. She didn't want to return. She wanted to stay where she was. Her protest was overruled, but she was promised that she would not have to stay on earth any longer than was absolutely necessary.

When she returned to her body, she later wrote, she felt very heavy and unpleasant, and she was accompanied by a demonic visitation that was cut short by the reappearance of her initial angelic beings, who protected her.

She immediately entered a long period of depression, which she later attributed to the fact that returning to an earthly life was, at best, anticlimactic.

For a long time, she wouldn't tell anyone about what had happened, but she slowly began a process of joining near-death support groups and giving talks to growing audiences. She volunteered at a cancer research center, working to comfort dying patients and their families. She studied hypnotherapy and opened a clinic, and she became involved with various Christian religious denominations, such as Catholicism, Methodism, and, for a short time, the Latter-Day Saints Church in Seattle.

Eventually she wrote *Embraced by the Light*. Its totally unexpected success changed her life completely. She gave up her hypnotherapy practice and began traveling extensively throughout the United States, Canada, Great Britain, and Ireland, giving talks about death and the afterlife.

Such fame is sure to attract criticism. In Eadie's case, it came from at least two fronts.

First, because she expressed her experience in distinctly Christian terms, non-Christians suspected she was merely repeating what they considered to be Christian platitudes, dogma, and doctrine.

But criticism came from Christians as well, because she didn't stick strictly to fundamentalist teachings. Although she claimed to have visited the Garden of Eden, for instance, and spoke favorably of the need to pray, she taught that although some Christian denominations and other religions express truth better than others, each individual was at a specific stage of spiritual development and needed to gather information appropriate to their level. Thus, they should not be judged. Considering the propensity for many conservative Christians to preach the doctrine of "my way or the highway," this didn't set too well in certain quarters.

She also developed the habit of referring to God with a lower case "g." To some believers, this was blasphemous. Her ideas concerning the Trinity and homosexuality ruffled feathers as well.

Her teachings on hell were likewise suspect to many Christians. She rejected the common image of hell as an eternity of suffering, believing instead that her life-review experience, in which

A visit to the Garden of Eden was, apparently, also on the itinerary during Eadie's trip to the other side.

she was made to process both the positive and negative consequences of her earthly actions, including their effects on others, in intense, personal detail was more than adequate retribution.

Although many who have experienced NDEs tend to believe in reincarnation, Eadie does not, except in some cases. She was told that only a few return to this earth more than once, and that they usually are sent back as teachers, to help others.

There is no doubt that *Embraced by the Light* and Eadie's subsequent work continued the impact that Moody's *Life After Life* had on the public's interest in NDEs. During the years between 1975 and 1992, enthusiasm about the subject ebbed and flowed, but it never went away.

Which might explain the tremendous impact the field of NDE research experienced in 2008, even though it was prompted by someone who had not experienced, technically at least, an NDE.

JILL BOLTE TAYLOR

TED (Technology, Entertainment, and Design) Talks began in 1984. They are a perfect example of how one field of study borrows from others, featuring experts in various fields who give talks on their specialty while mixing in a healthy dose of entertainment and technological effects.

Richard Saul Wurman and Harry Marks had noticed the convergence of the three arenas signified by the initials and designed a series of lectures to incorporate them. Among the first was a talk given by mathematician Benoit Mandelbrot, who demonstrated how to map coastlines using his developing theory of fractal geometry. It demonstrated the convergence of different fields of study quite well, but, as might be expected from the subject matter, was disappointing in terms of success. Equally unsuccessful were lectures demonstrating the relatively new invention of compact discs and e-book readers.

Needless to say, the event lost money.

Six years later, in 1990, they tried again. This time they held their program in Monterey, California, and it soon grew into an annual event. By then, people were ready to be entertained and educated at the same time.

A typical TED Talk is 18 minutes long. The time frame stems from both neuroscience and marketing strategy. It is based on the idea that 18 minutes is long enough to fully develop a single idea. The average length of a typical church sermon, for in-

Neuroanatomist Jill Bolte Taylor was studying how cells in the brain communicate when she had a stroke. She wrote about her long recovery in the best-selling book *My Stroke of Insight: A Brain Scientist's Personal Journey.*

stance, is 20 minutes. Preachers learned long ago that a shorter time doesn't work well and a longer time tends to put people to sleep. In 18 minutes, an average listener, unfamiliar with the content, can take in and digest the important points of a single topic.

By 2008 audiences were familiar with TED Talks, but that was the year they took off. The catalyst was a talk by Jill Bolte Taylor, based on her book, *My Stroke of Insight: A Brain Scientist's Personal Journey*. After publication the book had gone straight to the number-four slot on the *New York Times* Best Sellers list, staying there for more than a year.

Taylor's book was successful enough, but her TED Talk was so inspirational that it was the first to go viral on the internet. It is still readily available and has received almost 25 million views, becoming one of the most-watched TED Talks of all time.

Her success led to an interview with Oprah Winfrey, where she was the first guest featured on Winfrey's *Soul Series* podcast. She was also listed on *Time* magazine's 2008 TIME 100 list, which labeled her one of the 100 most influential people in the world.

Taylor had not experienced an NDE. She never "died." But her talk powerfully underlined what most near-death experiencers knew to be true. Her description of feeling "nirvana" resonated so deeply that it struck a powerful chord in the near-death community. She was able to put into words how what she called "brain chatter" can be stilled by "stepping to the right" of our left brains to discover a deep and fulfilling inner peace.

It all began on December 10, 1996. Taylor was 37 years old, a Harvard-educated brain scientist. She was struck by a massive stroke in the left hemisphere of her brain. As she recounts the experience, her first thought was that this was an opportunity to observe firsthand what previously she had only been able to study. Her harrowing story is riveting. For four long hours she went back and forth between what she called nirvana—a euphoric sense of well-being and peace—and the realization that she was suffering from a stroke that could take her life.

Thankfully, and heroically, she managed to navigate through the maze of confusion and get help. She got to the hospital on time, but it took a full eight years to recover to the point where she could think, walk, and talk.

In her live presentation she was able to laugh about the experience, bringing down the house with the observation, "How many brain scientists have been able to study the brain from the inside out? I've gotten as much out of this experience of losing my mind as I have in my entire academic career."

I emphasize again that this was not a bona fide NDE. Her heart never stopped, and she was never pronounced clinically dead. But it was so close to what some who have recovered from near-death experiences recognized that interest in the subject skyrocketed. Her TED Talk was so riveting, alternating between raw emotion and scientific reasoning, that it couldn't help but move people.

> What struck those who see similarities between her stroke and a near-death experience was the feeling that the intellectual part of our brain ... offers us an illusory experience of life.

What struck those who see similarities between her stroke and a near-death experience was the feeling that the intellectual part of our brain, the section that deals with day-to-day activities, offers us an illusory experience of life. We think we have a handle on what we see, feel, touch, taste, and hear, to the point where we call it reality and declare that nothing else exists. But a whole separate hemisphere operates on a different level, experiencing something quite different. Who is to say which is "real"?

If our experience of life is so tenuous and is subject to such drastic experiential differences, obviously there is much more to our existence than the illusion, albeit a very strong one, of reality.

When this fact of neurology echoes similar ideas from the field of theoretical physicists, some of whom say the whole universe is an illusion, it presents a strong argument that there is more going on in our existence than (pardon the pun) meets the eye.

Could it be possible that when we are freed from the filter/prison of our five senses, which is exactly what happens during an NDE, we experience the "real" reality, rather than the one that has so powerfully deceived us during our every waking hour?

There is no blame to be placed here. Our senses have been evolving ever since the first one-celled amoeba floated forth from some primeval ooze, or wherever it came from. If we had not had the advantage of them or been the recipients of their limiting filters, we would never have become whatever it is we are. We would have long ago been totally overwhelmed by the amount of information besieging us from all sides. Our physical bodies are dependent upon the fact that some impulses are more important than others when it comes survival.

> But when our consciousness is freed from the physical senses through the death of the material body, it observes, in the moment of its freedom, a reality otherwise hidden from us.

But when our consciousness is freed from the physical senses through the death of the material body, it observes, in the moment of its freedom, a reality otherwise hidden from us. That, in essence, is exactly what an NDE is. And although Jill Bolte Taylor never completely succumbed to death, her graphic and inspiring vision put words to the experience in a way few others have been able to do.

BRUCE GREYSON

From an article in the *New York Post* on February 2, 2020:

About fifty years ago, Dr. Bruce Greyson was eating pasta in the hospital cafeteria when his beeper went off. Greyson, a psychiatrist, was urgently needed in the ER to treat a college student who had overdosed. He called her name—"Holly"—and tried to rouse her. But she didn't stir. The next morning, Greyson returned to work at the hospital. Holly stirred. "I remember you from last night," she mumbled. "I saw you talking with Susan, sitting on the couch." Suddenly Holly opened her eyes, looked Greyson in the face and added, "You were wearing a striped tie that had a red stain on it."

The red stain came from the pasta sauce Greyson had spilled in his haste to get to the ER. That was when the doctor of neurobehavioral sciences, who is now the Chester Carlson Professor Emeritus of Psychiatry and Neurobehavioral Sciences at the University of Virginia, began to collect stories about near-death experiences. He told the story of his research in his book *After: A Doctor Explores What Near-Death Experiences Reveal about Life and Beyond.* He has also written hundreds of academic research papers.

His conclusion after all this research? "Near-death experiences are fairly common. Some 10 percent to 20 percent of people who come close to death report them—about 5 percent of the population."

Greyson was not religious. He grew up in a no-nonsense, scientific-minded household. But he now says that he "thinks the evidence overwhelmingly points to the physical body not being all that we are. There seems to be something that is able to continue after the body dies."

> **"Near-death experiences are fairly common. Some 10 percent to 20 percent of people who come close to death report them—about 5 percent of the population."**

In his book *The Handbook of Near-Death Experiences* he has gathered story after story to illustrate his point.

Consider this one, for example. Anita was a nurse who developed a friendship with one of the patients under her care. Unfortunately, the patient suffered cardiac arrest and died while Anita was away from the hospital, traveling. He was resuscitated and came back to life with a story.

On the other side, he said, he met Anita. She told him it wasn't his time to go, and that he must return.

But how could he have met Anita on the other side? What was she doing there?

Unknown to any of them, Anita had just died in a car accident miles away from the hospital.

Having heard this story and many similar ones, Greyson, with his background in the scientific method, began to collect more data and evidence, correlated a hypothesis, began to test the hypothesis, and eventually published it for peer review. He came to the personal conclusion that, in his words, "mind is not what the brain does." He began to see that "mind" exists separate from the brain. The brain is an *interpreter* of universal mind, not a *generator* of it.

Some of his observations seem very simple in theory but carry immense meaning:

· Time doesn't exist on the other side of death. It appears to function only in material space, as in Einstein's concepts of "space/time."

· But people have "experiences" there. Doesn't that imply some kind of time? Needless to say, this presents a classic paradox.

· Upon their return, when debriefed about their journey, they cannot adequately explain what happened, even though they are left with vivid impressions.

· In some ways, the experiences of an NDE and a psychedelic drug trip are similar. Does that mean the brain manufactures both, especially because drugs have often been given to patients who subsequently died?

· That couldn't be, because people under the influence of drugs on the operating table have statistically fewer NDEs than those who don't have any drugs in their system. Another paradox.

Because of these observations and many more, he began to consult with Dr. Raymond Moody and soon came to the conclusion that once you study NDEs with an open mind, following the evidence, your findings can change your life. They are not simply an academic exercise. In his words, "The problems of this bag of skin are not that important."

One of the things Greyson discovered was that some NDE researchers chose to ignore concerns about the dark side of NDE studies. How do we handle the few bad experiences that some people have?

In some ways, an NDE is like an experience after taking psychedelic drugs such as LSD. Could NDEs, then, be explained as merely some kind of reaction to chemical changes in the brain? Or maybe psychedelics just mimic NDEs.

Just because they are few in number, can we sweep them under the proverbial rug so as not to upset people or worry them too much?

Greyson refused to do that. He confronted the issue and made some important discoveries:

- Only about 1% of people who recount NDEs report a bad experience. But this figure, he believes, may be low, because most people don't want to talk about their negative experiences. It is simply too painful.

- Statistically, most of the people who experience a dark NDE story are Catholics and conservative Protestant Christians.

- Some of the negative experiences recalled by people raised in Western cultures involve blackness or emptiness. They interpret this as a fearful, terrifying place. Many people raised in Eastern cultures, however, such as

India, come back relating the same story but with a totally different interpretation. Their background in Hinduism or Buddhism prepared them for what they call the bliss of nirvana, and this is what they experience. Therefore, we have to take cultural background into account when we listen to NDE stories.

· Negative experiences are usually reported by people who have a personal history of wanting to be in control of their lives. They usually report that once they surrender to the experience, it immediately gets better. They carry this lesson with them for the rest of their natural lives.

> **Negative experiences are usually reported by people who have a personal history of wanting to be in control of their lives.**

The further Greyson dug into his research, the more he wanted to specialize in this field. In 1978, along with fellow researchers John Audette, Kenneth Ring, and Michael Sabom, he co-founded the Association for the Scientific Study of Near-Death Phenomena.

As we saw in an earlier chapter, in 1981 the organization changed its name to the International Association for Near-Death Studies (IANDS), and soon became a central clearinghouse for near-death research as well as the sponsor of many NDE conferences held around the world.

For 27 years Greyson edited the *Journal of Near-Death Studies*, and his continued importance to the field can be tracked by the many interviews he has recorded, now readily available on YouTube and other outlets.

EBEN ALEXANDER

If you are just starting to conduct even preliminary research into the current NDE phenomenon, you will immediately come across Dr. Eben Alexander, a neurosurgeon, author, public speaker, and NDE evangelist. He seems to be everywhere these days, and any interviewer or conference sponsor would be lucky to get him. He is personable, articulate, intelligent, and dynamic, but he wasn't always a believer. As a dedicated and talented neurosurgeon, he was much in demand, but in 2008 something happened to him that changed his life. In his own words:

> As a neurosurgeon, I did not believe in the phenomenon of near-death experiences. In the fall of 2008, however, after seven days in a coma during which the human part of my brain, the neocortex, was inactivated, I experienced something so profound that it gave me a scientific reason to believe in consciousness after death.
>
> I had somehow contracted a very rare bacterial meningitis that mostly attacks newborns. E. coli bacteria had penetrated my cerebrospinal fluid and were eating my brain. For seven days I lay in a deep coma, my body unresponsive, my higher-order brain functions totally offline.
>
> While the neurons of my cortex were stunned to complete inactivity by the bacteria that had attacked them, my brain-free consciousness journeyed to another, larger dimension of the universe: the same one described by countless subjects of near-death experiences and other mystical states. What I saw and learned there has placed me quite literally in a new world: a world where we are much more than our brains and bodies, and where death is not the end of consciousness but rather a chapter in a vast, and incalculably positive, journey.
>
> For most of my journey, someone else was with me. A woman. Without using any words, she spoke to me. The message went through me like a wind, and I instantly understood that it was true. I knew so in the same way that I knew that the world around us was real—was not some fantasy, passing and insubstantial. "You are loved and cherished, dearly, forever. You have nothing to fear. There is nothing you can do wrong."

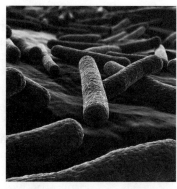

Dr. Alexander's brain was being eaten alive by E. coli bacteria, affecting his brain functions and, apparently, initiating a near-death experience.

Up until then, Alexander believed that a near-death experience was caused by the restriction of oxygen to the brain as a person transitioned from life to death. But no more. Eventually, his experience prompted Alexander to write the book that made him famous, *Proof of Heaven: A Neurosurgeon's Journey into the Afterlife*. Soon after publication, his life was changed. In that book, and countless interviews and lectures since, he tells his fascinating story.

The beginning of his experience was marked by rather dark images. He describes his surroundings as being semitransparent mud, or "dirty Jell-O," filled with "grotesque animal faces" that came to feel progressively more claustrophobic and frightening. But that was all to change. Something pulled him up into "the strangest, most beautiful world I'd ever seen."

A beautiful woman, riding on a butterfly's wing, approached him, telling him he was loved, and took him on a tour of a light-filled void. There he met a divine being who revealed many secrets of the universe to him. After his trip, he returned to the dark place where he first found himself, but this time he recognized that what he previously thought were "grotesque animal faces" were somehow replaced, or transformed, into people who were praying for him.

As with many who have crossed over, time ceased to be important, if it existed at all, but back in the hospital he spent seven days in a coma. His cortex ceased to function. Doctors began to wonder if they should unplug the equipment that was keeping his body alive. Then Alexander's eyes opened.

Eventually he was able to describe what had happened to him, referring to it as an "adventure." He believes that all the time he was in a coma, without any functions being carried out in his cerebral cortex, his "consciousness went on a journey."

His story was full of clouds and what he called "beings, streaking across a blue sky, leaving shimmering trails as they moved." He felt that they were "higher forms of life. There was a sound, a low booming noise that felt like an expression of joy. The noise was tangible, and [he] knew the beings were making it."

Typically, words failed him. How can those who never experienced such a thing understand a landscape "where it was all one," where a companion, the young woman, floated alongside him? He realized he was riding a carpet and saw a multitude of butterflies gliding through the sky. He was sitting on a butterfly wing. Colors were intense, iridescent, glowing like nothing he'd ever experienced on earth.

The woman looked at him, and he felt love—not romantic or friendly, but pure, whole love. "You are loved and cherished forever," she said without speaking to him. "You have nothing to fear. You can do no wrong."

The best he could do in describing what he saw was to paint a picture of "beautiful very lush forests and meadow water falling into crystal blue pools. Absolutely spectacular."

A beautiful woman floated by him, accompanying him and giving him a sense of pure love and benevolence.

He felt an intense feeling of relief, "as though I'd been previously misunderstanding the whole point of living. It was like being handed the rules of a game I'd been trying to play all my life."

For most people, this would be enough of an experience to last a lifetime, but it was just beginning.

As he and his guide traveled onward, every question he had was immediately answered "in a crashing wave of knowledge." A glowing orb of light accompanied them, and he realized his answers were coming from the orb. It was his interpreter, explaining the vast presence that surrounded him. He was able to understand concepts that would have taken a lifetime of study to grasp.

When he returned, finally opening his eyes just as doctors were considering pulling the plug on him, his meningitis was gone, and his cerebral cortex functioned normally.

Trying to get some kind of mental handle on all this was hard. His medical training told him that a person simply cannot dream when his brain is switched off. His colleagues, of course, wouldn't call him a liar by any means. They believed something happened. But they disagreed about what it was and what caused it.

Alexander is still a doctor, but he now spends a lot of time giving lectures and interviews, comparing notes with others, and fulfilling the role as unofficial spokesman for NDEs.

In February 2020, his alma mater published his story in *The Harvard Crimson*. Some of their descriptions are especially telling:

> *Alexander doesn't dispute that his brain had almost no activity during his coma; actually, it's one of the facts about his experience that he stresses most. He couldn't have been hallucinating, because his brain wasn't working. His apparent journey to the other side, he claims, is evidence that something about us—a soul, a consciousness, a spirit—is independent from our bodies: that we come from, and return to, the universe itself.*

> *This idea stands in direct opposition to materialism, the philosophical doctrine that everything, including our consciousness, is generated by the physical world. Materialism is the basis of modern science as we know it. Alexander, though, believes the spirit exists separately from matter.*

> *To Alexander, this conclusion is borne of logical reasoning, not of a disposition towards religiosity. He doesn't ask his followers to believe in what he says regardless of scientific evidence; he asks them to believe because of it.*

> **Plato … asserted that the physical world is not the "real" world. Ultimate reality, he declared, exists *beyond* our physical world.**

Anchoring his experience in history for those of intellectual bent, who need more prose than poetry, he sometimes references Plato, the Greek philosopher who asserted that the physical world is not the "real" world. Ultimate reality, he declared, exists *beyond* our physical world.

Refusing to be pigeonholed in any one religious concept, he writes that "Allah, Vishnu, Jehovah, Yahweh—the names get in the way, and the conflicting details of orthodox religions obscure the reality of such an infinitely loving and creative source."

Of course, such experiences have ramifications in this world as well. In a November 2022 interview with James Sengendo, titled "Doctor Who Experienced Afterlife Says It Was Like Plato's World of Ideals," he admits that his family wasn't ready for his new outlook on life.

"I think it really scared my family tremendously. They're all elated, but the first 36 hours I was in and out of my mind, kind of crazy at times." During a lengthy recovery process, Alexander said he spooked his sister by "sitting on the bed like this little Buddha just saying, 'All is well' [and] looking everyone deeply in the eyes."

To say that Alexander himself was transformed is an understatement. You can't blame him for wanting to reach out to help others who may be inspired and comforted by what happened to him.

To that end, he encourages others to prepare for death in every way possible. He counsels them not to wait until death for their life review, for instance, and to examine their lives minutely beginning right now. He encourages them to make choices today in regards to treating themselves and others with love and compassion.

This is not just about what happens when you die, but this is most importantly about how you make every choice today in treating yourself and treating others. Don't wait to do a life review at the end of your life. What a waste that is.

Dr. Alexander freely admits that he is no longer afraid to die. His busy speaking schedule reveals that he is making good use of every moment he has left and is in no hurry to go. But there is no doubt that he also doesn't want it to be put off forever.

In 2 Corinthians 5:8, the Apostle Paul voiced a similar feeling: "I am confident and willing rather to be absent from the body, and to be present with the Lord."

But because he felt he had unfinished work to do, he was willing to stay on and fight the good fight.

One gets the feeling Dr. Alexander would heartily agree.

St. Paul, while not fearing death, believed in living a life of good works and to focus on the present and not long for the afterlife, which would come soon enough.

PRACTICAL RESULTS

Deepak Chopra, Raymond Moody, Betty Eadie, Jill Bolte Taylor, Bruce Greyson, and Eben Alexander are not the only ones to have experienced or researched NDEs. They are not the only ones from the field of medicine who have reached across the academic aisle to borrow from the research of those in different fields. Their stories aren't necessarily different, more believable, or more developed than the thousands of stories that have been collected and, thanks to books, television, and the internet, are now readily available for anyone to peruse and study.

But their activities, viewed like this, in roughly chronological order over the last four decades, outline the progress the field of NDE research is making. It is no longer the product of an esoteric few, a metaphysical oddity, or the butt of jokes by those who consider themselves to be more sophisticated than others.

When highly regarded specialists like these demonstrate a willingness not only to stand up and be counted, but to risk their careers by seeking a deeper understanding of what it means to be human, others will surely follow. Because of their testimonies, we might be closer than ever to understanding what happens when each one of us sets out on a similar journey.

It will not happen, however, until we begin exchanging ideas from differing fields. No one area of study is big enough and comprehensive enough to encompass the subject. We need to borrow wisdom from each other, even if it means avoiding specialization and asking help from other experts.

Quoting again from the Apostle Paul, this time in 1 Corinthians 15:26: "The last enemy to be destroyed is death." That "enemy" will someday claim us all. Maybe we finally have it in our sights. When the fear of death is finally defeated, perhaps it will be because we will have discovered that our enemy has all along been our greatest friend.

PART IV
SOMETHING BLUE

Energy cannot be created or destroyed, it can only be changed from one form to another.

—Albert Einstein

Sometimes ideas come to us, to use a popular phrase, out of the blue. Concepts arrive full-blown right on the doorstep of our minds, without any careful preparation. Some of the greatest scientific theories of all time have arrived in this way.

Thomas Edison was a great proponent of deliberately seeking out times when he could stop intellectualizing and wait for an idea to arrive full-blown in his mind.

Einstein's Theory of General Relativity is now a fully developed mathematical equation, but regarding its initial conception, he claimed that it came to him all of a piece one day, while imagining a train ride.

The reason this is important for the study of NDEs is that many people, when questioned how they "heard" someone on the other side teaching them, say the information didn't come word by word and sentence by sentence. It arrived in what they often call a "block" of teaching.

The part of our brain that figures things out operates in time. It might be a very *short* period of time, but we usually learn by absorbing one fact, then another, then another, until a final "Aha!" moment occurs when the pieces fit together and we understand a concept. That's the way our brains have evolved and been trained. It's the way it has always been for us.

On the other side of material existence, free from the constraints of time, apparently it doesn't work that way.

Intuition is an important tool, one often neglected in this scientific age. Sometimes it is even a subject of patronizing slights, as in "woman's intuition"—meaning somewhat inconsequential, or inferior to intellectual importance.

But considering the number of NDE testimonies now on record, even though they are considered subjective in nature rather than objective, maybe it's time to take into account that our method of learning in this sensory perception realm might not be the only way. It might not even be the most reliable way.

Could it be that once we leave the world that exists as a construct in the intellectual hemispheres of our brains and enter an arena where time and space don't exist, we discover a reality that our consciousness remembers but whose practical use has atrophied from non-use?

In the tradition of Albert Einstein, try this thought experiment on for size.

If you lived in a world where no one could hear any sounds and this was considered normal, then a person who *could* hear and who tried to describe the sensation would likely be regarded as either insane or lying.

Imagine that you live in a world of sight, but you can't hear anything. In a very short time, you would come to believe, and believe deeply, that sound doesn't exist. Your science would prove, in a thousand different experiments, that sight is the only thing there is. You would teach this reality in your schools, and your vocabulary would evolve around metaphors of sight. You wouldn't say, "It doesn't sound right to me." You would say, "It looks suspicious."

You would probably ridicule anyone who suggested even the possibility of sound, because no one in your world could prove its reality. Why waste time even fooling around with the concept of sound? For all practical purposes, unless you could place sound under a microscope and study it, an impossible thing to do, you wouldn't believe it. You would ban its possibility from your laboratories and refuse to speculate on its existence at your scientific gatherings.

Then one day an archaeologist unearths some evidence that appears to indicate that a long-dead ancancestor from thousands of years ago believed that sound existed. Maybe he or she even claimed to have heard something. You would, most assuredly, chalk it up to primitive ignorance. If a "New Age" cult of sound sprang up, you would scoff and discount the whole thing as mere superstition. You would not allow it to be taught in your classrooms, and you would heap scorn on the idea, hoping that it would go away.

But you would never come to fully understand your universe, would you? Sound would remain undiscovered because you refused to even consider its existence.

Perhaps that's exactly what's happening with the testimonies of those who claim that on the other side of death there exists a world where things are different, where intellect formed by the reality of a stilted illusion won't cut it, and where teaching comes in blocks from "out of the blue."

The single most life-changing experience in my life came about in this fashion. A single block of teaching transformed me. Here is an account straight from my personal journal:

> As the twentieth century drew to a close, I spent time one summer at a cabin I had built in central Massachusetts. The idea was to commune with nature and get in touch with some issues that were on my mind.

> Five feet in front of the porch of the cabin was a rock, about four feet long, lying on its side. The best way to describe it is to recall the old "Weebles wobble but they don't fall down" craze. Remember Weebles? This rock looked just like that, right down to the flat face. Obviously, forces other than those found in nature had been employed to work the top smooth, and I had often wondered why it appeared to be almost face-like.

This was the setting where I spent afternoons for four days, meditating on whatever came to mind, trying to go deeper into myself than I normally do. By the second day I was conscious of sounds I first thought were caused by cars on the highway, about a mile away. It was not until the fourth afternoon that I realized I was hearing the sounds in my right ear, which is completely deaf.

> **It was not until the fourth afternoon that I realized I was hearing the sounds in my right ear, which is completely deaf.**

After a moment it came to me that what I was hearing was not highway noise, but drums. Suddenly I was aware that I had snapped my eyes wide open and was experiencing a fully formed sentence ringing in my head. My heart was racing. I didn't hear a voice, and I saw no apparition. I hadn't been thinking about dancing at all, but the sentence that seemed to appear, almost floating before my eyes, was, "It's not that you can't dance. It's that you won't dance."

As soon as I saw, heard, or somehow experienced that message I felt, rather than figured out, that the reason I could not dance was because at one time dance was so sacred, either to me or the people who once danced on this spot of ground, that I could not sully it by making it mere entertainment.

I am one of the most rational people you will ever meet. Back then I wasn't sure if I believed in reincarnation or not, and I only believed in spirits on the occasional second Tuesday. But in that instant, I looked down at the rock I had been contemplating for the last four days and knew, just knew, that it was meant to be standing upright.

Fearing that any minute I would have a perfectly acceptable psychological explanation for what was happening to me, I immediately got a shovel and began excavating around the rock. It took about an hour to dig

I am one of the most rational people you will ever meet. Back then I wasn't sure if I believed in reincarnation or not, and I only believed in spirits on the occasional second Tuesday.

down to bedrock, only about a foot deep on this ledge, clearing a six-foot circle surrounding the stone.

I knew long before I finished what I was going to find.

Hidden beneath the soil at the base of the rock was a tripod of stones, obviously placed by human hands, formed to exactly fit the bottom of the rock. And in a semicircle, spread fan-shaped to the east, were seven hammer stones that could only have been made by pre-European New Englanders.

Next day, when I used a hydraulic jack and ropes to stand the stone on its pedestal, the smoothed face of the stone swung just a fraction around toward the southeast, facing exactly the place where the sun peeked over a far-away ridge on the morning of the spring equinox.

In doing research about the indigenous people of my area, I later discovered a possible explanation for the rock. It stands on a natural divide. All the water from the stream to its east eventually flows into a huge reservoir to the south. The water draining from the swamp to the west flows out to the Connecticut River and the Atlantic Ocean at Long Island Sound. This would have made the area a natural place of power to the people who lived here. But the rock itself stood on a small plateau, a natural stage. On all four sides a tribe could have gathered to watch a religious ritual "in the round," so to speak.

One explanation for this particular stone being knocked over might be in unsubstantiated stories about religious disagreements between Indians and Europeans in early New England. When Indians watched Puritans burying their dead, they thought they must be worshipping a common deity. The Puritans used four-foot rocks as *grave headstones. Some Indian tribes had similar rituals, dancing around the rock as they prayed for the departed. But Puritans were taught that while their rocks were sacred, Indian rocks were heathen idols, so they knocked them down whenever they came across them.*

I had compiled a list with the names of every person who had owned that property since 1798, when the town was first settled. It is easy to believe the very first pioneer who farmed this land, which was awarded to his ancestral family as pay for participation in King Philip's War, came across this spot in his sheep pasture and, recognizing it for the pagan idol it was, knocked it down to the glory of God.

There it lay until I, his future town minister, put it back up, also to the glory of God.

The story doesn't end there. I was so impressed by the whole affair that I told some folks about it. One thing led to another, and we wound up having a dedication service there on the night of the winter solstice. Not knowing what to do, we drank some mead and burned some incense, hoping the spirit of the place would accept our good intentions.

And that was that until March. On a day of early thaw, I walked out to the place for the first time since December. The snow had melted back from around the base of the rock, just as it had around many other rocks in the area. But at the foot of this special rock lay the feathers, not the carcass, just the feathers, of a ruffed grouse.

My first thought was that a hawk had killed a grouse on this spot. Nine days out of ten I still believe that. But I called my daughter that day to tell her the story. She

> On a day of early thaw, I walked out to the place for the first time since December.... But at the foot of this special rock lay the feathers, not the carcass, just the feathers, of a ruffed grouse.

knows a lot about all things Indian, and I mentioned the grouse. She called me back a few minutes later and I could hear the excitement in her voice.

"Dad, I looked up the meaning of having the ruffed grouse as your totem animal." She then read to me, "When the Creator sends you the grouse as your spirit guide, it is a message to attune yourself to the dance of life. Its keynote is sacred dancing and drumming, both powerful ways in their own right to invoke energies ... rhythmic movement is a part of life ... all human activity is a kind of dance and ritual."

What do I make of all this? I don't have the faintest idea. My rational self accepts the coincidence of a grouse being killed by a hawk at this particular time and place. But why a grouse, with its ancient meaning relating to my own dance phobia? And why this particular time? And why this rock, out of all the many others? And why does it tie in to my discovering the secret of the rock after my time of meditation, exactly when I was attempting to let the woods sort out my confused mindset? And why just feathers, with no carcass?

I don't really know, but I once told this story to an Ojibwa teaching elder after an all-day seminar. We had spent the day sitting in a circle, learning about his tribe's creation myths. Much to my dismay, he appeared to be rather bored. As I told the story and commented on his seeming lack of interest, he said, "Okay, the grouse was on the west side of the rock. What next?"

"I didn't tell you it was on the west side of the rock. How did you know that?"

"Because that's where we would expect it to be. That's the direction the soul takes its leave when it departs. Honestly, why do you Christian preachers always expect your God to answer prayer, but act surprised when ours does?"

I was dumbfounded. "Do you mean to tell me I've been searching for an experience with God all my life and now I discover he's an Indian?"

The grouse feathers I had framed and that I keep on the wall on my back porch.

"No," he grinned back with a cherubic expression. "She's an Indian!"

I don't carry a medicine bag, but I had one of the grouse feathers laminated in plastic and I carry it in my wallet. And some more feathers are mounted in a picture frame on my back porch—just in case.

My life has never been the same since that day, when a block of teaching arrived in my head fully formed, out of the blue. It wasn't the result of an NDE, but for a moment I was traveling the same landscape discovered by those who have departed the life of the physical senses for a while before returning with a life-affirming story.

I was able to put the pieces together over the years, using my intellect and the usual method of gathering information together. I was able to consult with experts in other fields and eventually arrived at a reasonable explanation of what the teaching meant. But the bulk of the message arrived in a single block of insight. It has, quite literally, changed me, and remains to this day the most unforgettable experience I ever had.

People who have experienced NDEs are often told they must return to life because they have a mission, a message to convey, or an unfinished purpose to fulfill. Sometimes that purpose involves telling their story to a world that has forgotten what life is all about. Maybe it's time to start listening to them.

An old joke tells the story of a man trapped in a house by rising flood waters. Eventually he took refuge on his roof and prayed to God for help.

A man in a rowboat came by and the fellow at the oars shouted to the man on the roof, "Jump in, I can save you." The stranded man shouted back, "No, it's okay. God will take care of me." The rowboat went on.

Then a motorboat came by. The fellow at the helm shouted, "Climb aboard." But the stranded man said, "No thanks. God will save me." And the motorboat motored on.

Then a helicopter came by, and the pilot shouted down, "Grab this rope and I will lift you to safety." The stranded man yelled back, "No thanks. God will save me." So the helicopter flew away.

Soon the water rose above the rooftop, and the man drowned. He woke up in heaven. When he got a chance to talk about the manner of his death with God, he said, "I had faith in you but you didn't save me. You let me drown. I don't understand why!"

To this God replied, "I sent you a rowboat, a motorboat, and a helicopter. What more could you want?"

I wonder if we are being given signals and warnings through the testimony of those who have experienced NDEs and, like the drowning man, are ignoring them.

"Why doesn't God speak to us and alleviate our fears?" we ask.

Well, maybe God, or Source, or Brahman, or Manitou, or however else we want to label the mystical consciousness from which we sprang into material life, is doing just that.

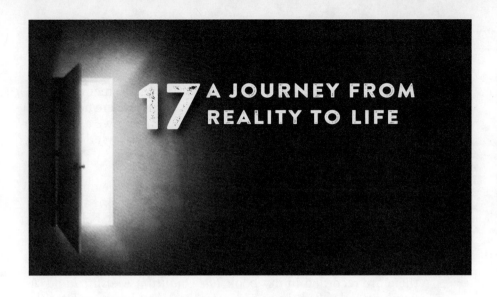

17 A JOURNEY FROM REALITY TO LIFE

Consciousness is something fundamental to nature—it is stitched into the very fabric of reality.

—Dr. David Hamilton, quoted by Sean Martin in
"End of Heaven? Quantum Science Says You ALWAYS
Have Existed and ALWAYS Will Exist,"
Daily Express, July 14, 2017

When people come back from an NDE with a story to tell, what have they seen? Was it a real "place"? Does it really exist? If so, where is it? What is it like? Or are they attempting to describe something beyond our experience, and therefore our ability to perceive?

There are paradoxes in every NDE story. Events seem to happen, which implies time. But we are told over and over that time does not exist there. The descriptions often include vivid pictures of parks, trees, gardens, and meadows. But how can such things be in a place where there are no rains to water the ground, death to enrich the soil with compost, or pollinating insects? How do we "fly" from place to place in a landscape with no atmosphere?

People often exclaim that things are more "real" over there than here, but how do we visualize "reality" if what we see and ultimately experience is an illusion? Are folks describing something that *is*, or what something *seemed like* to them?

It would probably be helpful to construct a way to conceive of all of this, but that's not an easy task. We need a mental image of some kind, but how can we trust that it's anywhere near accurate if we can't even trust the fact that the room we are in, the chair we're sitting on, and the view out our front window is not solid, or material in nature?

Over the years I've struggled with this. On the one hand, I firmly believe the experience of those I've talked to is real. They're not making it up or in any way lying to me. But I also believe that what they are trying to describe might possibly be beyond our intellectual prowess to really understand. I've never experienced an NDE, but I have had many out-of-body experiences. Some of them are recorded in my book *The Quantum Akashic Field: A Guide to Out-of-Body Experiences for the Astral Traveler*. The title reveals my prejudice. I have come to not only believe in, but to experience, the fact that what we call reality is not the *only* reality. Maybe not even the *real* one.

If this is off-putting to you, feel free to skip this chapter. It's totally subjective. It's my attempt to prescribe parameters in a boundless world. You might even call it a crutch—something to lean on until you find your own footing while traveling through landscapes our language was never invented to describe or explain. If you are firmly invested in your current perception realm, you might have difficulty conceiving of anything else. You will be, metaphorically speaking, a fish out of water—out of your natural element.

The concept of the Akashic field was developed by the Hungarian philosopher Ervin László, who described the cosmos as a field of information in his book *Science and the Akashic Field: An Integral Theory of Everything.*

But perhaps what follows might help. I developed this construct 15 or 20 years ago, wrote about it in three or four books, and explained it on numerous podcasts and interviews, each time trying to get a little closer to what might be called a crude attempt to answer two big questions, "Where do we come from?" and "What happens when we die?"

I'm a left-brained, "seeing-is-believing" kind of guy, so this is a visual image of something that I've used, over the years, to help understand the answers to life's big questions. It works for me. To my mind it harmonizes theology and philosophy, as well as quantum theory.

This will probably not prove to be the ultimate answer. It is certainly simplistic. But it might serve as a place to start. Maybe you can modify it and take it further than I've been able to go. Although it is based on my own study, research, personal experience, and interviews with those who have had NDEs and OBEs, it's only meant to serve as a metaphor. Don't get too literal with it.

Picture your life as a river, flowing downhill to the sea. You are usually contained within banks that mark the boundaries of your day-to-day existence. Thus, your life is predestined to flow in one direction, within certain parameters. Once in a while, however, when pressures build up, your free will asserts itself and you rampage out of the banks, angrily flooding the surrounding landscape while asserting that sometimes you simply *must* have your own way. Eventually, though, you return to flow within your normal banks.

Along the way you gather experiences and influence others you encounter along the course of your existence. Sometimes you merge with other rivers. Sometimes you give birth to small creeks, which then begin their own journeys, eventually becoming full-fledged rivers themselves.

Finally, you reach the sea and merge with other rivers into that vast space that gathers all the rivers of the world into its embrace. You meld into one great body.

But consider this. Where is the source of your river?

"Up in the mountains," you say. "I began as a single drop of water somewhere high in the hills where I started my downhill run that led inevitably to the ocean."

Was that really your source?

No, it wasn't. The drop of water had its own source. It began in the sea, was taken up on high where it became water vapor, was blown by the winds into the atmosphere, and eventually fell to earth as solid snow or liquid rain. It was transformed into ice, or water, and only then did it begin to return to where it came from.

That's right. The sea is both the source and the destination.

When water from a river flows into the sea, it is really returning to its source just as we return to our source when we die.

Now translate the metaphor into your reality. Substitute the reality of your life for the river. Your *source* ("Where did I come from?") is also your *destination* ("What happens when I die?").

What is the Source? Well, we don't know. Traditionally, we call it God, but we might as well use Cosmic Ocean, or Consciousness, or Great Mystery, or Ultimate Unknown, or even Great Spirit. Call it whatever you find most comfortable, but for purpose of this illustration we'll use the term Source.

Now picture yourself as a wave of some kind of energy within that Source—an amorphous vapor of water that will eventually become a particle, like a single drop of water. As yet, you have no shape or form. You take up no space but contain infinite possibility. You travel at no speed and exist in perfect rest, but have infinite potential.

Along with you in the Source there are an infinite number of other such energy waves, but that isn't apparent because all waves are One Wave.

You certainly can't say there exist anything approaching individual droplets because all is one, but you cannot grow and personally develop through such oneness. You can't become a river because you are still in the source. You can't gather experience in that environment. The only way to do so is to develop uniqueness. And the only way to do that is through individuality. You've got to become your own river.

So it begins. You are taken up as an amorphous vapor and blown gently inland to a foreign landscape. A single wave breaks out, beginning its journey toward uniqueness, toward individuality, toward singular experience. When every wave in the Source undergoes such transformation, each on its own journey, total potentiality becomes possible. All it requires is space and time for every single possible experience to become realized. When all such waves finally unite back home, the Source will then have become, and personally experienced, everything. Every potentiality will have been realized. The Source will have become infinite, realized possibility.

There are, of course, problems inherent in this process. *Realized* possibilities are not always *nice* possibilities. To put it simply, potentiality has a downside. Good and bad, peaceful brooks and raging floods, yin and yang—pairs of opposites now enter the picture. Physical manifestation requires a world of duality. At the material source of your river grows a tree whose fruit contains the knowledge of *both* good *and* evil.

Whatever the Source is, religions all over the world tell us that love is at the center of existence. We might even say that the Source is love. The Bible and many holy books agree—"God is love."

But when you begin a journey out from the Source, out from Love, out from Unity and toward individuality, you begin the process of establishing your "self," which, by definition, is separate from Unity. You are now your own river, in charge of your own experience.

This is where things get interesting.

Because I am a clergyman, I have been trained to visualize this separation from Source by employing metaphors from the Bible. In this case, the third chapter of the book of Genesis provides a good reference point. It tells the well-known story of the banishment from Eden.

Perhaps whoever wrote this story experienced a similar vision to the one we've been using in the last few paragraphs. He or she wouldn't have expressed that vision in the scientific terms we tend to use. Instead, the writer would have employed thought-expressions drawn from their own culture.

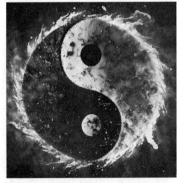

The beginning of the Genesis story finds our first parents living in a state of blissful unity. They are one with each other, one with nature, and one with God, with whom they "walk in the cool of the evening." They eat whatever nature pro-

The problem with becoming individuated from the Source is that it does not guarantee a good result. Individuals have the potential for both good *and* evil.

vides and enjoy each other's company. They live in the Source—Oneness, unity, perfect contentment, peace, and love.

But this unity is about to be broken. In order to experience individuality—the "river"—they need to leave Eden, the place of perfect unity. Thus it was that Eve ate the apple from the tree of the knowledge of good and evil. She offered some to Adam and they "became as gods, knowing good and evil." They entered the world of duality. No longer would they experience perfect bliss for all eternity. They now knew what it was to be two "selfs" standing side by side, rather than united in perfect harmony.

Their individual rivers began to flow downhill.

We all know the outcome of the story. Both rivers began to cut their own course back to the Source.

There were moments of bliss, especially when the two rivers joined together for a few minutes and became one. But they contrasted with times of pain and anguish.

When life is good, we feel a vestigial memory of the unity of the Source. When life is bad, we feel cut off and lost. But we keep flowing downhill.

There can be no question that the primary result of disunity, of leaving Eden, of leaving the Source, is pain. "All life is suffering," said the Buddha. And he was right.

Life consists of having to gather a full mixture of experiences. Even in the best of times, we still buy insurance policies. The threat of pain is always with us.

This is probably where the concept of the devil came from. It is the sense of self, our own ego. The ego wants and desires. The ego cannot always have its own way.

Selfishness is the root of all evil—the devil himself. In other words, the experience of "selfishness," the devil we created when we ventured out of the Source, seeks the very experience that leads to so much heartache in the world. We, ourselves, are the source of our own dissatisfaction.

Can real love, real "self-less-ness," be experienced only when we enter into harmony with one another? Is that a memory of the good times back in the Source?

Even more interesting, is such "self-less-ness" the ultimate goal of the whole evolutionary process? Are we moving toward what now seems impossible—the experience of individuality within unity?

If this is true, then all the world's heartache, which ultimately stems from some expression of selfishness, may be the necessary stage we are now experiencing.

Think of it this way. We cannot become emotionally mature as adults without experiencing the pain of separation from first our mother and then our family. There is no other way to grow.

Thus, if we can learn lessons from our current stage of adolescent selfishness, we may finally grow into a fully evolved species that can experience individuality within unity.

Think of it! Not only will we experience bliss, we will retain our individuality while doing it. The many shall become one, and the one will have become many. The rivers will flow together. We will have grown up.

With this in mind, let's get back to our journey outward from the Source.

Picture again that wave of potential that is, ultimately, you. Your journey begins. You move out from the Source. Where do you find yourself? What environment do you now inhabit?

I call it Consciousness. It is what both Albert Einstein and Stephen Hawking once called "the mind of God."

Although you still have no mass, either physical or metaphysical, you are now what I might describe as being a little "thicker" or "heavier." You are on your way to becoming a water droplet. You haven't yet visualized where you are going or what you will look like, but you are aware that eventually you will.

In order to grow up, we need to leave the home of the Source and learn to become individuals and experience life on our own.

In the "mind of God" there is still complete unity. There is also an awareness that something we can only call uniqueness or individuality exists. What's it like to be different from every other wave? What does it feel like to be alone, for instance? How will you react to an experience no other wave has ever known?

There's only one way to find out. You must travel onward.

Your journey now takes you through your first defining field. It's a place wherein you begin to take on shape. Not mass. Not yet. You are not yet a bona fide river. You're not even a rivulet. But you grow a little heavier as you begin to transform yourself into something truly unique and separate.

Ervin László coined the term "Akashic field" from the Sanskrit word *Akasha,* meaning "space." Everything that we know and experience around us, every rock, tree, and flower, every person, every animal, every bird, and every fish, was first conceived in Akasha. Akashic consciousness is the observer that creates all things.

Here, the water droplet begins to conceive of a river. You have gathered metaphysical mass. You now understand the concept of individuality expressed both in final form and in idea. You understand that unique individuality leads to unique experience. You pass through the Akashic field and become something different. You now have some direction.

When you emerge from the Akashic field you find yourself in a totally different realm. You have now entered quantum reality. This is the world discovered by theoretical physicists about a hundred years ago. We are just now beginning to explore it with mathematics and particle accelerators.

Those who have experienced an NDE, mystics, gurus, and shamans have known about it for thousands of years.

English mathematician, physicist, astronomer, and idealist James Hopwood Jeans was noted for his calculations of the James length and the James mass, which predict whether an interstellar cloud will collapse to form a star.

Sir James Hopwood Jeans was a brilliant English physicist, astronomer, and mathematician. One of my favorites among his many great quotes was his observation that "humanity is at the very beginning of its existence—a new born babe, with all the unexplored potentialities of babyhood; and until the last few moments its interest has been centered absolutely and exclusively on its cradle and feeding bottle."

But by far his most famous quote, appearing in almost every physics textbook and quoted in hundreds of lectures throughout the world of quantum physics, was this: "The universe begins to look more like a great thought than a great machine."

For this reason, I call the world of quantum reality the place of "Thoughts and Intentions."

You're still not a full-fledged river. You're not human yet. You still have a way to go. But here in this world you can now form what might be called a thought as to what "human" is, and form an intention that you're going to be one.

Quantum reality is a place of potential. Humans don't really live here. Not yet, anyway. But what might be called "humanness" now exists. The potential for any one human is here, and that potential will soon be realized. But for "humanness" to become "a human" it must first "collapse" into the environment humans experience. To do that it must pass through the newly discovered Higgs field.

No one quite knows how to describe the Higgs field. Many have tried, but it is so counterintuitive that it takes some pretty complex mathematics to even begin. Suffice it to say that when energy passes through the Higgs field it emerges on the other side with, for the first time in its journey from the Source, physical mass. In other words, it becomes material.

Metaphorically, water *vapor* collapses into water *drops*. It is now within our perception realm. We've come home.

This is the world of our five senses, within the material realm of the scientists. They now have something to measure, study, dissect, and put under a microscope. This is the world I call our perception realm. It's the world we see around us.

But even this world has its hidden realms. When I say "perception realm," I'm referring to the cosmos in all its many manifestations. Here lies the multiverse in its infinite capacity for creativity. Here dwell all possible manifestations of every single possibility. Here lie an infinite number of "yous," each living their own life in woeful ignorance of their doppelgangers in parallel universes.

> **Our particular universe seems to be supported by mysterious dark matter that pushes it out toward infinity. Here we find the mysteries inherent in the mathematics of modern physics.**

Our particular universe seems to be supported by mysterious dark matter that pushes it out toward infinity. Here we find the mysteries inherent in the mathematics of modern physics. This is the home of fantastic ideas circulating around the great universities of the world, eventually flowing out to television's Discovery Channel. Here we find everything that intrigues and mystifies us.

This is the world of the river as it makes its way back to the sea—the Source of all that is. Its journey to conception was airy and light. Its route to the sea cuts through tough, seemingly unyielding, physical landscape.

Hopefully, this rather simplistic metaphor will help us see the world that those who experience NDEs are trying to describe. For a moment, they are able to rise up and peek out over the banks of their personal river. They glimpse the distant sunrise over the ocean, the bright light that waits us all upon our return. They see fellow travelers in various states of existence—those who inhabit the shores of life along the course of the river's journey, perhaps to offer unseen assistance along the way. Free from the pain of ego's self-inflicted separateness, they feel embraced by the love that they vaguely remember was once their normal habitat.

If this metaphor helps at all, I hope it will aid you until you cross the bar in confidence and return home to the Source with joy and contentment in your heart.

If NDEs can instill some of this into our daily lives—well, okay!

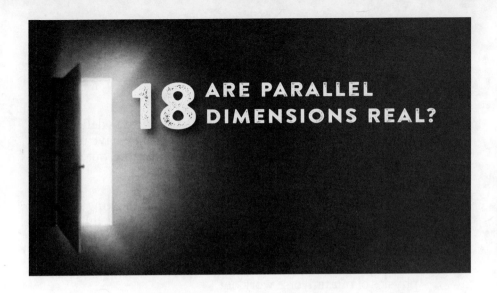

18 ARE PARALLEL DIMENSIONS REAL?

All my life I have been strangely, vividly conscious of another region—not far removed from our own world in one sense, yet wholly different in kind—where great things go on unceasingly, where immense and terrible personalities hurry by, intent on vast purposes compared to which earthly affairs, the rise and fall of nations, the destinies of empires, the fate of armies and continents, are all as dust in the balance.

—Algernon Blackwood in *The Willows*, 1907

Do those who undergo a near-death experience see other realities, or what might be called "parallel dimensions"? Do glimpses of these dimensions sometimes come to the rest of us "out of the blue," seemingly conjured from the recesses of our minds? Are they illusions? Or are we *living* in the illusion, and catching sight of reality? Are parallel dimensions waking dreams, or are we living in a parallel dimension to another dream, perhaps even our own?

What is the nature, expressed in scientific terms, of the reality, if it *is* a reality, that someone sees when they come back from death?

If you want to drive a theoretical physicist crazy, make him or her attend a metaphysical seminar during which they are forced to listen to pseudoscientific psychobabble about the existence of parallel universes.

Parallel universes are a science-fiction writer's delight. Ever since Superman discovered Bizarro World, they have proved to be a staple of stories where everything is the same, but radically different.

Relatively recently, however, scientists are taking seriously the idea that other worlds, other universes, other differences, might exist, in which the laws of physics so familiar to theorists might not apply. The existence of such dimensions seems to be the only thing that makes much of the math undergirding the physics of our universe work out.

It's a tough spot to be in, but almost every modern theory about how the universe came to be seems to have loose ends that can be tied up only by projecting hypothetical universes that, according to the theories themselves, cannot even be comprehended, much less measured, observed, and replicated in compliance with the scientific method. It forces a physicist to rely on what seems, from the outside at least, unproven and unprovable speculative "belief." That's not a comfortable place for a scientist to be.

To make matters worse, there is not one single theory of parallel universes. There are many. Do beings or entities, maybe even human beings of some kind, exist in these parallel dimensions or universes?

Perhaps death or an NDE brings us into contact with a parallel universe rather than a dream or an afterlife.

According to the theories, they do!

Are these beings the ones who communicate with a person who dies and moves away from earthly reality? Does a near-death experience unite a person with his doppelganger with whom he is entangled in a parallel world?

Maybe.

Hugh Everett, for instance, came up with what was considered a radical theory for his time. It was rejected by his peers, and Everett was exiled from physics into the world of government bureaucracy. He died thinking he was a failure. Now his ideas are lauded by many of the physics community.

Here's how Nick Herbert describes the theory in his book *Quantum Reality*:

American physicist Nick Herbert is best known for his book *Quantum Reality*, published in 1985.

> *Of all the claims of the New Physics none is more outrageous than the contention that myriads of universes are created upon the occasion of each measurement act. For any situation in which several different outcomes are possible (flipping a coin, for instance) some physicists believe that all outcomes actually occur. In order to accommodate different outcomes without contradiction, entire new universes spring into being, identical in every detail except for the single outcome that gave them birth. In the case of a flipped coin, one universe contains a coin that came up heads; another, a coin showing tails. Paul Davies champions this claim, known as the many-worlds interpretation.... Science fiction writers commonly invent parallel universes for the sake of a story. Now quantum theory gives us good reason to take such stories seriously.*

Everett developed the Many-Worlds theory in 1957. Before you question his brilliance, consider this tidbit. He wrote a letter to Einstein when he was only 12. Einstein replied.

Niels Bohr hated the theory. Of course, for a long while he didn't want to believe in even *one* quantum reality, let alone an infinite number.

Max Tegmark, a professor at MIT, in his book *Our Mathematical Universe*, called Everett's work as important as Einstein's theory of relativity.

It sounds like a crazy idea, but it is important because it solves the measurement problem. How can a conscious being have the power to change a universe simply by choosing one method of measurement over another?

The answer is, he or she can't. The wave doesn't "collapse" into a single piece of cosmic "stuff." It collapses into *every possible* piece of cosmic "stuff." All possible outcomes occur. If it's you making the decision, you don't realize it because you're stuck in one backwater universe and experience only one outcome. But if it's any consolation, other versions of "you" exist in parallel dimensions. In one universe you're standing there wondering why you made the choice you made, while in a parallel universe your counterpart is standing there wondering why *she* made the choice *she* made. Both are unaware of the other, of course, and continue on as if nothing special has happened.

Think of it this way: When a particle (a quantum) is measured (or observed) it can become manifested in many different ways. Each manifestation is dependent on an observer or a measurement device. If we are the observer, we see one such random manifestation.

But what about the others? What happened to them?

Everett's explanation is that they all occurred, but outside our sensory experience. In other words, there are other "yous," each existing in their own space, and each observing a different result. All possible "real" states are manifested, but each in its own universe.

> Everett's explanation is that they all occurred, but outside our sensory experience....
> All possible "real" states are manifested, but each in its own universe.

In this universe, you may have died. When that happened, you collapsed into another "you" that didn't. Eventually, all the "yous" will be gathered together and all your experiences merged into one. You will have accomplished your mission and will return to the Source.

Think of it as an extension of quantum entanglement. When measured, an electron has a 50% chance of rotating clockwise and a 50% chance of rotating counterclockwise. Which will occur when you check it out?

Only one. At least, you can measure only one at a time. Suppose you get a clockwise rotation and notate it in your log. Then you're done for the day.

But what about the other possibility?

Everett says there is another "you" who got a counterclockwise spin, wrote it down in *his* log, and then was done for the day.

Like ships that pass in the night, you both remain unaware of the other's existence. You live in parallel universes, separated, perhaps, by less than the width of an electron, but you are completely oblivious to your other, quantum self. The two outcomes, caused by two measurements, both transpire, but in different universes, so you never know it.

How many such universes exist? Who knows? For that matter, who's counting?

Another possibility of parallel realities is also a science-fiction staple. You invent a time machine and travel back in history. There, you make some small change in something. When you return home, everything is different. You have altered the time-space continuum. Perhaps the cascading change of events even means that you were never born.

This is not as far-fetched as it seems. The latest projections of Einstein's space-time theories seem to indicate that it might be possible to travel back in time, though probably not forward.

What might that mean? If a future time traveler went back to pay our ancestors a visit, he might have changed the reality we are currently enjoying. What if someone already launched a new timeline, an alternative reality, and we're living in it? Is the unique story we are forging subject to change because of some future bungler?

We won't know until we somehow learn that time travel is possible, but that won't happen if the discovery of time travel is someday postponed by a malcontented time traveler who comes back to either delay the discovery or somehow "make things right," according to his or her ideas. Arnold Schwarzenegger (*The Terminator*), Michael J. Fox (*Back to the Future*), and *Star Trek*'s Borg have all made a lot of mileage out of that one.

If all this keeps you up at night, scientists as famous as Neil deGrasse Tyson have already declared that it is theoretically possible, given the open-ended aspect of eternity, that this has already happened an infinite number of times, and will continue

Neil deGrasse Tyson is an American astrophysicist who is well known as a popularizer of science through his books, lectures, and TV appearances. The prominent scientist has said it is legitimate to entertain the possibilities proposed by Everett.

to happen until all possible alternative realities are lived out in time.

In other words, every possible universe that *could* ever be, *will* be. All we need is time to bring it about.

From that kind of statement, it's not preposterous to say that a near-death experience is nothing more than a glimpse outside our reality. For a moment, an NDE lets us rise above our programming to glimpse the hardware at work, or maybe look across the aisle to another program running in the same time slot. It sounds silly, but in these days of quantum physics, a lot of things do.

Let's look at one more idea. This one comes from none other than the brilliant Richard Feynman.

Picture a particle that decides to travel from point A to point B. There are, of course, an infinite number of paths the particle could follow. Each of these paths can be given a mathematical probability of being one the particle will choose, based on things like ease of travel, shortest distance between two points, and so on.

But don't forget, particles are also waves! Unlike particles, waves spread out as they move. The individual "particle path" now becomes what is called a "probability amplitude."

As the waves spread out, they take up more space and bump into one another, either canceling others out or amplifying each other. If you carry this idea to its logical conclusion, at the end you will be left with one, and only one, possibility. That's the possibility we're living in, called the sum-over-paths theory.

According to this theory, we live in a universe that exists only after all other possible universes were given their time on stage. Our path is what *we* call reality. We can never experience any of the others because they are outside our realm of possibility. We can deduce that they existed as very real possibilities, but we can never know for sure their nature or their aspects.

This is where Feynman leaves it, but we might choose to consider the possibility that an NDE is a glimpse across the space from one path to another.

Or we might not.

While we're on the subject of paths and distances, consider one more theory.

The universe is infinitely large. The elements that compose it are finite. What this means is that if you mix the finite components together there will be a limited number of ways to combine them, but infinite space in which to do it. Sooner or later some "mixes" are going to start to look similar to others, so if you travel "out" far enough, you're bound to come across areas that look very much alike.

Nobel Prize–winning physicist Richard Feynman deduced that our reality is the result of the interactions of all other reality paths interacting with each other in what is called the sum-over-paths theory.

If you consider this idea and take it to its logical conclusion, somewhere out there a bunch of chemicals and cosmic stuff came together in a way that is very similar, if not identical, to the way the chemicals and cosmic stuff that make up your body formed you. In other words, there is a nearly identical "you" way out there somewhere that thinks he or she is unique and that "you" are simply a mathematicians' dream.

Take apart a fine Swiss watch, put all the pieces in a paper bag, and shake them up. Will they ever reform in their identity as a fine Swiss watch?

"Never!" you exclaim.

But do it an *infinite* number of times and mathematically, no matter how improbable it seems, they will. The chances are one in an astronomical amount, but that one chance will happen eventually.

The key is found in the word *infinite*.

Does an NDE consist of waking up from the material identity you identify as "you," breaking free, and perhaps glimpsing other possibilities? Who knows?

Cosmologist and theoretical theorist Alan Guth led a team of researchers to develop a theory of cosmic inflation based upon elementary particle behavior.

Here's a final idea. Current thinking in cosmology involving the birth of the universe revolves around an idea called inflation. It was developed in the 1980s but described in mathematical detail in 2002 by physicists Alan Guth, Andrei Linde, and others.

Before we go too far into this concept, however, we need to point out that as I write these words, images from the new James Webb Space Telescope are already tearing it apart. By the time you read this, the Big Bang theory might be considered a quaint, but rejected, idea.

The basic concept is that at the very beginning of the universe, right after the Big Bang, the universe expanded exponentially at a rate much faster than the speed of light. This period of expansion is called the inflationary epoch.

I wrote about it at length in my book *Hidden History*, so I'll just summarize things here.

The theory speculates that during the inflationary epoch, which lasted less than even a split second (to be precise, it began at 10^{-33} second and lasted all the way until 10^{-36} second), the universe hugely expanded. It's still expanding, but not nearly that fast.

According to the Big Bang theory, the beginning of the universe consisted of an infinitesimal point of unimaginable energy that existed only as potential. Somehow, something triggered the event that caused space and time to grow, virtually instantaneously, into material that built the universe we view today.

If the explosive expansion took place in one part of space, it must have also happened in other parts. In other words, bubbles formed. Each one became a potential universe. Ours is just one of many.

Think of sitting in a bathtub and watching soap bubbles form on the surface of the water. Some are big and some are small.

They merge. They become bigger. Some of them pop right away. Others take longer.

Each bubble is a variation of our universe. No one living in any one bubble can possibly be aware of anyone living in another one.

> **Each bubble is variation of our universe. No one living in any one bubble can possibly be aware of anyone living in another one.**

Or can they? Is that what an NDE might be? Is it a glimpse a-cross to another bubble, once we are freed from the perceptions that make us think we're living in the only one? We can't reach across the gap and touch another bubble. That's scientifically impossible.

But is there another way to do it?

What if the bubbles form in a sea of something that we call consciousness? The bubbles aren't forming on their own. They're forming on the surface of the water. "Water," in this metaphor, is consciousness. If human beings can discover ways to separate their individual consciousness from the barriers caused by their five senses—the barriers that separate us from a greater reality—they might be able to peer across the vast divide that is now im-possibly far away from us and experience realities existing in other "bubbles."

We can't physically travel such extreme distances, even at the speed of light. But what if we could somehow travel at the speed of thought? If consciousness is the water that supports ev-erything—all the "bubbles" floating on the surface of conscious-ness—then consciousness itself is the unifying reality. And once we leave the bubble and wake up to universal consciousness, or whatever we choose to call it, this idea conjures up the possibility of an underlying unity upon which an infinite number of uni-verses float, expand, experience their time on the surface, and then pop away into oblivion.

This is very close to a Hindu religious concept. It goes back thousands of years, but NDEs are even older than Hinduism.

This kind of thinking is fun. It probably doesn't explain anything, but if it leads to another way to consider the stories of those who have died, left this reality, seen visions of a completely different landscape, and returned to tell the tale, it might open our eyes to new possibilities. For too many years, NDEs have only been seen through one lens—that of mystical, paranormal experience. Maybe it's time to change the prescription of our glasses.

19 THERMODYNAMICS AND NDEs

Energy can be converted from one form to another with the interaction of heat, work, and internal energy, but it cannot be created nor destroyed, under any circumstances.

—First Law of Thermodynamics

Heat always moves from hotter objects to colder objects, unless energy in some form is supplied to reverse the direction of heat flow.

—Second Law of Thermodynamics

The field of NDE research is deeply divided. On one side there are fervent believers who have experienced one, are thoroughly convinced of its validity, and really don't care much about what, how, or why it happened. They are very much entrenched in the seeing-is-believing camp.

On the other side are those, mostly of a materialist viewpoint, who have pretty much decided that nothing exists outside of physical reality. If they can't measure it, taste it, see it, dissect it, or put it under a microscope, they don't believe it exists. If NDEs are real, it would totally disrupt their worldview.

I find it somewhat amusing that many now in the first camp once solidly identified with the second. All it takes to make one a believer, it would seem, is to have a near-death experience.

That being said, some people from both sides try pretty hard to buttress their argument with faulty reasoning. Scientists tend toward explaining NDEs away by citing study after study that uses so-called medical principles, such as the overused oxygen deprivation or drug-induced arguments that are prevalent today. Neil deGrasse Tyson has even gone so far in an interview as to say that eyewitness testimony is the weakest form of argument, so anyone who has had an NDE and tells the story should not be believed unless they can produce some sort of evidence from the other side.

From the believer's camp, the tendency, after telling their story, is to try to boost their argument by quoting so-called scientific principles. If they can use science against scientists, they think it will bolster their credibility.

I can relate to both sides, but the gap between them seems to grow ever wider. It would be much more reasonable, I believe, if the scientist could open his or her mind to possibilities of a nonmaterial nature at the basis of life itself, and if the NDE enthusiast would respect the need of those trained in the scientific method to ask for more than vivid stories.

British Nobel Prize–winning physicist, mathematician, and philosopher Roger Penrose is a giant among today's scientists contributing to the fields of cosmology and general relativity.

There are those who attempt to bridge the gap. Recently, no less an authority than Sir Roger Penrose, the British mathematician, mathematical physicist, philosopher of science, and Nobel laureate in physics, has made waves by suggesting that our understanding of consciousness must move from the locality of the brain to the field of unified quantum mechanics.

That is an earthshaking suggestion. I can make that argument and no one, quite rightly, will pay me much attention. When he says it, with his credentials, the world of physics listens. They might not agree, but they listen.

This brings us to the argument that NDEs are "real" because of the first law of thermodynamics. The idea is this: If energy does not disappear but only changes form, then the energy of our body cannot disappear either. It remains but in a different form.

It sounds logical. And it is. But if you use this line of thinking with a real scientist they will look askance and probably ignore you because they will despair at the idea of teaching you a whole course in general science before you will see your mistake.

But hold on. It's not that easy.

It's true that the first law of thermodynamics doesn't support the idea of a nonphysical, continued existence after death. It is simply a law of physics describing what happens to the energy of an isolated, closed system. It has nothing to do with life or consciousness at all, and it does not indicate that a physical object of any kind will continue to exist.

The typical example goes something like this. Picture in your mind a sealed box with a small bomb contained in it. The box will contain an explosion without letting matter or energy either in or out. It is perfectly insulated.

That is not possible in real life. This is only a thought experiment.

The box has a certain amount of energy already inside it, plus the potential energy of the bomb, which is wired to a timer.

After the box is sealed, the timer reaches zero and the bomb goes off. It ceases to exist *as a bomb*. Its organization and pattern are gone, even though the air inside the box, like the walls of the box themselves, are now hotter.

The total amount of energy in the box is the same. The first law of thermodynamics sees to that. But there is no more bomb, no more organized object, and no continued existence of the bomb that used to hold energy.

Even if a living person was inside the box, the first law of thermodynamics would hold true. The person's energy would still be present, but there would be no identifiable object that would in any way resemble a person. You could measure the body's energy, but you couldn't reconstruct the body.

The only way the person could continue after death would be if you somehow found a way to maintain a system of a continuous pattern of energy-information without a physical body.

The only way the person could continue after death would be if you somehow found a way to maintain a system of a continuous pattern of energy-information without a physical body.

This isn't just a hypothetical thought, by the way. Biologists are beginning to explore this concept, which is called negentropy. But as yet, there is no way to come close to make the process work.

Don't lose hope, however. They can't define either life or consciousness, either.

That doesn't end the matter. There's a lot more of interest to consider.

It seems obvious, using this chain of reasoning, to assume that after our body dies, its energy continues to exist. If we are cremated, for instance, our physical material will transform to ash and carbon dioxide. If we are buried, our corpse will disintegrate or be eaten by animals or bacteria, thus becoming part of those animals or bacteria. But the fact that the matter continues to exist in no way means that *we* continue to exist.

The same thing happens with the energy within us. When the body dies, the energy in us continues. If we are cremated, it becomes heat. If we are eaten, it becomes the energy of the animals who eat the body where we used to live.

What this means is that neither matter nor energy can be destroyed. But it says nothing of continuing as a human being. If a living human being were a unique, ongoing pattern of energy-information, it *could* continue after bodily death, but it's not. It is a part of an evolutionary pattern of biology, not physics.

The first law of thermodynamics, then, deals with a quantity of energy. It is neither created nor destroyed.

This is a limited definition, however. To go any further, we must delve into the second law of thermodynamics. That's the one that addresses the *quality* of the energy. In other words, even though the same amount of energy still exists before and after death, what is the *state* of that energy?

Stay with me here. This gets complicated, and it may have a surprising ending.

The second law of thermodynamics deals with entropy. In other words, heat always moves from hotter objects to colder objects, unless energy in some form is supplied to reverse the direction of heat flow. When an ice cube melts in your glass, it will gradually disperse out to the liquid. The ice will become warmer and the liquid cooler, until everything in the glass is a uniform temperature.

Consider this fact, which usually doesn't occupy our thoughts during the normal course of our daily lives. The energy that exists in our bodies came into existence some 13.8 billion years ago, during the first nanoseconds after the Big Bang. That's when all the energy in the universe began.

The second law tells us that this energy has been dulled and dispersed for all that time, seeking to align the temperature of the cosmos to a unified whole. What this means is that the energy in you is the very energy that emerged into the universe when the universe was first born. In effect, what powers you is a 13.8-billion-year-old ghost. You are heat energy that is constantly sloughing off to bring the universe to a uniform temperature.

Our bodies don't *contain* energy. Energy flows *through* us. It's in constant flux.

Now, what does this tell us about life and afterlife? We are powered by a seemingly immortal essence, and it's the same essence that powers the whole universe.

Here's how rocket scientist Wernher von Braun put it: "Nature does not know extinction; all it knows is transformation. Everything science has taught me, and continues to teach me, strengthens my belief in the continuity of our spiritual existence after death."

The energy and mass that makes up the present you has its origins in the Big Bang some 13.8 billion years ago. The qualities of that energy and mass have changed, however.

With that quote we come right back full circle. *Now* we can say that the laws of thermodynamics *do* support the idea of a non-physical, continued existence after death.

In a very real sense, we are children of the stars. We were conceived in the first nanosecond of creation, and we have been evolving and transforming ever since. Our bodies do not possess *an* energy. They are the conduit by which *all* energy constantly flows. If energy existed *before* the Big Bang, we were there. If energy was created *by* the Big Bang, that was the moment of our physical creation. If energy underwent transformation *after* the Big Bang, it eventually became part of us.

And when we die, the energy of our material bodies will continue to transform the universe.

If life is energy, then who is to say we don't live forever?

20 THE MUSIC OF THE SPHERES

I have the sense of being drawn upward. Then comes the surprise. I hear my physical voice saying, "It's music!" I don't have the words to express the visual sensation, but it felt like being inside music. I hear a voice saying, "Stay in the music," but even though I really want to stay, I hear myself saying, "I can't." Immediately I am back in my body.

—Jim Willis: Out-of-Body Experience
on September 1, 2012

When we looked at parallel dimensions in an early chapter, I deliberately left one theory out. I wanted to devote a whole chapter to it because I have had personal experience with it. It's called string theory. The ancients used to call it the Music of the Spheres.

When I say that I have had personal experience with string theory, I need to make clear that I am not, by any stretch of the imagination, a string theorist. I'm not even a particularly qualified layman. I don't understand physics in terms of the complex math it requires. All I can put forth is an explanation that stems from a lot of reading and the experience of talking to a lot of people who have had NDEs.

What I now offer are the musings of someone who has had numerous insights that seem to come out of the blue, but correspond amazingly well with what I understand string theory to be, as interpreted by a reasonably well-read layman.

Michio Kaku is an American theoretical physicist, futurist, and author of science books for general readers. A professor of theoretical physics at the City College of New York and CUNY Graduate Center, he makes regular appearances on the BBC, the Discovery Channel, the History Channel, and the Science Channel as a science expert explaining difficult concepts to average audiences. In 2021 his book *The God Equation: The Quest for a Theory of Everything* became a *New York Times* best seller.

One of his endearing quotes is that according to string theory, strings play the notes, biology and chemistry produce the phrases, and the multiverse is the song. In other words, string theory is about tiny strings, each vibrating to its own frequency. To my ears, that sounds like music, which is, at its core, vibration.

Without going into too much detail, the basis of this theory is that at the root of everything in the physical world lie vibrating, one-dimensional objects called string particles. They interact with each other in specific ways.

We're used to thinking in terms of particles that have both mass and charge. That's basic physics. But string theory is different. String vibration produces gravitational force. Conventional theories of gravity don't harmonize with the other theories provided by quantum theory, involving the electromagnetic and the strong and weak nuclear forces. If string theory works out, it will connect all four, making it a candidate for the illusive Theory of Everything.

Professor Michio Kaku is a theoretical physicist, futurologist, author, and television personality who has worked to make scientific theories and principles accessible to the general public.

So far, gravity is the force that gives scientists fits. For various technical reasons it doesn't play well with the other three forces (electromagnetic and the strong and weak nuclear forces). But string theory made allowances for it and manages to tie them all together. It was so promising that it soon matured into a proposition called superstring theory. It is currently the best attempt so far to unify what are called the "natural" forces that govern our universe.

(If your eyes are starting to glaze over about now, stick with it just a little longer. We're almost at the end.)

For reasons known only to very gifted nerds, superstring theory works if you posit 11 different hypothetical dimensions. It's almost impossible for people like you and me to picture these in our heads. We do well with up and down, side to side, and time. But after that we get easily lost.

> For reasons known only to very gifted nerds, superstring theory works if you posit 11 different hypothetical dimensions. It's almost impossible for people like you and me to picture these in our heads.

Theoretical physicists, however, aren't as limited. They exist in a mental world that honors powers far beyond those of mere mortals.What happened was that some very gifted people began to think about string theory so much that the whole idea morphed into what is now called M-theory. ("M" stands for membrane, although some scientists substitute "mystery" or even "magic.")

Let me turn the podium over to Andrew Zimmerman Jones and Daniel Robbins for a minute. They wrote about this in the famous *Science for Dummies* books:

In string theory, the Multiverse is a theory in which our universe is not the only one; many universes (called Membranes or 'Branes) exist parallel to each other. These distinct universes within the Multiverse theory are called parallel universes. A variety of different theories lend themselves to a Multiverse viewpoint.

In some theories, there are copies of you sitting right here right now reading this in other universes and other copies of you that are doing other things in other universes.

Other theories contain parallel universes that are so radically different from our own that they follow entirely different fundamental laws of physics (or at least the same laws manifest in fundamentally different ways), likely collapsing or expanding so quickly that life never develops.

Forty years ago, physicists began to understand that string theory had the potential to incorporate the four natural forces, and thus all matter, in a single quantum mechanical framework. So far, it is still a controversial area of research. As many scientists swear *by* it as there are who swear *at* it. It remains to this day a mathematical construct. After all, how do you observe and replicate something so small?

As far back as 1905, Einstein unified space and time with his special theory of relativity. He proved that motion through space affects the passage of time. Ten years later he included space, time, and gravitation with his general theory of relativity. He showed that curves in space and time are responsible for the force of gravity. Most of us have seen the well-known image of a grid like a bed sheet that slumps in the middle when a bowling ball rolls around and around toward the center. He thought this was how gravity worked.

This wasn't enough for him, though. As monumental as these achievements were, he wanted more, and he dreamed of one powerful mathematical framework that would tie together space, time, and all of nature's forces. He called it a unified theory and tried, for the rest of his life, to decode it.

He never did, but since then a host of others—Gabriele Veneziano, Leonard Susskind, Holger Bech Nielsen, and Yoichiro Nambu—continued the work. John Schwarz, Joël Scherk, and the École Normale Supérieure joined the quest, as have many others.

Why is it so elusive?

Well, one reason is that for reasons known only to some brilliant mathematicians, the math demanded that the universe doesn't have just the three spatial dimensions we're all used to but at least six, maybe seven, or even more. Now the estimate is up to 11.

Albert Einstein famously united the concepts of time and space with his special theory of relativity and also predicted the existence of gravitational waves, but he was never able to unify the four forces of nature.

How do we get our minds around dimensions that we simply can't experience with our typical sense perceptions? Maybe this will help.

We live in what we perceive to be a three-dimensional world. There are actually four, but we'll get to that in a minute.

Think first about a dot on a piece of paper. That's what we'll call the first dimension. It has width, but that's about it. There's not a lot of room for a person living in one dimension to move around.

But suppose we add a second dimension by making the dot into a line. Now we have two dimensions—width and length. Someone who lives in the second dimension, if so inclined, can reach out a hand to his first-dimensional buddy and introduce him to a whole new world. They can now travel around and actually go someplace. It's a brand-new world, albeit flat. Many new possibilities and experiences await.

Now we'll go one step further. We'll add height. People who live in two dimensions look up and see someone above them. They realize their world is not flat at all. They can go to the right and left for some distance, but a third dimensional being now says, "Welcome to a new world," holds out his or her hand, and introduces them to something they can barely understand. From right to left, they can now move up and down.

We live in the third dimension. Like our counterparts in the first two dimensions, we can't conceive of anything else.

We have observed something interesting, though. Our three familiar dimensions are contained within a box, and we have experiences that occur one after the other. We have now added both space (the box) and time (the experience of sequential events). This adds, in effect, a fourth dimension. Einstein connected them for us and called it space-time.

Now comes an important question. Why stop there? We can't conceive of any more dimensions any more than the poor guy who lived in width could conceive of length, or the two-dimensional residents could conceive of height. They didn't believe that anyone could live in a third dimension, that of height bounded by space and time, but here we are, looking down on them from our third-dimensional perch.

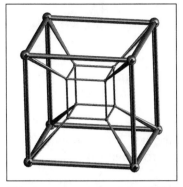

This shape represents a "shadow" of a four-dimensional object appearing in three dimensions. Imagine all the lines in this illustration are at right angles to each other and you get how difficult it can be to imagine higher dimensions—especially since this illustration is in only two dimensions!

Now, what if there are beings who inhabit dimensions we cannot fathom? And what if they can look in on us and introduce us to dimensions yet undreamed of in our reality?

This is rather crude, but I hope it serves the purpose.

What are these dimensions made of? How are they constructed?

Think in terms of musical instruments. A French horn is coiled up into a lot of ever-decreasing circles, but it's really quite a long instrument when you unfurl it.

It's the same with the strings of string theory. They vibrate in such small dimensions that they have been hidden from sight all these years. But these vibrations spark the energy (the poet in me wants to say "music") of the material universe.

Once again, I need to beg your indulgence. We'll soon tie all this into NDE research. Hang on. The end is in sight!

As the 20th century drew to a close, a new idea began to percolate among the few scientists who still stuck with string theory. A number of different concepts began to coalesce into what is called M-theory. "M" stands for membrane, or 'brane for short.

Picture everything we know and experience, the well-known dimensions of height, width, breadth, and time, as existing on a flat hypersurface. This is a 'brane. Right next to us is an extremely thin layer of another dimension, and on the other side of that is another 'brane that could conceivably have evolved just like we did, filled with sentient beings who are also wondering about the makeup of the multiverse. Once in a great while, measured in billions of our years, these 'branes fluctuate enough to touch at one point, causing a big bang to ripple through both universes. The last time this happened was 3.8 billion years ago.

Get the idea?

Here is where we get back to NDEs. What brought these universes into existence? According to NDE theory, it was a universal field called consciousness. Each 'brane is a field in which consciousness plays out its never-ending game of observing itself in the pursuit of life and experience. During an NDE, consciousness moves out of a body that is now lifeless and, for a time, is able to peer across to the 'branes in parallel universes.

In that sense, NDEs are pictured in a similar fashion as that which we discussed in the chapters about parallel universes and biocentrism.

We'll never know what Einstein thought about all this, of course. And most string theorists don't equate their highly scientific work with anything resembling NDEs. But it's an interesting crossover between science and metaphysics.

The work has just started. Who knows where it might lead?

CONCLUSIONS: NEW LANGUAGE FOR OLD EXPERIENCES

*We live in a world where there is more and more infor-
mation, and less and less meaning.*

—Jean Baudrillard in *Simulacra and Simulation*, 1981

Joe Thompson is a typically great guy who, like most great
guys, is anything but typical. He is a man's man in that he loves
to laugh, hunt, fish, and spend time with his friends. He is also a
sensitive man who deeply cares about others. On Sunday morn-
ings you will probably find him in church, singing in the choir
or fulfilling the duties of any leadership position he happens to
hold at the time. He is devoted to his wife and family and right-
fully proud of their accomplishments. Even though I moved
away from the town where he lives and have not seen him in person for some 15 years, I am still proud to call him my friend.

For five years before I retired from the ministry, I served as
pastor to the church in which he was very active. In that capacity,
I visited him one day soon after he got out of the hospital, following
a serious episode in which he either died or came very close to it.

That same hospital was where Joe worked in a highly technical position. I once asked him what he did, and in his typical
understated and humorous way he replied, "You know how joints
these days are sometimes replaced by a mechanical apparatus?
My job is to make sure that after the operation there are no left-
over parts lying around."

I suppose that my reasons for visiting him were normal ones. He had just come out of the hospital. He was a parishioner and my friend. Talking was what pastors and friends did. "How was it? How are you doing? Do you need anything? How do you feel?" The usual. I had done it thousands of times over the previous 40 years.

Little did I know that what he was about to tell me would stay with me as long as I lived.

It's been a little more than 17 years, but I remember it as if it were yesterday. We sat at his kitchen table—Joe, me, and his mother-in-law. I thought I sensed in him a bit of eagerness to tell me something, but a hesitancy as well. There was something a little off. Joe wasn't completely himself.

Now I understand. He had not told this story before and wasn't completely sure how it would be received. He had experienced something profound, but did he dare share it?

To his credit, he did. Many thousands of people before him have been through a near-death experience but kept it quiet for years because they were afraid of how they would be perceived. *They* knew it was real, but would their friends? Or even their family?

There was also a very real sense of self-doubt. Had it actually happened, or had he just imagined it? Was it simply a vision of some kind, brought on by hospital-administered drugs or an overly active imagination?

NDEs are, if nothing else, out of the ordinary. They are not something you casually share with friends and family around your kitchen table.

Over the course of my ministerial career, I'd heard stories such as this, but only on rare occasions have I personally experi-

> Time doesn't exist on the other side of the veil. Things seem to happen in blocks, arriving full-blown all at once.

enced anything of this nature. Since then, I have known out-of-body experiences during which I witnessed similar things, but back then I was, to paraphrase the Bible, listening "by faith and not by sight."

When Joe told me the story it came out without a lot of literary niceties. It was an example of stream-of-consciousness thinking, words tumbling over themselves without a lot of punctuation and well-manicured sentences. This is typical of NDE accounts. Time doesn't exist on the other side of the veil. Things seem to happen in blocks, arriving full-blown all at once. It's hard to describe this kind of thing in a world where we usually proceed with a "first this happened and it led to that" type of narrative.

Because that kind of story is hard to follow, I've edited things like periods, commas, and paragraphs into his account. But in his own words, this is what happened.

Joe had collapsed while doing his job. If you must suffer a heart episode of this severity, it's probably best to do it at a fully equipped hospital with a very competent staff, most of whom know you very well. The fact that it happened when it did, where it did, probably saved his life. Here's his story:

After being diagnosed with three coronary arteries that required bypass surgery, I waited and thought to myself, "What if I don't make it?"

I thought of my dad who had passed away back in '93 and was now in heaven. Did he see me? Did he see my kids and my wife?

I remember being rolled into the surgical suite where they gave me some medication. I wanted to say thank you to the people I knew, because I worked in the operating room. As I lay down on the bed, I prayed, "Your will, not mine be done."

I started to drift off to sleep. I felt very peaceful, and I remember floating along, but having the feeling of walking. There was no weight on my feet, however, and I was in complete darkness. The farther I went, the easier it was to walk, surrounded by colors that are unimaginable. I started toward a light and found myself moving at a

SOMETHING BLUE

faster pace as I came closer. Things turned to light brown around me, and I felt a presence behind me. In my right ear I heard the words, "Do not fear."

I remember walking on perfect sand. Everything around me had a pearlescence, a beauty that is really beyond description. I came to a huge gate that reached up into the sky, a bridge with water underneath—beautiful water.

> I remember walking on perfect sand. Everything around me had a pearl-essence, a beauty that is really beyond description.

The voice said to me, "Behold, your question is answered," and I had a magnificent view across a river to a beautiful city.

At first it didn't look like anything, but then I started to notice that there were people singing every song of praise you've ever heard. It was beautiful! Like a hawk, I started to have distance vision, and the music was getting louder.

Then the voice behind me said, "You can see with your own eyes." There was my father, beautiful, well, and happy!

I don't know how anyone could see me or talk to me, but I had knowledge and wisdom that was beyond compare. I knew every math problem that I've ever studied. I knew the answers to any of the questions anybody could ask. I was in the presence of the Holy Spirit.

They looked like they were waiting for me. I felt as though they were waiting for me to make a choice. The voice behind me was so kind and so sweet, and said, "You must not take one more step or you can't go back. Now, I give you a choice. The choice is yours."

I said to them in my most convincing voice, "Lord, I want to be with my children. They have to know, all people have to know, that this is not just real, it's beautiful."

230   NEAR-DEATH EXPERIENCES: AFTERLIFE JOURNEYS AND REVELATIONS

The voice behind me felt like it was touching me and said, "Go in peace, my son. Go in peace."

Unbeknownst to me, I'd had an excellent triple bypass surgery—not one hiccup, not one burp. It couldn't have been better.

Upon awakening, though, I learned that my breathing tube had become 95% clogged, so I was only pushing 5% of my total volume of air. I was dying after a successful triple bypass surgery.

The anesthesiologist was one of my friends and told me later that I was leaving after they had all worked very hard. "We couldn't figure out why you were dying," he said, "but I took a little flexible scope and I couldn't get it down through your airway. I have a loud voice, and said, 'May God help me! I can't give you up!'"

As I emerged from my anesthesia, he took his right hand and pulled the plug tube out almost completely.

I breathed my first breath after being in heaven.

He was concerned watching my numbers, and asked, "So how are you doing?"

I said, "I'm doing fantastic!"

Then he left because it was too stressful for him. The other anesthetist said, "You sure had us scared for a couple minutes. Where did you go?"

I looked right at them and I said, "Up to heaven. I got to see the gate, and I chose to turn away."

He said, "I believe you!"

The one thing that happens when you die is that you have total consciousness and total clarity. There is no gray area in the world.

He told his mother-in-law and me the story two days later with, in his words, "the conviction of the Apostle Paul," and finished with these words:

> The one thing that happens when you die is that you have total consciousness and total clarity. There is no gray area in the world. You know what's right, and you know what's wrong. The longer I was awake, the more that knowledge stayed with me. I was left with a feeling of pure love.

> I know that when it comes my time to go, I will pray to God that I'll be allowed to take that step across the bridge. There will be many people there to greet me, and there will be much joy.

A few years after I retired and moved away, Joe told this story in church on a Sunday morning. I was assured by some who attended that service that when he finished, there wasn't a dry eye in the house.

Let's compare this account to other typical NDE accounts on record, and study them one event at a time.

THE OUT-OF-BODY EXPERIENCE

In Joe's words:

> I started to drift off to sleep. I felt very peaceful, and I remember floating along, but having the feeling of walking.

If all NDEs have one thing in common, it is the OBE, or out-of-body experience. The person experiencing an NDE has the distinct impression or feeling of somehow separating from the body and moving away from it. Sometimes they describe hovering over the scene of death, observing their body from near the ceiling of the operating room. As we have seen throughout this book, they are often able to describe in minute detail what went on and recount conversations couched in medical-speak, using terms with which they are not familiar.

How can they "see" without eyes? How can they "hear" without ears? How can they "move" without limbs?

The person experiencing an NDE has the distinct impression or feeling of somehow separating from the body and moving away from it.

If we accept these experiences as bona fide—and there is simply too much evidence not to do so—then we are led to believe that our eyes, ears, and limbs have evolved to be material manifestations of something that is an eternal reality; that the body is a vehicle for the soul, to be discarded when it has served its purpose.

If this is true, we can say that when our consciousness separates at death, we still exist in an eternal state and experience the now-familiar stages of what is to come. When our brains are revived, they go back to doing what they do so well—organizing and interpreting what our eternal consciousness experienced in the interim.

In the meantime, however, during the OBE you feel that everything is real. It seems more vivid than the reality you live in, day to day. And it is! Your normal life consists of deciphering an illusion produced by your five senses. Of course an OBE will feel more real than that.

But when you "return" to your senses, they will immediately convince you that what you experienced while "out" was just in your head.

How could it be otherwise? Your memory of that trip is interpreted by your physical brain, which will select past experiences to produce an image of what just happened in order to make sense of it. But by the time that takes place you are *remembering* something, not *experiencing* it.

This is extremely important. When you return from an NDE and your physical brain kicks back in, you are remembering what it *felt like at the time*. By the time you tell the story, it will be only memory, similar to remembering a dream. That's how physical brains, steeped in the passage of time, operate. They relate incidents one step at a time, in a logical sequence.

But time doesn't exist on the other side, so language is insufficient to describe that kind of reality.

No wonder so many people come back from an NDE and report, "It felt so real!" That's because it was!

LIFE REVIEW

Joe's experience didn't include a life review, except for one small quote that may reveal volumes:

I thought of my dad who had passed away back in '93 and was now in heaven. Did he see me? Did he see my kids and my wife?

Joe's mind was definitely on the accomplishment that he most hoped would make his dad proud. The important thing to him at that moment was not how much he had done professionally, or how much he had accumulated. At that time the most important thing to him, so important that it canceled out everything else, was his family.

Although full-blown life reviews are very common, they are not always part of the NDE experience. But many people report seeing their whole life flash before their eyes, a process that somehow reveals to them how their actions influenced others. Usually it's not the big things, the important things, they remember, but rather small, seemingly insignificant things that stand out. They might remember their arguments with siblings, their ego-influenced activities that they thought were life-changing but really weren't, the kind words spoken when a friend needed to hear them.

What is the purpose of this process?

It's been said that you can't judge a book by its cover. Publishers go to great lengths to supply a book with just the right title, just the right picture on the cover, in order to promote what they call "shelf appeal." Real estate people will do the same thing to ensure what they call "curbside appeal." First impressions are often the most important.

That doesn't seem to be the objective of a life review. It's more interested in the content than the cover—the underlying motives rather than the superficial events.

Think of it this way. When a music reviewer reports on a performance of a Beethoven symphony, he doesn't report on the music itself. That's a given. It's understood that the music of Beethoven is above the fray and doesn't need to be critiqued. It stands alone, in and of itself.

No, he reports on the *performance* of the music. Was the violin section playing together? Were the trumpets in tune? Did the conductor select the best tempo?

> That's what a life review seems to be. It doesn't ask the question "Does love exist?" Instead, it says, "How well did you live a life of love?"

That's what a life review seems to be. It doesn't ask the question "Does love exist?" Instead, it says, "How well did you live a life of love?" That seems to be the emphasis. Your performance is more important than your content. Things that we call emotions, such as love, compassion, goodness, and humility, are assumed to be the reality up against which we measure our earthly experience. As such, we can assume those are the things that compose the very bedrock of the universe. They stand alone, without question. The only thing we review is how well we carried them out in our actions and motives. It doesn't matter if we are successful in the eyes of the world. What counts is our interior motivation.

I really can't call the movie *Meatballs* one of my favorites. It is fun and funny, but not something I would carry with me to a desert island if I had only a limited number of films to watch for the rest of my life. But it contains a poignant scene that will probably stay with me as long as I live.

Actor and comedian Bill Murray had a poignant line in the movie *Meatballs* in which he told his young camper charges that, when it comes down to it, winning or losing "doesn't matter!"

For those not familiar with the film, it is a quintessential summer camp movie starring Bill Murray in the kind of role he was born to play. The campers, perpetual "losers" in the opinion of their peers, full of angst and displaying the awkwardness of teenagers everywhere, are depressed because they are about to enter into an athletic event with the camp across the lake, populated by privileged, wealthy, gifted, and talented kids who always win the annual event.

In a wonderfully funny scene, Bill Murray gives them a motivational speech, delivered as only he can do it. In effect, he liberates them when he gives them a slogan we all could take to heart. When it comes to winning and losing, he tells them, "It just doesn't matter! It just doesn't matter!"

Winning is not, in the words of Vince Lombardi, "everything," or even, as the great coach continued, "the only thing." It's how you play the game that counts. To review your actions and motivations seems to be the purpose of the life review. There is no judgment. The life review, as reported by those who experienced it during an NDE, seems to be for your benefit, not some judgmental God. If the purpose of life is to gather the flowers of experience for the benefit and growth of eternal consciousness, it is during the life review that we arrange the bouquet. It will forever be on display in the sacred halls of the cosmic Akashic record.

In a few minutes, when we sum up our ideas about the primacy of consciousness, we'll go into why this should be so. For now, it's enough to know that according to thousands of those who have been through the process, it's nothing to fear.

THE TUNNEL

Joe didn't specifically *mention* a tunnel, but he *described* one in great detail:

There was no weight on my feet ... and I was in complete darkness. The further I walked, the easier it was to walk in shades of color that are unimaginable.

Some far-fetched theories have arisen to explain another common feature of most NDEs. One of them, for instance, put forth by otherwise knowledgeable people, is that when we die, our last memory is that of the trip through the birth canal that we experienced when we were born.

That one raises more questions than it answers, so we won't pay much attention to it.

Another explanation, which might have more validity, features a theory from the field of cosmology. The tunnel, according to this view, is a wormhole that connects two separate dimensions. It comes from the fertile mind of Albert Einstein and is called an Einstein–Rosen bridge. It even has its own equation: $ER = EPR$, or *Einstein–Rosen* equals *Einstein–Podolsky–Rosen*, or "EPR pair." It signifies the conjecture that two entangled particles are connected by a wormhole. It's thought to be a possible theory for unifying general relativity and quantum mechanics, resulting in a Grand Unification Theory (GUT)—the so-called Theory of Everything.

The idea inherent in this speculation is that if particles can be entangled through time and space, always in instant communication and connected by a sort of tunnel through time and space, can the same be said of bodies, one departing the dimension of physical reality while in the process of joining its astral counterpart in a nonphysical realm?

Maybe, but is there a less esoteric explanation? Wormholes and black holes are fun to think about, and science fiction writers love them, but they are still hypothetical.

Here's the one I prefer. It's a lot more down to earth. I adapted it from Bob Costas, the famous sportscaster, in an article he wrote for the *AARP Bulletin* in May 2023. AARP is not noted for its work on NDE research, but this works for me.

When I was a kid, I liked to play baseball. I even watched some on TV, but not a lot. TVs back then featured tiny screens and black-and-white pictures. There was no spectacle, no instant replay, or much else that we're used to today. Fewer commercials, too!

Some games were then played during summer afternoons, and one day my dad took me to my first live baseball game in Detroit at what was then named Briggs Stadium (later, it was renamed Tiger Stadium, which was demolished in 2008).

Back then we entered the stadium through a long tunnel that ran underneath the seats. When we came out of the tunnel

Perhaps journeying to the afterlife is like passing through a wormhole, and that is why so many NDE experiencers see some kind of tunnel.

the sight took my breath away. It was huge. The bright green field, impeccably mowed in crisscrossed stripes, the light-colored dirt of the infield, pitcher's mound, and outfield warning track, the impossibly white chalk marking the diamond, a brilliant blue sky overhead, and the uniforms of my heroes on the home team.

Remember, now, that I had only seen games on a tiny black-and-white screen. This was magic.

If you've ever seen the original movie version of *The Wizard of Oz*, you'll remember the part where Dorothy and Toto are transported from black-and-white Kansas to Technicolor Oz. That was my experience. From gray to full color when we exited the tunnel. From everyday life to full-blown reality.

Maybe that's what the NDE tunnel is all about. We leave the usual gray life we have lived for our whole lives and walk, or, in Joe's case, kind of float, up into reality. It seems like a tunnel that leads from a gray normalcy into vivid Technicolor. "Things turned to light brown around me," he remembered, and then to "shades of color that are unimaginable."

Maybe that's the only way to describe it.

THE LIGHT

I started toward a light, and found myself moving at a faster pace as I came closer.

I don't think I've ever interviewed someone, or read any NDE accounts, that didn't feature a light, usually at the end of a tunnel. Again, we can only guess what it means, but almost everyone describes it using the same words. That's why Betty Eadie named her book *Embraced by the Light*.

There is the usual academic opinion about it: "A sudden surge in brain activity at the time of cardiac arrest may be what causes people to perceive a bright white light when having a near-death experience."

Okay. We've come to expect such prosaic opinions. I prefer the opinion of Bruce Greyson, a foremost specialist in the subject who interviewed thousands of people before expressing an opinion:

Many people who encounter NDEs experience an overwhelming sense of peace and well-being. People sometimes describe it as a living entity radiating tremendous love, acceptance, and warmth. They feel enveloped by it; it permeates their being, and they don't know what to call it, so they simply name it the light.

Greyson continues:

When you talk to near-death experiencers, and you ask them, "What happened to you?" the first thing they say is, "Well, there aren't words to express it. I can't really describe it for you."

People who have NDEs often describe meeting an entity of some sort that radiates pure light and love.

The questions that come up with the near-death experience probably can't be answered with our limited language and our limited logic. In other words: The light is a feeling that can't really be explained.

So what is it? I have no idea. Again, I fall back on the difficulty of putting it into words. But perhaps we can say that the light is generally associated with positivity and warmth, whether you see an actual beam or not. Maybe that's why people who experience NDEs typically come back less afraid of death. People consistently, from all over the world, say that the near-death experience leads you to a place that is not something to be feared. Seeing the light can be a deeply moving experience associated with peace and tranquility. It's not just a ray of sunlight or electric bulb [in an operating room]. While some people do see such brilliance, it's more about the feeling of light itself: warmth, positivity, and freedom.

We can speculate, hypothesize, or talk about the importance of light in the field of particle physics, but I expect that when we come to the end, we will discover that, like most things that exist outside our sensory experience, it probably consists of something we really are not equipped to fully understand.

RELAXING INTO ACCEPTANCE

As I lay down on the bed, I prayed, "Your will, not mine be done."

In an earlier chapter we talked a little about bad near-death experiences. They are few and far between, and they usually dissipate when people relax and accept the fact that they have no control over what is happening to them.

Joe was one whose faith allowed him to instinctively do this right at the beginning. He experienced a brief time of darkness. That was only natural, something to be expected in a transition from one kind of reality to another. But he was never afraid.

Perhaps that's something we can all take from a study of NDEs. Acceptance will make our transition into death less fearful and more exciting.

> **I recently discovered firsthand that there are powers outside our experience that can and do lend a helping hand from time to time, even before we make our transition.**

I recently discovered firsthand that there are powers outside our experience that can and do lend a helping hand from time to time, even before we make our transition. Having lived now for 78 years, I am fully aware that the world around me has changed a great deal. I confess that I simply cannot keep up, and sometimes it scares me. I am a bit of a control freak when it comes to life in general. I like to think that I at least understand and have a handle on the basics, but modern technology sometimes terrifies me.

Take cell phones, for instance. I don't understand them. I'll bet you don't either, no matter how tech-savvy you think you are. Oh, I know how to push the buttons. Usually. But that doesn't mean I have the faintest idea how I can hit "send" on my end, launch a signal off to a tower somewhere, which transfers it to some satellite, which contacts something called a server, which selects your phone out of the millions that are all working somewhere, somehow, and accomplishes all this in less than a second or two.

As I get older, my apprehension and feeling of powerlessness increase. As a result, I have, for the last few years, experienced terrifying nightmares. They usually consist of me trying to get home from somewhere but losing my way or forgetting where I parked my car. Sometimes I find myself trying to navigate a noisy, dirty factory, filled with lots of loud machines and people who don't seem to want to help at all.

I won't go into too much detail, but I often wake up with a cold sweat, and can't seem to get it through my head that it was a dream. I usually must get out of bed, turn on the lights, and walk around the house until I understand where I am.

I've heard about meds that claim they will dull the dreams, but that doesn't make any sense to me. After all, the dreams are not the problem. They are the symptom of a problem. Life makes me feel out of control and is extremely terrifying. I feel that I am lost in a world I don't understand, trying to find my way home.

I knew I needed to attack this situation at the source, but I didn't know how.

One night I had two of these nightmares, equally frightening, within a matter of four hours. I got up at 3:30 in the morning, afraid to go back to sleep, where I had no control over my dreams.

> Having had a lot of experience with OBEs by this time in my life, I was sure that unseen powers were available.

The next night, bedtime came and went, and I was still uncomfortable about going to sleep. I went out on my back porch, surrounded by deep woods and natural sounds, and meditated.

Well, not really. I called it meditation, but I was praying to "to whom it may concern"; to the powers that be; to God; to anyone or anything that would listen. Having had a lot of experience with OBEs by this time in my life, I was sure that unseen powers were available. I just didn't know how to make use of them. But in my meditation, I felt an assurance that help was on the way.

I went to bed, somewhat comforted, and fell asleep. Four or five hours later, I experienced another dream, but this one was very different. I was lost again, just as before. I was trying to get home. But this time, I saw a peaceful river flowing in the direction I knew I needed to go. There was a raft, with no manual oars or paddles, waiting for me near the bank. All I had to do was get on the raft and let the river carry me along.

I awoke with a powerful message ringing in my head. I didn't "figure it out." It came as a single block of teaching, and I knew it was a message from outside, rather than something I thought of myself. It was an answer to my prayer. I was told I needed to relax and go with the flow. I had to surrender.

Our lives are filled with what the old writers called "unseen angels," "spirit guides," waiting to assist us on our life's journey if only we let them. When the time comes for me to die, I hope I will have learned to relax and just ride the raft home. It will make the journey so much easier.

Was this an NDE?

No. I didn't die.

Was it an OBE? Maybe. I've had them before.

Was this a message from beyond my perception realm? Definitely!

As Joe put it, "Not my will, but thine be done."

THE PRESENCE

I felt a presence behind me. In my right ear I heard the words, "Do not fear." The voice said to me, "Behold, your question is answered," and I had a magnificent view across a river to a beautiful city.

Another very common component of NDEs is what I call The Presence. Someone, some entity, some being, appears to act as a sort of welcoming agent and guide.

In the West, among people who have grown up within a monotheistic culture, this person is often identified as Jesus, or

Moses, or an archangel of some kind. In the East, it is usually described as a Buddha, or Vishnu, or an entity from the pantheon of Hindu gods. Even atheists identify The Presence according to their cultural surroundings.

It is not uncommon at all for some experiencers, at this point, to remind listeners that they were raised in a household of unbelievers and had no expectations of there being anything but annihilation waiting for them. Rarely, however, do they remain atheists. Nonbelievers invariably return from an NDE with a strong spiritual belief system. Not necessarily a religion, mind you. But what they prefer to call spirituality.

It is almost universal in nature.

MEETING PEOPLE

Almost every NDE story I have ever heard involved meeting someone, usually a loved one who has already died. In Joe's case it was no different:

> Then I started to notice that there were people who were singing every song of praise you've ever heard. It was beautiful! Like a hawk, I started to have distance vision, and the music was getting louder.
>
> Then the voice behind me said, "You can see with your own eyes." There was my father, beautiful, well, and happy.

Given the number of people who swear they met loved ones during their NDE, we must assume that our consciousness survives death, along with our individuality. If it were otherwise, if we were simply absorbed into a nebulous whole, we would not be able to recognize specific people, especially those who were dear to us.

Personal experience leads me to believe that individuality is important, and often not surrendered lightly. Let me share with you my own story. This wasn't an NDE. It was an out-of-body experience I

Meeting friends and family who have passed away before us is also a common element of NDEs.

had in 2012 that might explain how much control, or lack of it, we can experience if we are not prepared when death comes knocking.

It began with a time of what had by then become "normal" vibration and a pleasant expanding of consciousness, before I simply exploded out of my body.

There is no other way I can describe it. I exploded into color, but "color" doesn't do it justice. I seem to remember seeing my body as a black shadow form against a backdrop of brightness. I felt an enormous, wonderful, powerful, fulfilling surge of energy, and I just expanded—kind of like what the Big Bang must have been like during the inflation period.

There was what might be described as a loud "pop," and then I just expanded into rainbow colors surrounding my body as a kind of halo, though they were just a small circle of familiar hues close to my body. They quickly faded into a brightness that I can't describe.

> I felt an enormous, wonderful, powerful, fulfilling surge of energy and I just expanded— kind of like what the Big Bang must have been like during the inflation period.

It was wonderful, and I remember thinking, "If this is death, bring it on!" The rest is lost. It felt as though time passed, but I have no idea how much.

Then the strangest thing happened. I thought I was back in my body, walking toward the bedroom, my nighttime meditation over. When I got there, I saw a woman lying on the side of the bed like my wife does while leaning over to pet our dog.

I couldn't see her face, and she was wearing unfamiliar, strange clothes. Maybe even clothes from a different period. I wasn't sure.

She was crying, and I went over to comfort her. That's when I realized I was still out of my body. I wasn't walking, I was floating. It was *my* body, for sure, but different.

I was full of confusion, never having experienced anything like this. I wondered if the woman was someone who was "stuck" in an astral plane between this life and the next.

The experience ended there for a few days. I needed time to think and prepare. But I couldn't let it go. I felt sure the woman had died before I was born, but was still stuck in the "wherever" her belief system had limited her to experiencing.

This might be pure speculation, of course. But my pastor's heart kicked in. Even in my waking hours, I couldn't forget that she seemed to need help. I almost felt as though I had a new ministry. Call it serving "Christians without a Country."

In my experience, some conservative Christians form rigid ideas about heaven and hell. Those ideas form the basis of what they expect to find on the other side. I'm sure that when some of them die and return with a tale about what heaven looks like, those beliefs shape their narrative. The consensus religious consciousness of the last few hundred years probably creates such a place, which is reinforced by the similar beliefs of so many who shared that earthly experience of traditional Christianity.

Thus, when some Christians have an NDE, many report seeing the so-called pearly gates, just as they have been taught. Some report meeting Jesus. Could it be that what they are experiencing is an astral projection of what they expected to find?

If that is the case, it will be difficult for them to proceed beyond that expectation. Maybe they need an "astral evangelist" to take them further. Who better than a recovering Christian pastor like me?

Whatever the case—and remember, this is sheer speculation—I felt I had a great deal to learn and experience before any of this could come to pass.

People raised in the Christian tradition have certain expectations of the afterlife, so if they see the classic pearly gates, perhaps they see them because that is what they *expect* to see.

Then came November 23, 2012. I learned her name. She told me it was Sarah Hines.

I got up to meditate that morning at about 5:00. My intention was to somehow find her again and try to offer some help.

Right away, I knew something was going to happen because very soon after I began to relax and concentrate, I felt a small surge of energy in my right temporal lobe. It was followed shortly by a similar surge in my left temporal lobe.

I've felt this before, but only on the left. It happens sometimes when I try to step out of my "busy-mind" mode and become the Watcher. Sometimes it feels as though I'm outside my body, on the left side, watching myself meditate. I had never felt it on the right side before that morning. But my impression, after both energy surges, was that I felt balanced. My whole brain, or head, or whatever, was soon surrounded by the energy glow, or circle, that I've felt before.

Now it gets difficult to describe. For a long time, I felt disoriented. My body was asleep. I could even hear myself snoring a little bit. But my mind was fully awake, fully functioning, and floating. An hour passed. All I could do was drift and experience the feeling.

I finally was able to focus enough to try to find the woman I was looking for from yesterday's OBE. As soon as I thought of her, I saw her again. She was lying on the bed, just like before. But this time she became aware of my presence, sat up, and turned toward me so I could see her face.

She was scared. I could tell. It was as though she was seeing an apparition or a ghost. Her eyes were wide, and she had a frightened look on her face.

She seemed European and had a round face with a small pug nose. Her hair was a dirty blond with a kind of Little Orphan Annie cut. She was wearing a skirt that looked like burlap but was a finer material. It had straps that went up over her shoulders. She had a shirt on that was like cotton, and a lighter color than her skirt. She was wearing stockings of some sort, and no shoes.

I had the impression that there was a fireplace behind her as she lay on the bed, and the room she was in seemed to be built with heavy, dark beams. It reminded me of an English pub, though now that I think of it, I had never been in one up to that time of my life. I guess it reminded me of scenes in movies I've seen set in English pubs.

When she became aware of me, her brown eyes opened wide and she just stared, somewhat withdrawn. I asked her to please tell me her name; then, without her speaking it, I knew it was Sarah Hines. (This seems strange. I definitely talked to her, and she answered, but neither of us said anything. "Telepathy" doesn't sound right, but there's no other word I can think of that's better.)

It all felt very real. I was monitoring all this from my fully conscious left brain, and it felt as though I was talking to a real person, but on another plane of existence, and in another form that was more spirit than matter.

All this thinking, mixed emotion, and analyzing began to bring me back to my body. I felt as though I was being drawn back away from her, and I only had time enough to say, "Sarah, you don't have to stay here. You can go on ... you can go farther." She just watched me, her expression never changing. Then I was back in my body.

Now came the final mediation, a few days later, while I was attending a seminar at the Monroe Institute. I discovered that she lived in Germany, late 19th century, and spelled her name Sarah Heinz, not Hines. We had an emotional reunion. She was waiting for me.

I led her to the exit for the next level, where she said, "You're sad!" I told her I was. Truth be told, I wanted to go with her. She stayed for a while to hold my hand and comfort me. Then I returned and she, presumably, went forward. Somehow, I didn't believe this was the end.

A person like Sarah Heinz is someone who might get stuck in their earthly identity, carrying it with them when they go. They believe in their senses, even after death has quieted them. It's like waking from a dream and feeling that the dream is still real.

It's a frightening thing. I think people like Sarah experience that. They are so deeply into the illusion of life that when their body dies, they continue in that illusion. They need to be shaken awake.

What's the purpose of this rather long narrative? Just this.

> **I have come to believe that when we die, we keep our identity, at least for a while.**

I have come to believe that when we die, we keep our identity, at least for a while.

Does the phrase "for a while" have any relevance in a place where time does not exist? I don't know. This leaves a lot of questions, but that is the nature of a dream.

After we dream, we sometimes retain the reality of the dream, bringing it with us back to our waking reality. Perhaps that happens after death as well.

Consider, for instance, the appearance of aging. People who return from an NDE often describe the relatives they met there as being younger than they were when they died.

Perhaps we are seeing them in their prime. Who knows for sure? Our soul, our essence, doesn't age. It's eternal. But who knows what our memory is doing?

Remember that the NDE experience, when later recalled after the return to physical life, is a memory. While we *experience* it, it's reality. When we *describe* it, it's not the reality, it's our *memory* of reality, and it probably suffers during the translation.

In Joe's case, the memory seems perfectly clear. He saw his father, and he saw a lot of beautiful people. I, for one, believe they were real.

THE FEELING OF LOVE AND ACCEPTANCE

Another universal testimony of those who have experienced NDEs is that when the physical body is shed, along with its limited senses and intelligence, they are left with a feeling of total acceptance and complete understanding. The body that we inhabit, even if it came equipped with the brain of an Einstein, Hawking, or Sheldon Cooper, is a crude instrument. When consciousness is released and entangled with every other metaphorical "cell" in eternity, it is nothing short of omniscient.

This is how Joe put it:

I don't know how they could see me or talk to me, but I had knowledge and wisdom that was beyond compare. I knew every math problem that I've ever studied. I knew the answers to any of the questions anybody could ask. I was in the presence of the Holy Spirit.

A quick search of YouTube videos done by those who have experienced NDEs reveals that almost every one of them has the supposed answer to our purpose, future, reason for being, eventual end, or place in the universe. When I use the words "supposed answer," I'm not implying that the experiencers are making things up, or under delusions of grandeur, or egocentric. I'm sure they really believe they received a message to bring back. Probably most of them did. But once again, we need to remember that we are listening to the *memories* of people who, having returned from a realm beyond our senses and intelligence, are again dealing with the limitations of human language.

> **The near-death experience produces insight, to be sure, and probably profound wisdom. But there is a huge gap being *knowing* and *doing*.**

Answers to life's biggest questions are difficult, possibly even impossible, for us to understand. The near-death experience produces insight, to be sure, and probably profound wisdom. But there is a huge gap being *knowing* and *doing*.

We all know, for instance, that if we could follow the golden rule and treat others as we wish to be treated, if we were to love one another, and if we would show compassion to our neighbors, we could eliminate every police position and disband the armies of the world. If any truth is noble and right, this is it.

But does anyone think that's even remotely practical? If all we had to do was pass a law that says "Love one another" and obey it, the world would change in an instant. Would you be willing to give me odds on that happening?

I don't wish to denigrate anyone's testimony, no matter how many views it has on YouTube. But life is under the influence of the human brain, not eternal omniscience.

That's one of the things that struck me so forcefully about Joe's story. He said that when he was *on the other side,* he "knew the answers to any of the questions anybody could ask." He didn't claim that was the case after he returned. That illustrates both honesty and humility.

This is not to say that insight doesn't sometimes arrive "out of the blue" to gifted individuals who are ready to receive it. From Thomas Edison to Johannes Brahms, from Picasso to Nikola Tesla, their work illustrates art, not just craft. Art comes from "the muse." Craft comes from hard work. There is a vast difference.

In music school I spent two years studying the chorales of Johann Sebastian Bach. I learned every one of his rules and could write music based on the techniques he both invented and manipulated. But my music didn't sound like his. Not even close. His was inspired. Mine was clever. That's the difference between art and craft.

> Leaving knowledge aside, however, there is another aspect to the NDE that I find not only practical but comforting. Almost everyone who returns from an NDE ... talks about love and acceptance.

Leaving knowledge aside, however, there is another aspect to the NDE that I find not only practical but comforting. Almost everyone who returns from an NDE, including Joe, talks about love and acceptance. They all struggle to find descriptive adjectives. The most common word used is "total": *total* love, *total* joy, *total* acceptance.

We looked at this in depth in an earlier chapter, so we won't go over it again here. Suffice it to say that we can take a lot of comfort in the fact that what we all "know" to be true about what is right and good, what we all "know" could solve the problems of the world, is the common standard of existence on the other side.

That's probably why we know it. It's not something we *learn*. It's something we *remember*. We once lived within that standard of excellence. Is it any wonder that our return to it is joyful and comforting?

THE CHOICE

This is a stage that I find the most intriguing of all. It makes me believe that we all chose to come here and live the life we did. Joe's experience was typical:

> *I felt as though they were waiting for me to make a choice. The voice behind me was so kind and so sweet, and said, "You must not take one more step or you can't go back. Now, I give you a choice. The choice is yours."*
>
> *I said to them in my most convincing voice, "Lord, I want to be with my children.*

If, as I speculated in an earlier chapter, we chose to leave the Source and journey out into physical life, if we made the choice to live the lives we are now leading, if physical manifestation is a means to gather experience that is not possible within the parameters, or rather *lack* of parameters, of unity and wholeness, then it makes sense that when we leave here before our allotted time, we are often given the choice to return and finish the task we set out to do.

Granted, this is sheer speculation, and it might very well raise more questions than answers. Why would someone *choose* to live in pain and misery? Why would someone *choose* to die in the Holocaust? Why would someone *choose* to live in slavery?

The Christian metaphor of Christ choosing to die a horrible death on a cross answers those questions by declaring that the end justifies the means—that there is a greater good to achieve. But it appears questionable that there is a greater good to achieve when someone dies alone and afraid, after suffering a painful death from cancer or a wasting disease of some kind. Christian doctrine may declare that Christ died for the sins of the world. That's a noble goal and worth any pain and anguish, but I doubt seriously

As with Christ, it can make sense to suffer and die for a great and noble cause, but what about innocent people who die sick, alone, and afraid for no good reason?

that someone born with a horrible physical defect or incurable disease can make the same claim.

No, platitudes and sanctimonious speeches aside, the truth is that there are no answers to these questions, but the fact remains that countless NDE experiences include such a choice.

On some occasions I have experienced such a choice myself during OBE experiences. This is just one example from few years ago, pulled from my dream journal:

I seemed to walk through a vast, seemingly infinite field of white light, conscious of being in the vibrational state all the time. When I pushed through the field of light, I "saw" only darkness. But it was extremely peaceful and very comfortable. I stayed there a long time, even though there was a small pull to return. I felt that this time the choice was mine to make. I probably could have decided to stay right there forever if I had wanted. I remember asking if there was anyone else around. I saw nothing and nobody, but it was a wonderful, peaceful place to be. Finally, and almost reluctantly, I came back.

I emphasize again that this was not an NDE. It was an out-of-body experience, but it involved the choice to stay or return.

What I call "the Choice" implies that our lives have purpose. If accepted as a working hypothesis, it provides some comfort during hard times. Perhaps all things happen for a reason. Our job is not necessarily to "live happily after." It is to endure and get through, and hopefully to be grateful that we did it.

But this stage is closely associated with the next, so we'll get right to it.

THE MISSION

Joe felt very strongly that upon his return he had a job to do, a mission to fulfill. This is very common to all who, given the choice, return to their bodies:

They have to know, all people have to know, that this is not just real, it's beautiful. The voice behind me felt like it was touching me, and said, "Go in peace, my son. Go in peace."

In short, he felt an obligation to tell people about what had happened to him.

I've known Joe for a long time, both before and after his NDE. Trust me when I say that he did not become an obnoxious evangelist. He doesn't try to push his religious views, and he is a guy anyone would want to spend time with. He doesn't insist on dominating conversations or ruining parties with grandstanding. He is still, pardon the pun, "a regular Joe."

But having gone through what he experienced, and having seen what removing the obstacle of fear from someone who faces death can accomplish, he is not hesitant to do what he can to be a helpful witness.

He has not changed his profession or greatly altered his lifestyle. But who knows? Maybe his mission was to ultimately help someone through a tough time by having his experience recorded for posterity in a book such as this.

It's only fitting, then, that we give him the last word:

The one thing that happens when you die is that you have total consciousness and total clarity. There is no gray area in the world. You know what's right, and you know what's wrong. The longer I was awake, the more that knowledge stayed with me. I was left with a feeling of pure love.

I know that when it comes my time to go, I will pray to God that I'll be allowed to take that step across the bridge. There will be many people there to greet me, and there will be much joy.

> **I have come to believe that the body evolved to be the organ through which consciousness can perceive itself.**

Let's try to encapsulate this in a commonsense, practical way.

I have come to believe that the body evolved to be the organ through which consciousness can perceive itself.

Here's an example. Without our eyes, the body cannot see, but the eye is not independent unto itself. It cannot say, "Today I don't feel like going to work." It is a small part of a larger organism. Working in conjunction with our ears, nose, tongue, and skin, it helps us experience the world around us and form patterns that make sense of our environment.

In the same way, biological chemicals and electronic impulses generated in our brains form feelings that we interpret intellectually, such as love, fear, pleasure, pain, and loss.

Together, all this information forms the experiences that make up what we call life. But our individual lives are all "organs," for lack of a better word, that together make up a vehicle for the real manipulator behind the scenes, called consciousness, *in order to experience life in a material world.* This is the essence of the word "God." Returning to the Bible, in both the Old and New Testaments, "Know ye not that *ye* are Gods?" (Psalms 82:6 and John 10:34).

Consciousness is eternal and omnipresent. We are its eyes, ears, and all the rest. The eye doesn't say, "I am separate from the body and can work on my own." It is a part of a larger whole, just like we can't really say, "I choose to be separate from consciousness and work on my own." It doesn't work that way.

We may *feel* separate, but that's an illusion. As a matter of fact, feeling separate, feeling like an individual, is part of the process. It is a necessary part. It is the purpose of consciousness. We call it ego. Individuality is something that universal consciousness, which is a wholeness of unity that many people call God, can never achieve without such a body.

> When the physical body dies, and its senses with it, individual consciousness, sometimes called Soul or Spirit, is released to return to wholeness rather than separateness.

When the physical body dies, and its senses with it, individual consciousness, sometimes called Soul or Spirit, is released to return to wholeness rather than separateness. That, in essence, is what an NDE is. In the moment of death, consciousness returns to its real form—eternal, immortal, omnipresent, and omniscient.

In secular-speak, the dreamer wakes up from the dream.

In religious terms that many are familiar with, the soul returns to heaven; the spirit returns to God; atman returns to Brahman.

That is probably why people so often report spiritual/psychological changes, and even physiological ones, after returning from a near-death experience.

Spiritual/psychological changes usually include a loss or decrease of the fear of death, an increase in generosity and charity, an increased desire for knowledge, the resolution of issues from childhood, and an increase in childlike wonder and joy.

Physiological changes include different patterns of thought processing, becoming more creative and inventive, increased light or sound sensitivity, changes in food preferences, lower blood pressure, and increased metabolism. The person may even become younger-looking.

In short, an NDE usually makes us more "godlike." At least for a while. Lifelong habits are tough to break, and old ways of thinking die hard. It's easy to return to the status quo. But most people keep at least a vestige of their NDE memories with them until the day they die ... again.

Consciousness is eternal and omnipresent, but human intelligence evolved within space and time. Thus, we might never attain an intelligence great enough to fully understand the reality that becomes known through an NDE.

In the end, we must return to the words we used at the beginning. Science or metaphysics, religion or spirituality, materialism or "otherness," maybe this is the best way to say it:

The song that we all learn as children might be correct: "Life is but a dream." An NDE happens when we mo-

mentarily wake up from that dream. We soon fall back to sleep when we re-enter our bodies and return to materialistic existence. But for the rest of our lives, we usually long to return to the embrace of the Dreamer.

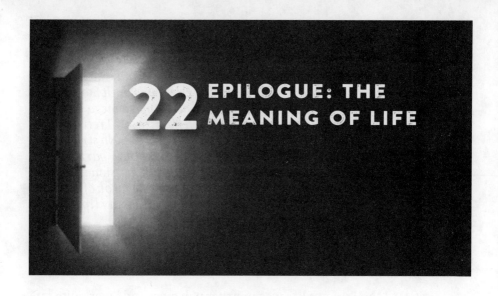

22 EPILOGUE: THE MEANING OF LIFE

Synchronicity: the coincidental occurrence of events and especially psychic events ... that seem related but are not explained by conventional mechanisms of causality....

—Merriam-Webster's Unabridged Dictionary

Whatever else eternity holds, certainly the gift of potential is among its greatest treasures. If we can imagine it, its reality must be out there somewhere, just beyond our present grasp. All it takes is space and time. There are plenty of both in the Cosmos. Sooner or later, we'll get there.

—Jim Willis, in *Savannah: A Bicycle Journey Through Space and Time*

In 2013, I wrote *The Dragon Awakes: Rediscovering Earth Energy in the Age of Science*. At the time of its publication, I thought it was a fitting way to finish a life that had been quite fulfilling. Over the course of the previous three years, I had discovered and nourished a worldview quite different from the Christianity that formed the parameters of my life in ministry and teaching. I had moved from religion to spirituality.

As I expressed it on the home page of my website, www.jim-willis.net:

> When I retired to the woods of South Carolina I wanted
> to experience a passion similar to those who built Stone-
> henge—strong enough to inspire me to move mega-ton
> boulders halfway across England. That is to say, I retired
> with an agenda. "Okay God, it's you and me. No struc-
> tures No restrictions. No theology. No holds barred.
> Twenty-four hours a day. You are my only passion. You
> say you like a challenge? Bring it on!" Like Jacob of old
> who wrestled with God, I had one prayer on my lips: "I
> will not let you go until you bless me!"

> Imagine my surprise when, in a totally unexpected way,
> God answered and did just that!

I thought my life was pretty much over, and I was quite satisfied with the results. My bucket list had been ticked off, including a wish to spend my final year alone in the woods, preparing
for my transition into eternity. That was my childhood dream,
and it had been more than accomplished. By then I had been
given not one year, but three.

Even though I was starting to notice health problems, along
with a reduced capacity to confront life on my own terms, I was
a happy camper. Self-publishing what I thought was a final book
about this last chapter of my life was the icing on the cake.

I had even been given a bonus. Over the course of daily med-
itations, I had begun having out-of-body experiences that revealed much about what to expect when I drew my final breath.

Little did I know that on December 16, 2014, a whole new chapter in the unfinished novel of my life would open for me. A new career was about to begin. Quite unexpectedly, I became an author.

Out of the blue, I received a contract to write *Ancient Gods*
in 2017. It was followed by *Supernatural Gods* in 2018, *Lost Civilizations* and *The Quantum Akashic Field* in 2019, *Hidden History* in 2020, and *Censoring God*, the *Individual and Primal Unity
Trilogy*, and *The Wizard in the Wood* in 2021. *American Cults*, the
final book of my *Bicycling Trilogy*, and *Cosmo and Me* all followed in 2023, and now this latest book about NDEs in 2024.

Twelve books in 10 years. They summed up much of what I
have learned over the course of a life that saw almost eight decades come and go.

When the gods answer your prayers, however, it seems as though they expect something in return.

When the gods answer your prayers, however, it seems as though they expect something in return. I was granted a longer life, extending into what I now call Eldership, but I was asked to give something back. That was what the writing was all about.

The days of being an author alone in a room, punching away at the keys of a manual typewriter before sending a written manuscript away to a publisher, are long gone. Because I couldn't handle both the writing and the new technology needed to navigate the chores of marketing, publicizing, scheduling, interviewing, and all the rest that goes with being a writer these days, my daughter, Jan, moved next door to handle that side of what was rapidly becoming a business. Not a lucrative one, to be sure, but a business just the same. We seem to have formed a nonprofit enterprise, though not by design.

What happened on that momentous day in December was barely noticed at the time. It was only after I finished writing the first draft of this book, 10 years later, that I had occasion to reread words I wrote in the dream journal I kept at the time.

To say the least, they took my breath away.

Serendipity? Coincidence? Luck?

Sure. All of that. But to those words, add one more: obligation.

As I read my long-forgotten entry, I came to understand that I had been given a new lease on life, and a new career, for a reason.

Joseph Campbell used to say that he didn't think people were searching for a *meaning* to life. Instead, he thought they sought an *experience of being alive*.

That might be true. At least, I agreed with him for many years.

Now I'm not so sure. Perhaps we *are* searching for the "experience of being alive," but maybe that search is what gives our life *meaning*.

Throughout this book I have emphasized that I never have been through the physical process of a near-death experience. I have never technically died. But I have enjoyed, on numerous occasions, out-of-body experiences. Without feeling any need to prove it to others, I am convinced that I have traveled through the veil and seen the other side.

> **Without feeling any need to prove it to others, I am convinced that I have traveled through the veil and seen the other side.**

I want to share that experience with you who have stayed with me thus far. If it brings any comfort, I will be content, satisfied that I fulfilled the obligation I took on a decade ago to make my final years count.

On that fateful day, I hadn't had my accustomed afternoon nap. I was too busy with work after a long season of frustration. There had been no spiritual breakthroughs, and my OBE connections were few and far between.

The choice between meditating or a brief session on the couch was a tough one, but I decided to meditate, even though in the back of my mind I didn't expect much. I was too distracted by busy-ness. But immediately upon starting some meditation music, I seemed to physically dissolve, leaving only my non-material self, my essence, freed from the body.

I felt my astral being pulled outward to an ancient stone circle, the first one I had excavated and restored after moving to this property. I had discovered, through dowsing, that it was the oldest sacred circle in the area. It was the place where I first met my spirit guide and learned his name. I also learned that he was the first in a long line of sacred shamans who lived and worked here, starting probably some 25,000 years ago.

In spirit, he was waiting for me, and he immediately took me to a place I now call the Shaman's Circle, a long-displaced ancient stone effigy that was only a brief walk uphill through the woods.

There, after I took what was by now my accustomed place, Grandfather, the teacher, appeared to talk to us. These were his words. They came to me in a block of teaching that I hastened to record as soon as I re-entered my body at the close of the meditation.

At the time, I didn't fully understand them. Now, 10 years later, having written this book, I think I do:

The lesson today is about the meaning of life.

A rich man entered a village and offered a reward to anyone who could reveal to him the meaning of life.

A prominent teacher came forward and said, "The meaning of life is found in love."

"That may be so," said the rich man, "but I cannot make myself love what I consider to be unlovable. The best I can do is pretend to feel what I do not feel. Surely the meaning of life cannot be found in falsehood."

And he dismissed the prominent teacher.

A successful businessman then stepped forward.

"The meaning of life," he said, "is to be found in activity. Busy people are successful people, and successful people are happy."

"But I find happiness in leisure as well," said the rich man. "Surely the meaning of life is not to be found only in activity, for many active people know deep down that they live lives without meaning, despite their success."

And the businessman walked away.

Then a poor man approached the rich man. He was a beggar, despised by all.

"The meaning of life," he said, "is found in the knowledge of the certainty of death."

"Explain," said the rich man.

The poor man continued.

"Only when you know that death is imminent, when you know it is at your very doorstep, can you come to really feel the moment you are in right now, for you realize it may be your last experience of life. The present moment becomes crystal clear, sharp, and vivid. The meaning of life is to be found in fully experiencing the clarity of every living moment. That, after all, is why we choose to be born in the first place."

The poor beggar won the reward. He had revealed the meaning of life.

As *you* draw *your* final breath, as you cross the boundary into a world that is your home, your source, and your destination, may you have found both the meaning and the purpose of your life.

Namaste!

FURTHER READING

Alexander, Eben, MD. *Proof of Heaven: A Neurosurgeon's Journey into the Afterlife.* New York: Simon & Schuster Paperbacks, 2012.

Ashton, John, and Tom Whyte. *The Quest for Paradise: Visions of Heaven and Eternity in the World's Myths and Religions.* New York, NY: Harper Collins, 2001.

Atwater, F. Holmes. *Captain of My Ship, Master of My Soul.* Charlottesville, VA: Hampton Roads Publishing, 2001.

Atwater, P. M. H. *We Live Forever: The Real Truth about Death.* Virginia Beach, VA: ARE Press, 2004.

Buhlman, William. *Adventures Beyond the Body.* New York: Harper Collins, 1996.

———. *Adventures in the Afterlife.* Millsboro, DE: Osprey Press, 2013.

———. *The Secret of the Soul.* New York: Harper Collins, 2001.

Campbell, Joseph. *Transformations of Myth through Time.* New York: Harper & Row, 1990.

Campbell, Joseph, with Bill Moyers. *The Power of Myth.* New York: Bantam Doubleday Dell Publishing Group, 1988.

Chopra, Depak, and Leonard Mlodinonow. *War of the World View: Science Versus Spirituality.* New York: Harmony Books, 2011.

Eadie, Betty. *Embraced by the Light.* Placerville, CA: Bantam Books, 1992.

Ellwood, Robert S., and Barbara A. McGraw. *Many Peoples, Many Faiths: Women and Men in the World Religions,* 7th edition. Upper Saddle River, NJ: Prentiss Hall, 2002.

Fisher, Mary Pat, and Lee W. Bailey. *An Anthology of Living Religions.* Upper Saddle River, NJ: Prentiss Hall, 2000.

Gaskell, G. A. *Dictionary of all Scriptures and Myths.* New York: Gramercy Books, 1981.

Greyson, Bruce M. *The Handbook of Near-Death Experiences.* Santa Barbara, CA: Praeger, 2009.

———. *After: A Doctor Explores What Near-Death Experiences Reveal about Life and Beyond.* New York: St. Martin's Essentials, 2021

Grof, Stanislav, and Hal Zina Bennett. *The Holotropic Mind: The Three Levels of Human Consciousness and How They Shape Our Lives.* San Francisco, CA: Harper Collins, 1993.

Hancock, Graham. *Supernatural.* New York: Disinformation Company, 2007.

Harner, Michael. *Cave and Cosmos.* Berkeley, CA: North Atlantic Books, 2013.

———. *The Way of the Shaman.* San Francisco, CA: Harper & Row, 1980.

Harper, Tom. *The Pagan Christ.* Toronto, Canada: Thomas Allen Publishers, 2004.

Hick, John. *Classical and Contemporary Readings in the Philosophy of Religion.* Edgewood Cliffs, NJ: Prentiss Hall, 1964.

Highwater, Jamake. *The Primal Mind: Vision and Reality in Indian America.* New York: Harper & Row, 1981.

Ingerman, Sandra, and Hank Wesselman. *Awakening to the Spirit World: The Shamanic Path of Direct Revelation.* Boulder, CO: Sounds True, 2011.

Kapra, Fritjof. *The Tao of Physics: An Exploration of the Parallels between Modern Physics and Eastern Mysticism.* Boston: Shambala Publications, 1975.

Lanza, Robert, with Bob Berman. *Beyond Biocentrism: Rethinking Time, Space, Consciousness, and the Illusion of Death.* Dallas, TX: BenBella Books, 2016.

———. *Biocentrism: How Life and Consciousness Are the Keys to Understanding the True Nature of the Universe.* Dallas, TX: BenBella Books, Inc, 2009.

Lanza, Robert, with Nancy Kress. *Observer.* The Story Plant, 2023.

Laszlo, Ervin. *The Akashic Experience: Science and the Cosmic Memory Field.* Rochester, VT: Inner Traditions, 2009.

———. *Science and the Akashic Field: An Integral Theory of Everything,* 2nd edition, Rochester, VT: Inner Traditions, 2007.

———. *The Whispering Pond: A Personal Guide to the Emerging Vision of Science.* Rockport, MA: Element Books, 1996.

Macrone, Michael. *By Jove!: Brush Up Your Mythology.* New York: Harper Collins, 1992.

Mails, Thomas E. *Dancing in the Paths of the Ancestors: Book Two of the Pueblo Children of the Earth Mother.* Cambridge, MA: Da Capo, 1999.

McMoneagle, Joseph. *Remote Viewing Secrets: A Handbook.* Charlottesville, VA: Hampton Roads Publishing, 2000.

———. *The Stargate Chronicles: Memoirs of a Psychic Spy.* Charlottesville, VA: Hampton Roads Publishing, 2002.

Miller, Hamish. *The Spirit of the Serpent.* Reality Entertainment, 2008.

Miller, Hamish, and Paul Bradhurst. *The Sun and the Serpent.* Cornwall, UK: Pendragon Partnership, 1994.

Mitchell, Edgar, and Dwight Williams. *The Way of the Explorer: An Apollo Astronaut's Journey through the Material and Mystical Worlds*, revised edition. Newburyport, MA: New Page Books, 2008.

Moody, Raymond A. Jr. *Life after Life.* New York: Harper One, 2001.

———. *The Light Beyond.* New York: Random House, 1988.

———. *Reflections on Life after Life.* New York: Bantam Doubleday Dell, 1978.

Monroe, Robert A. *Far Journeys.* New York: Doubleday, 1985.

———. *Journeys Out of the Body.* New York: Doubleday, 1971.

———. *Ultimate Journey.* New York: Doubleday, 1994.

Moorjani Anita. *Dying to Be Me: My Journey from Cancer, to Near Death, to True Healing.* Carlsbad, CA: Hayhouse, 2012.

Peterson, Robert. *Out of Body Experiences.* Charlottesville, VA: Hampton Roads Publishing, 1997.

Radin, Dean. *The Conscious Universe: The Scientific Truth of Psychic Phenomena.* San Francisco, CA: Harper Collins, 1997.

———. *Entangled Minds.* New York: Simon & Schuster, 2006.

———. *Real Magic: Ancient Wisdom, Modern Science, and a Guide to the Secret Power of the Universe.* New York: Harmony Books, 2018.

———. *Supernormal: Science, Yoga and the Evidence for Extraordinary Abilities.* New York: Random House, 2013.

Ritchie, George G. *Return from Tomorrow.* Minneapolis, MN: Chosen, 1978.

Sartori, Penny. *The Wisdom of Near-Death Experiences: How Understanding NDEs*

Can Help Us Live More Fully. London: Watkins Publishing, 2014.

Selbie, Joseph. *The Physics of God*. Wayne, NJ: The Career Press, 2018.

Shushan, Gregory. *Near-Death Experience in Indigenous Religions*. New York: Oxford University Press, 2018.

Stevenson, Ian. *Children Who Remember Past Lives: A Question of Reincarnation*. Jefferson, NC: McFarland & Company, 2021.

Strassman, Rick. *DMT and the Soul of Prophecy*. Rochester, VT: Park Street Press, 2014.

———. *DMT: The Spirit Molecule*. Rochester, VT: Park Street Press, 2001

———. *Inner Paths to Outer Space: Journeys to Alien Worlds through Psychedelics and other Spiritual Technologies*. Rochester, VT: Park Street Press, 2008

Targ, Russell, and Harold R. Puthoff. *Mind Reach: Scientists Look at Psychic Abilities*. Charlottesville, VA: Hampton Roads Publishing Company, 1977.

Taylor, Albert. *Soul Traveler: A Guide to Out of Body Experiences and the Wonders Beyond*. Covena, CA: Verity Press Publishing, 1996.

Tucker, Jim B. *Life Before Life: Children's Memories of Previous Lives*. New York NY: St. Martin's Press, 2005.

Weiss, Brian L. *Many Lives, Many Masters*. New York, NY: Simon & Schuster, 1988.

———. *Same Soul, Many Masters*. New York, NY: Simon & Schuster, 2004.

———. *Where Reincarnation and Biology Intersect*. Westport, CT: Greenwood Publishing Group, 1997.

Willis, Jim. *Ancient Gods: Lost Histories, Hidden Truths and the Conspiracy of Silence*. Detroit: Visible Ink Press, 2016.

———. *The Dragon Awakes: Rediscovering Earth Energy in the Age of Science*. Daytona Beach, FL: Dragon Publishing, 2014.

———. *The Religion Book: Places, Prophets, Saints and Seers*. Detroit: Visible Ink Press, 2004.

———. *The Quantum Akashic Field: A Guide to Out-of-Body Experience for the Astral Traveler*. Rochester, VT: Findhorn Press, 2019.

———. *Supernatural Gods: Spiritual Mysteries, Psychic Experiences and Scientific Truths*. Detroit: Visible Ink Press, 2017.

Wolf, Fred Alan. *Parallel Universes: The Search for Other Worlds*. New York: Simon & Schuster, 1988.

Wright, Patricia C., and Richard D. Wright. *The Divining Heart*. Rochester, VT: Destiny Books, 1994.

INDEX

Note: (ill.) indicates photos and illustrations

A

AARP (American Association of Retired Persons), 237

AARP Bulletin [magazine], 237

Abraham, Prophet [biblical], 19

acceptance, feeling of in NDEs, 51, 61, 64, 114, 124–25, 239–42, 248–51

Across the Frontiers (Heisenberg), 115

Acts, Book of, 9–12

Adam [biblical], 19, 198

Adana–Mersin, Turkey, 9

Africa and Africans, 35

After: A Doctor Explores What Near-Death Experiences Reveal about Life and Beyond (Greyson), 173

afterlife experiences
common era, NDE testimonies from the, 39
IONS, NDE research at, 85, 90
medicine, NDEs and the field of, 61
parallel dimensions, reality of, 204
philosophers, NDEs of the, 4, 7
photos and illustrations, 123 (ill.), 237 (ill.), 245 (ill.)
researchers, top NDE, 163, 165, 168, 181
shared-death experiences, phenomenon of, 155

thermodynamics and NDEs, 217

TMI, NDE stories from, 94–95

world, NDE stories from around the, 25

Age of Enlightenment, 43–44

Akashic Field Theory, 194, 200, 236

Alcock, James, 164

Alexander, Eben, 87, 90, 176–82

Alexander the Great, 3

All Souls' Day, 86

Allah, 20, 180

Alps, Swiss, 113–14

American Association of Retired Persons (AARP), 237

American Cults (Willis), 258

Ananias [biblical], 11–12

Ananke (Lady Necessity) [goddess], 4

Ancient Gods (Willis), 258

Andromeda, 125

Anecdotes de MÈdecine (Monchaux), 17

anesthesia, NDEs' relation to, 145, 145 (ill.), 150, 156, 231

"Angel Band" (Suffern), 18–19

Annie, Little Orphan [character], 246

anoxia, NDEs' relation to, 56, 59, 150, 156

Antioch [historical], 9

Antiquity, 1–2

Apollo 14 mission, 83

"Are Near-Death Experiences Real?" [radio episode], 55

Aridaeus. See Thespesius of Cilicia

Aristotle, 3

Army, U.S., 69, 73–74, 77, 99

Association for the Scientific Study of Near-Death Phenomena, 103, 176

Astellas Institute for Regenerative Medicine, 133

The Atlantic [magazine], 89, 103

Atlantic Ocean, 187

Atlantis, 5

atman, 139 (ill.), 139–40, 255

Atropos, 4

Attanasio, Natale, 131

Atwater, Lt. Frederick Holmes "Skip," 69, 71–75, 77, 91, 93, 99

Audette, John, 103, 176

The Awakening Heart (Eadie), 165

Awakening to the Spirit World: The Shamanic Path of Direct Revelation (Ingerman and Wesselman), 27

Ayer, Sir Alfred Jules "Freddie," 35, 115–16, 116 (ill.)

Aztec tribe, 86

B

Bach, Johann Sebastian, 27, 250